T0322885

THE
GREAT PYRAMID
VOID
ENIGMA

"With some of the best forensic reporting, Scott Creighton looks again for answers to the most intriguing questions ever to emerge from the Great Pyramid. The mysterious and unexplained 'Big Void,' revealed in 2018 by subatomic-particle physicists, has baffled everyone so far, but now, with a wealth of facts and details unavailable from any other single source, Creighton makes stunning connections between cutting-edge science and esoteric tradition, and he backs it all up with some very impressive detective work. If you want to know the facts—and be thoroughly enthralled—you must not skip this terrific read."

J. Douglas Kenyon, author of *Ghosts of Atlantis*

"Everyone loves a mystery, and the mystery of Giza's Great Pyramid is perhaps the most enigmatic mystery known. Who built it? When, and why? These three questions have tantalized researchers and historical chronologers seemingly forever. Recently, the scientists of the ScanPyramids project discovered a large void as long and wide as the Grand Gallery itself; another large chamber hidden within an enormous, incredibly ancient structure. It's a mystery, of course. In *The Great Pyramid Void Enigma*, Scott Creighton digs deep into the history and the most pertinent of legends surrounding Egypt's pyramids and the Great Pyramid in search of answers to the big questions of 'who, when, and why.' Creighton sifts through the legends and explores the landscape of one of the most tumultuous times of our past, a time of climatic chaos and mass extinction 12,000 years ago. Most of all, he spins a marvelous story around a complex topic that the best of mystery writers will surely envy, and he links a 12,000-year-old catastrophe to the beginning of our own history. A fascinating and enlightening book. I couldn't put it down."

EDWARD F. MALKOWSKI, HISTORICAL RESEARCHER,
AND AUTHOR OF *ANCIENT EGYPT 39,000 BCE*

"In true whodunit style, Creighton transports the reader on a journey of exploration, skillfully weaving powerful themes with clear emotional expression, endeavoring to reveal the truth behind Egypt's fabled Hall of the Ancestors. A comprehensive blend of history, archaeology, and ancient pyramid lore, it will undoubtedly rouse your curiosity."

LORRAINE EVANS, ARCHAEOLOGIST,
HISTORIAN, AND AUTHOR OF *BURYING THE DEAD*

"Scott Creighton casts fresh eyes on one of the world's oldest mysteries, shattering the expectations that there is nothing new to be revealed about the marvelous megaliths of Egypt's Giza Plateau. Go inside the Great Pyramid void, and you'll emerge looking back with reawakened wonder."

RAND FLEM-ATH, RESEARCHER AND COAUTHOR OF
THE ATLANTIS BLUEPRINT AND *THE MURDER OF MOSES*

THE
GREAT PYRAMID
VOID
ENIGMA

The Mystery of the
Hall of the Ancestors

SCOTT CREIGHTON

Bear & Company
Rochester, Vermont

Bear & Company
One Park Street
Rochester, Vermont 05767
www.BearandCompanyBooks.com

Text stock is SFI certified

Bear & Company is a division of Inner Traditions International

Copyright © 2021 by Scott Creighton

All rights reserved. No part of this book may be reproduced or utilized in any form or by any means, electronic or mechanical, including photocopying, recording, or by any information storage and retrieval system, without permission in writing from the publisher.

Cataloging-in-Publication Data for this title is available from the Library of Congress

ISBN 978-1-59143-402-3 (print)
ISBN 978-1-59143-403-0 (ebook)

Printed and bound in the United States by Lake Book Manufacturing, Inc. The text stock is SFI certified. The Sustainable Forestry Initiative® program promotes sustainable forest management.

10 9 8 7 6 5 4 3 2 1

Text design and layout by Debbie Glogover
This book was typeset in Garamond Premier Pro with Cyan, Gotham, Gill Sans MT Pro, and ITC Legacy Sans used as display typefaces

To send correspondence to the author of this book, mail a first-class letter to the author c/o Inner Traditions • Bear & Company, One Park Street, Rochester, VT 05767, and we will forward the communication.

This book is dedicated to the memory of my beautiful niece,

Stacey Diane Creighton

(1982–2020),

who was called from this earthly realm much too soon.

She could sing like an angel, and the angels will surely

embrace her as one of their own.

* * *

The ideas in this book would likely never have seen the light of day were it not for the many other authors, researchers, scientists, and thinkers who have gone before me and upon whose shoulders many of the ideas in this book stand. To those great and maverick thinkers and researchers who paved the way—Graham Hancock, Robert Bauval, Robert Schoch, the late, great John Anthony West, and last but by no means least, Rand and Rose Flem-Ath—I thank and salute you all.

Writing a book such as this is, for the most part, a lonesome endeavor and not without its problems and setbacks. Without the daily encouragement of my wife, Louise, this book might never have been completed. I cannot thank you enough for always being there, Sweets. We had some exhilirating and fun-filled days at the height of the research, none of which was at all easy during a global pandemic.

My children were very young when I began my writing adventure. They are young adults now, studying at university and making their own way in the world. But in both of them I see young minds that are willing to question, a characteristic that will, I'm sure, stand them in good stead in the years to come. Thank you, Jamie and Nina for all your questions.

Gary Osborn, coauthor of my first book, *The Giza Prophecy,* deserves a special mention here. He has always been willing to look over my work with a critical eye and has, in this book, added a quite brilliant insight which helped make better sense of some of my findings.

Kayla and Jeffery, my tireless and brilliant editors at Inner Traditions • Bear & Co., also deserve much credit and plaudits here. Their attention to detail is truly astonishing, and it is through their skill and dedication that this book is what it is. Thank you both.

And finally, to my critics. Without you there would be few questions for which to seek answers. Thank you all for driving me to dig ever deeper into the mysteries of our past.

Contents

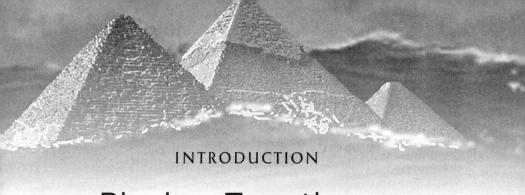

Piecing Together a Bigger Picture

History is like a multidimensional jigsaw puzzle: we know that an overall picture exists, but often, particularly with our most ancient prehistory, the picture is but the faintest of outlines because while some of the pieces of the puzzle have been correctly placed, many others have been set down in the wrong place; sometimes the pieces we have are mixed up with pieces from other puzzles; and worst of all, sometimes pieces are simply lost, preventing us from ever completing the picture. With no "box cover" to guide us and with only a few of the pieces of the puzzle in the correct place, we can only ever make an educated guess as to what the partially completed picture truly represents. Similarly, in archaeological research, we can perceive but a faint sketch of our remote past from the clues we piece together.

And so it is with the early, giant pyramids of the Old Kingdom of ancient Egypt. They rise out of the desert sands like some giant, geometric jigsaw puzzle, a puzzle in which we cannot even be certain that we have all of the pieces, and of those that we *do* have, we cannot be sure that we have placed them in the correct place in order to make sense of and build the true history, the correct picture, of these ancient monuments.

Of the pieces that we do possess, they were found by many different individuals, often centuries apart, making the progress toward building a true, complete picture of these monuments frustratingly slow. But gradually, enough pieces were found to allow us to come to a consensus as to what the partially completed picture is showing us. And this is essentially where we find ourselves today with mainstream Egyptology, whose consensus view of these ancient monuments is that they were built as tombs of the pharaohs, that they were "devices" constructed in monumental stone architecture that would ensure that the pharaohs could journey to the heavens and to an everlasting afterlife among the gods residing there, the stars.

How Egyptology came to this view is a story in itself, for it wasn't always the case that the prevailing tomb theory was the accepted purpose for these ancient structures. The purpose of the pyramids is but one small part of the overall picture that we are trying to piece together. Compounding this particular issue and making the puzzle almost impossible to solve is the fact that unscrupulous individuals have placed some pieces of their own making into the mix, pieces that simply do not belong to the puzzle at all but that have the effect of completely blurring and confusing the true picture, resulting in incorrect interpretations and conclusions being reached.

But the true picture of these monuments—the picture on the front of our puzzle box—has, in fact, always been available to us. And it shows us, in fairly clear terms, how the pieces of this ancient puzzle *should* be fitted together. This particular picture, however, has long since been cast aside by mainstream Egyptologists who insist that the picture of these monuments presented to them by the ancient Egyptians themselves has little or nothing to do with the puzzle they are trying to piece together today. They prefer to work without the box picture, working in the dark, believing the few pieces they have put in place are enough for them to see the picture of our past in full.

Everything seemed fairly settled until 2016 with the publication of *The Great Pyramid Hoax,* which showed that some of the pieces of the puzzle used by Egyptologists to construct their history of these monuments were, in fact, fabrications—false pieces of the puzzle that served only to distort and obscure the overall picture. Since the publication of that book, even more false pieces have been uncovered, and like the earlier false pieces, these need to be removed from the puzzle in order to clarify the picture. More recently, in November 2017, another piece of the puzzle was discovered: a potentially massive new chamber deep within the Great Pyramid that calls into question the picture the Egyptologists have so painstakingly created over the past two hundred or so years. And once again, it was a piece of the puzzle that the ancients had already told us about but that was effectively dismissed and ignored by Egyptology.

And so, with these new discoveries, we find that parts of the puzzle we had already assembled will have to be removed and discarded, making space in the picture for the placement of the newly discovered pieces, the correct pieces. With these recent finds, the picture of our ancient history is gradually beginning to change. No longer are we looking at a simple "tomb of the pharaoh" picture so beloved by the Egyptologists. There is more—much, much more—to the story, to the picture, of these ancient monuments.

The picture was always available to us—on the cover of the puzzle box—to guide us to correctly complete the puzzle. So, with this picture in hand, let us now remove the false pieces of the puzzle, insert the recently found pieces, reorganize the remaining pieces, and reveal the true picture of our past. In so doing, a picture emerges that better correlates with that on the box cover, better matches the ancient legends that tell us when these timeless monuments were built and, more importantly, better fits *why* they were built.

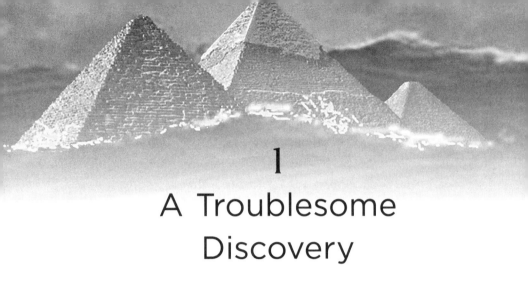

1

A Troublesome Discovery

It seemingly came from nowhere, the proverbial bolt from the blue: the discovery of a massive new "void" or space deep within the superstructure of the Great Pyramid of Giza—a possible new pyramid chamber that is equal in size to the pyramid's enormous Grand Gallery (fig. 1.1). The

Figure 1.1. The Grand Gallery within the Great Pyramid. The gallery is almost 30 feet in height, 154 feet in length, and is inclined at an angle of 26.5°. (Photo: Keith Adler)

discovery of the "Big Void," as it was dubbed by its discoverers, was an instant media sensation and one that reverberated all around the world. Indeed, such was the magnitude of this discovery that even people with little interest in ancient Egyptian history were openly discussing it and, naturally, speculating on what, if anything, might be found within.

On November 2, 2017, an international team of around thirty-three scientists from the ScanPyramids project published the results of their two-year-long Great Pyramid research project in the journal *Nature*. Using a technique known as muon tomography (or simply muography), the ScanPyramids team set up their muon detectors inside and outside the Great Pyramid. Similar to X-rays, which are used to show different densities of matter within the human body, muons (which are by-products of cosmic rays) can be used to detect different densities of matter within solid rock, thus revealing areas where there are cavities or possible hidden chambers within the structure. The technology was first successfully used in the 1970s and since then has been used to probe the interiors of structures as diverse as volcanoes, glaciers, and even nuclear reactors.

The ScanPyramids project team was split into three separate groups, with each group working independently of the others using a different muography technique. All three groups reported identical findings with a confidence level of 99.9999 percent that the Big Void within the Great Pyramid truly is a real structural anomaly within the monument

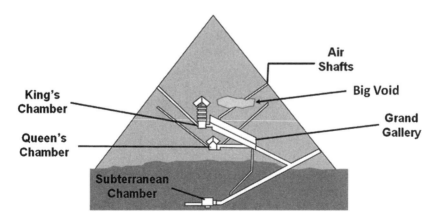

Figure 1.2. The interior chambers of the Great Pyramid, including the Big Void above the Grand Gallery. (Image: Scott Creighton)

and not simply a statistical anomaly. In short, the scientists detected a massive space almost as large as, and a short distance above, the Grand Gallery of the Great Pyramid (fig. 1.2), a space that could turn out to be a truly massive hidden chamber.

And with this discovery, a new chapter in our understanding of this most ancient monument was about to begin.

Or was it?

WORLD REACTION

The reaction to the discovery of the Big Void from leading Egyptologists and other academics around the world was perplexing, to say the least, with some people talking about the "discovery of the century" while others suggested that the data the ScanPyramids team presented was actually in error and that no new space exists in the Great Pyramid at all.

Zahi Hawass, former head of the Supreme Council of Antiquities in Egypt (now the Ministry of Antiquities), took the academic "no mystery, nothing to see here" attitude toward the ScanPyramids project's data. Hawass led the ScanPyramids science committee overseeing the project and said:

> This is not a discovery. The pyramid is full of voids and that does not mean there is a secret chamber or a new discovery.[1]

In another article, Hawass stated:

> Now to build the Grand Gallery inside the Great Pyramid, they cannot build the Grand Gallery with a solid structure, they have to have hollows around it to build it. And therefore, the 30-meter void is already existent. It's already mentioned by Dieter Arnold 25 years ago.[2]

The Egyptologist Aidan Dodson of the University of Bristol in the UK, was equally dismissive of the find, stating:

> There's zero chance of hidden burial chambers.[3]

The current head of Egypt's Ministry of Antiquities, Mustafa Waziri, was of a similarly cautious mind, and he seemed to be more critical of the preemptive manner in which the news of the Big Void discovery was released to the world's media, stating:

> The project has to proceed in a scientific way that follows the steps of scientific research and its discussion before publication.[4]

A leading American Egyptologist, Mark Lehner, who is on the ScanPyramids project's review panel, also waded into the controversy, stating about the discovery:

> Right now it's just a big difference; it's an anomaly. But we need more of a focus on it especially in a day and age when we can no longer go blasting our way through the pyramid with gunpowder as [British] Egyptologist Howard Vyse did in the early 1800s.[5]

While Hawass and other Egyptologists insist on caution in making any official pronouncement as to what the Big Void actually is (or may be), other investigators in the project have been more forthcoming with their views.

> Sébastien Procureur, from CEA-IRFU, University of Paris-Saclay, emphasized that muography only sees large features, and that the team's scans were not just picking up a general porosity inside the pyramid.
> "With muons you measure an integrated density," he explained. "So, if there are holes everywhere then the integrated density will be the same, more or less, in all directions, because everything will be averaged. But if you see some excess of muons, it means that you have a bigger void.
> "You don't get that in a Swiss cheese."[6]

Mehdi Tayoubi of the Heritage Innovation Preservation Institute in France and codirector of the ScanPyramids project believes this massive cavity within the Great Pyramid to have been a deliberate construction.

When you know the pyramids, and the perfection of the pyramids, it's hard to imagine that it's an accident. . . .[7]

He also said:

We don't know whether this big void is horizontal or inclined; we don't know if this void is made by one structure or several successive structures. What we are sure about is that this big void is there; that it is impressive; and that it was not expected as far as I know by any sort of theory. . . .[8]

And further:

It's not a false start, where they tried something and abandoned it. The engineering and design of this structure was carefully planned. It's not an irregularity of construction. We leave the door open to discuss this with Egyptologists.[9]

Tayoubi makes an important point here, and it is one that is unlikely to have been missed by the Egyptologists: the discovery of the Big Void "was not expected as far as I know by any sort of theory . . . and . . . this structure was carefully planned." In other words, this discovery is a troublesome one for Egyptology, for if this anomalous void truly *does* turn out to be another giant chamber deep within the Great Pyramid, then its presence simply does not fit with the carefully constructed "tomb of the pharaoh" narrative we have all read in our school textbooks for the better part of two hundred years.

All of which may go some way to explaining the clear reluctance of leading Egyptologists to even acknowledge that there is anything at all to the anomaly and the willingness of others to assert that the project data indicating the presence of the Big Void may actually be in error. For the Egyptologists, the scenario here is akin to having pieced together a substantial part of a large, complex jigsaw puzzle only to find much later that there's another big piece in your puzzle box you had completely overlooked, and no matter how hard you try, it is a piece that simply will not fit into the picture you have hitherto created, a picture that you were convinced was correct but that may now have to be taken apart in order to insert the new piece.

THEORIES ABOUND

Naturally, with a discovery of this magnitude (especially one with such profound implications), we find that ideas and theories as to what the ScanPyramids project data might mean and how it should be interpreted come thick and fast. Everything from a treasure chamber, the fabled Atlantean Hall of Records, the location of the Ark of the Covenant, the true burial chamber of Khufu,* a natural vug, or an artifact of the pyramid's construction process have all been suggested. Here we will take some time to consider some of the more plausible ideas that have entered into the public debate as to what the ScanPyramids project's data might ultimately reveal.

Data Misinterpretation

Misinterpretation of scientific data happens—and more often than most of us realize. Could the ScanPyramids team have made a terrible mistake with their interpretation of the data? The editor of the *Journal of Ancient Egyptian Architecture* expressed such concerns, writing:

> The form of the anomalous particles forming the supposed void image seem to have the same characteristics as the Grand Gallery: long, tall and narrow. Could it be possible that the Grand Gallery is in some way influencing the measurements made because of its very particular geometry? Perhaps creating a kind of ghost image or reflection in the scans?
>
> These are questions that we raise to try to find an explanation for

---

*Throughout this book, we will sometimes use the names Cheops, Khufu, Suphis/ Saophis, or Surīd. According to Egyptologists, these different names all likely refer to the same historical person.

the singular announcement made this week that contradicts much of what we know about the funerary architecture of this period. Our concern is that the conclusions that have been drawn from the data are not supported by that data, but we remain open and attentive to the progress of the mission, and results that might justify more definitive interpretation.[10]

Following on from this, the British Egyptologist David Lightbody considers data misinterpretation to be a distinct possibility. In a working paper analyzing the ScanPyramids project's data, Lightbody presents a hypothesis that offers an alternative interpretation of the data that suggests that no Big Void actually exists at all. In his paper, Lightbody writes:

The "big void" may in fact be the result of two zones containing many small construction voids which flank the Grand Gallery. Geometric calculations . . . indicate that the new features on the scans which were interpreted as produced by a single "big" void viewed from two directions, located 40m out towards the north face of the structure, could in fact have been produced by two smaller void zones closer to the center of the pyramid, one on either side of the Grand Gallery structure.

Due to the offsets of the two Nagoya nuclear emulsion detection plates from the center line of the Grand Gallery, which were of a similar magnitude . . . and the inward slope of the sides of the Grand Gallery structure, only one such void zone would be clearly visible on each Nagoya scan. On one side the small voids would be aligned with the detector and would form a zone that was almost a continuous void directed at the plate. On the other hand, the opposing void zone signals would not align with the detector and so the effect of the signals would not be cumulative. In addition, most of them would be hidden behind the signal of the main gallery structure. . . .

It is not intended to suggest that this second interpretation is definitive, as some of the same methodological problems raised by the previous interpretation would then be revisited, but it is proposed that it is another plausible interpretation of the data set that should be carefully evaluated. . . . The interpretation of scan results for ancient and singular structures like the Great Pyramid must take place within a context that includes historical, archaeological, and architectural knowledge, experience, and expertise, and a methodical approach.[11]

Lightbody certainly makes valid points and a compelling argument that the Big Void may be some kind of scanning artifact, a ghost image or reflection from the Grand Gallery itself. However, the muography scanning of the Great Pyramid was carried out by three independent teams working not from two but from *three* different locations (inside and outside the monument). Lightbody's theory may explain two of those convergences but not the third. The independent results from each of the three teams converged to the same location within the structure—around ten to fifteen meters *above* the Grand Gallery. It is difficult to see how measurements taken from three different locations could all project a ghost image to the same location within the monument.

However, in consideration of this possibility, in 2019 the ScanPyramids project team performed further scans from several other locations within the Great Pyramid, including the Grand Gallery, the King's Chamber, and also the small compartments* high above the King's Chamber (and thus *above* the Grand Gallery) in order to eliminate the possibility of any discovery being the result of a reflection or ghost image of the Grand Gallery, as per Lightbody's theory. The new scans confirmed the 2017 results: the Big Void is a real, massive space located above the Grand Gallery (and not a reflection or ghost image), and its length, previously thought to be thirty meters, is now thought to be closer to forty meters. The team continued to scan up to the pyramid's apex but did not detect any other significant unknown voids within the monument. As a result of the new findings, Hawass and Lehner have apparently changed their view

---

*Discovered in 1837 by the British pyramid explorer Colonel Richard William Howard Vyse.

of this discovery. Larry Pahl, director of the American Institute for Pyramid Research, said:

As I write this (December, 2019), the Egyptian government has the Scan Pyramids team back in the relieving chambers above the King's Chamber doing more scans and probing to find the best way to try and access that large void. The team has been quiet for several years after the discovery and worldwide announcement of the void. It took a while for the Supreme Council to be convinced of that void, but now Dr. Zahi Hawass and Dr. Mark Lehner are talking openly about it, as a possible store of something significant.[12]

Stress-Relieving Chamber

Although accepting that the project team's data is sound and that it indicates a void of some kind within the pyramid, Lehner remains skeptical that the Big Void has any meaningful significance beyond perhaps being a "legacy" of the pyramid's construction process, stating: It could be a kind of space that the builders left to protect the very narrow roof of the Grand Gallery from the weight of the pyramid.[13]

This theory by Lehner is similar to that of the so-called chambers of construction (known also as the relieving chambers or Vyse chambers) that were discovered by Vyse above the King's Chamber in 1837 (see much more on Vyse in chapter 5 and the appendices). It is believed that to relieve the immense weight and stress on the flat roof of the King's Chamber, a series of five small chambers or "compartments" were constructed above the King's Chamber, with the topmost of these compartments possessing an inclined, gabled roof in order to deflect the immense downward pressure laterally into the body of the pyramid.

This idea, however, does not stand up to scrutiny since the Queen's Chamber, which is located much farther down within the body of the pyramid and, as such, has much greater weight bearing down on its roof, has none of these stress-relieving chambers. Lehner's proposal seems also to have been rejected by one of the ScanPyramids project's team leaders, Hany Helal of Cairo University, who believes that the Big Void is simply too large a space to act as a pressure-relieving device.[14] And, of course, the corbelled design of the Grand Gallery forms a great arch, which itself can be considered a stress-relieving design, which then prompts the question: Why would you require a stress-relieving chamber to relieve another stress-relieving chamber? The arched design of the Grand Gallery suggests that whatever might be found within the Big Void might be of considerable weight.

The Iron Throne of Osiris

One of the first theories to emerge as to the purpose of the Big Void, proposed by the Italian mathematician and archaeoastronomer Giulio Magli of the Politecnico di Milano, suggests that the Big Void will be found to contain a throne made from meteoric iron that would accompany Khufu on his journey through the *duat* to his everlasting afterlife among the stars.

> For the moment, the prospections are too approximate to allow us any definitive conclusion; however, the existing information— together with what we know about the funerary religion of ancient Egypt—are sufficient to attempt at an explanation of the void which has been shown to exist inside the Pyramid of Khufu. It appears indeed that this void is not a failure in the construction, neither can [it] be interpreted as a structural feature such as a relieving chamber. We proposed here that the void corresponds to a nonfunctional "copy" of the Great Gallery beginning at the egress of the northern lower shaft and built to contain a symbolic object located under the apex of the pyramid. This object might be a throne endowed with sheets of meteoritic Iron, in accordance with some "resurrection" passages of the Pyramid Texts.[15]

WHAT NEXT?

Now that the existence of the Big Void has been verified with another series of scans, science can now consider how best the space can be investigated. Some ideas on how this might be done have already been proposed. For the BBC News, Jonathan Amos wrote, "Jean-Baptiste Mouret, from the French national institute for computer science and applied mathematics (Inria), said the team had an idea how to do it, but that the Egyptian authorities would first have to approve it. 'Our concept is to drill a very small hole to potentially explore monuments like this. We aim to have a robot that could fit in a 3cm hole. Basically, we're working on flying robots,' he said."[16]

An initial investigation may be even simpler. A small hole could be drilled into the roof of the Grand Gallery deep enough to reach into the Big Void, and then an endoscopic camera pushed up through the hole to look inside the space. This idea would not be unlike the method used to explore the small cavity discovered behind Gantenbrink's Door at the top of the south shaft of the Queen's Chamber in the 1990s.

THE PICTURE ON THE BOX

While the Big Void has clearly wrong-footed Egyptology, the fact of the matter is that it really shouldn't have. This is because the Coptic-Egyptian texts that have come down to us from ancient times—texts, it has to be said, that are mostly ignored by Egyptologists as being purely myth and legend—actually tell us of this chamber or, at the very least, strongly imply its presence within the Great Pyramid. These texts present to us the guiding picture on the front of our historical puzzle box, and are our guide to piecing together and revealing the true picture of our ancient past and, in particular, the true nature and purpose of the Big Void, including why it was absolutely vital for the ancient builders to place this inaccessible chamber high up within the Great Pyramid.

So what *are* these ancient texts, and what is it they tell us?

2

Examining the Legends

The past of humanity is quite literally littered with thousands of myths and legends, fantastic tales passed down to us in countless languages from just about every corner of the world. Most scientists today dismiss such literature as nothing more than the unscientific, wild fantasies and folklore of deeply superstitious and primitive peoples. Some scientists, however, take a different approach, viewing many of these myths and legends as accounts of actual historical events, albeit couched in a deeply symbolic and often highly embroidered language. They concede that many of these stories may, in fact, contain elements of truth, that they may actually have been attempts by ancient people to explain unusual events occurring in their natural environment using such literary devices as metaphor, allegory, and simile to create explanations that made perfect sense within their own cultural tradition's view of the world and its place in the cosmos. These fanciful stories would sometimes be written down using an assortment of media (stones, palm leaves, parchments, etc.), but more often than not—since most ancient people could not read or write—they were passed down only by oral means for hundreds and even thousands of years and were finally committed to the written form only in relatively recent times.

The oldest oral tradition we presently know of comes to us from the indigenous people of Australia.

For Aboriginal hunter-gatherers in Australia, the imperative of passing on precise information about the nature and possibilities of the continent's harsh terrain was clear. Without such information, painstakingly accumulated by generations of ancestors, the children within a tribe might not survive. Careful story preservation seems to have been an effective strategy. . . .

The island of Fitzroy, which is some 3 miles off the east coast of northern Queensland, offers an example. The Yidiɲɖi Aboriginal name for the island is "gabaɻ," meaning the "lower arm" of a former mainland promontory. The term describes a situation that could have only been true when the sea level was at least 98 feet lower than it is today . . . 9,960 years ago. If the original naming of Fitzroy Island as "gabaɻ" dates from a time when it was visibly attached to the mainland—and there is no good reason to suspect otherwise—then this memory is almost 10 millennia old. That means this story has been passed on orally through some 400 generations. . . .

Humanity has direct memories of events that occurred 10 millennia ago. This conclusion runs against what many anthropologists and others have inferred about both the factual basis and the longevity of such oral traditions. Science more broadly has generally been dismissive of these, largely considering them anthropological curiosities, minutiae that define particular cultures. Now many of us are forced to look at ancient stories as potentially more meaningful. The preservation of extant oral traditions, in whatever cultures they may still be found, is imperative—they help define us all.[1]

Here we see the importance of the oral tradition. Where a stone or a piece of parchment can be lost, destroyed, or simply deteriorate over time, the human memory endures. And these "stories" were more than fables or moral tales; they often contained vital information within the narrative to ensure the tribe's survival in one of the harshest environments on the planet. These Aborigine legends were essentially "survival guides," containing much factual information, though perhaps expressed in story form for ease of teaching to children and to assist the memorizing process. What is truly extraordinary here, of course, is how intact these Aborigine stories have remained over this lengthy period of ten thousand years! But then, when your very survival is at stake, such stories will never be forgotten; they are literally a matter of life and death.

The Coptic-Egyptians had a similar imperative to adopt the oral tradition to transmit much of their own ancient history, even although their ancestors were among the first in the world to invent and use written accounts. The members of this long-persecuted group (presently about 10 percent of the Egyptian population) insist that they are the direct descendants of the ancient Egyptian civilization, the custodians of the history of the pyramid builders of the Old Kingdom. The word *Copt* is a derivative of the ancient Egyptian word *Ptah,* which simply means "Egypt." There are a number of reasons why much of the ancient history of the Coptic-Egyptians was only ever transmitted across time through the oral tradition.

In her doctoral dissertation, "The Vision of Theophilus: Resistance through Orality among the Persecuted Copts," the Egyptian professor Fatin Morris Guirguis explains why the oral tradition was so important to the Coptic-Egyptian people.

> The Copts are the direct descendants of the ancient Egyptians, one of the first civilizations to introduce writing to the world. And yet, throughout much of their history, they have reverted to preserving and transmitting their literature primarily through oral means. . . . We can identify oral transmission of narrative as a covert strategy of resistance against the erosion of religious identity and the erasure of historical practices. . . .
>
> Oral transmission of narrative not only helps preserve and define certain aspects of a culture, such as its bonds to its language, location and history, but is also a particularly resilient tool with which a culture might defend itself against extinction during conditions of persecution. Hence, we might expect to find that the oral tradition will resist change to the core message of a key narrative, but will nevertheless welcome, or at least tolerate, necessary or peripheral additions and deletions to accommodate changes over time. . . .
>
> Not only can orality preserve and save a threatened culture's

history from corruption by the colonizers and those who are in power, but it can also accrue political benefits through lack of incriminating written evidence. Orality's ability to preserve secrecy, as well as collective history and identity, explains why the Copts as descendants of the ancient Egyptians, a highly literate society, and one of the earliest in human history to be credited with inventing writing, historically reverted to oral transmission to preserve their history and identity.[2]

Throughout their history, the Coptic-Egyptians were subjected to three major waves of invasion and persecution by outsiders: the Macedonians under Alexander the Great, circa 323 BCE, the Romans under Augustus Caesar, circa 31 BCE, and finally the Arab invasion, circa 639 CE. Of these conquests, Morris Guirguis further tells us:

> This brutal persecution achieved its effects; by the end of the eleventh century, the overwhelming majority of the Copts no longer used Coptic in their everyday exchanges. Manuscripts provide further evidence of this massive linguistic shift: By the twelfth century most of the Coptic manuscripts had to be translated into Arabic while the original physical Coptic manuscripts were neglected; today most of these originals have been lost or destroyed.[3]

With their culture suppressed from the time of Alexander the Great, it is little wonder that the Coptic-Egyptian people were effectively forced into memorizing their history and passing it on through the generations purely by oral means. Fragments of this oral history relating to the pyramids of Giza were eventually committed to the written form in early medieval times by a number of Arabic scholars (obviously keen to learn of the origins of these remarkable structures). The earliest Arabic translation of these Coptic-Egyptian legends seems to have been translated at some time between 840 CE and 874 CE. The most complete of these translations was included in the *Akhbār al-zamān* (The history of time) and tells us of the builder of the pyramids, King Sūrīd, and the reason for their construction. While the authorship of this early medieval tome is uncertain, some scholars believe it to have been the work of the Arabic historian al-Masudi. Later versions of the pyramid legend were also written by Murtada ibn al-Afif, Al Maqrizi, Ibn Abd al-Hakam, Abu Mashar, and Ibrahim ibn Wasif Shah, among others. The scholar Sándor Fodor tells us, "This Arabic text of the Surīd legend was translated from Coptic . . . the translation was made in A.H. 225, i.e., in 840/841 AD."[4]

In his published account of his pyramid explorations, Vyse (quoting the scholar Aloys Sprenger), states:

> It appears from M. Quatremere's dissertation, that the traditions of the antient Egyptians were preserved by their descendants, the Copts, who were held in great respect by the Arabs. It is also said, that, in the reign of Ahmed Ben Touloun, who conquered Egypt about 260 A.H. [874 AD], a learned man, above one hundred years old, and of either Coptic or Nabathaean extraction, lived in Upper Egypt. This person had visited many countries, and was well informed of the antient history of Egypt, and was, by order of Ahmed Ben Touloun, examined before an assembly of learned Maliometans; and Masoudi's [al-Masudi's] account of the Pyramids is said to have been given upon the authority of this learned man. . . . Masoudi affirms, in the Akbar-Ezzeman, that he wrote his account of Surīd from a Coptic modern history.[5]

And so, in this Arabic translation of the original Coptic-Egyptian tradition, we read of a quite different purpose for the pyramids. Vyse, continuing to quote Sprenger's comments on the Surīd legend given by Al-Masudi, states in the appendix of *Operations,* volume II:

> That Surīd, Ben Shaluk, Ben Sermuni, Ben Termidun, Ben Tedresan, Ben Sal, one of the kings of Egypt before the flood, built the two great Pyramids . . . that the reason for building the Pyramids was the following dream, which happened to Surīd three hundred years previous to the flood. It appeared to him, that the earth was overthrown, and that the inhabitants were laid prostrate upon it;

that the stars wandered confusedly from their courses, and clashed together with a tremendous noise.

The king, although greatly affected by this vision, did not disclose it to any person, but was conscious that some great event was about to take place. Soon afterwards in another vision, he saw the fixed stars descend upon the earth in the form of white birds, and seizing the people, enclose them in a cleft between two great mountains, which shut upon them. The stars were dark, and veiled with smoke. The king awoke in great consternation, and repaired to the temple of the sun, where, with great lamentations, he prostrated himself in the dust. Early in the morning he assembled the chief priests from all the nomes of Egypt, a hundred and thirty in number; no other persons were admitted to this assembly, when he related his first and second vision. The interpretation was declared to announce, "that some great event would take place."

The high priest, whose name was Philimon or Iklimon, spoke as follows:—"Grand and mysterious are thy dreams: The visions of the king will not prove deceptive, for sacred is his majesty. I will now declare unto the king a dream, which I also had a year ago, but which I have not imparted to any human being." The king said, "Relate it, O Philimon." The high-priest accordingly began:—"I was sitting with the king upon the tower of Amasis. The firmament descended from above till it overshadowed us like a vault. The king raised his hands in supplication to the heavenly bodies, whose brightness was obscured in a mysterious and threatening manner. The people ran to the palace to implore the king's protection; who in great alarm again raised his hands towards the heavens, and ordered me to do the same; and behold, a bright opening appeared over the king, and the sun shone forth above; these circumstances allayed our apprehensions, and indicated, that the sky would resume its former altitude; and fear together with the dream vanished away.

The king then directed the astrologers to ascertain by taking the altitude whether the stars foretold any great catastrophe, and the result announced an approaching deluge. The king ordered them to inquire whether or not this calamity would befall Egypt; and they answered, yes, the flood will overwhelm the land, and destroy a large portion of it for some years.

He ordered them to inquire if the earth would again become fruitful, or if it would continue to be covered with water. They answered that its former fertility would return. The king demanded what would then happen. He was informed that a stranger would invade the country, kill the inhabitants, and seize upon their property; and that afterwards a deformed people, coming from beyond the Nile, would take possession of the kingdom; upon which the king ordered the Pyramids to be built, and the predictions of the priests to be Inscribed upon columns, and upon the large stones belonging to them; and he placed within them his treasures, and all his valuable property. . . . He also ordered the priests to deposit within them, written accounts of their wisdom and acquirements in the different arts and sciences.[6]

So here we have an entirely different picture as to the original purpose of the first pyramids of ancient Egypt—that they were constructed as some kind of repository or ark to help preserve all that was essential to ensure that the ancient kingdom could "reboot" itself after an anticipated, devastating deluge. These first pyramids, according to the Arabic translations of the Coptic-Egyptian oral tradition, were not constructed as the tomb of the king* but rather as the womb of the kingdom, as recovery devices or instruments of revivification that would ensure the rebirth or afterlife of a kingdom that was soon to be laid waste by some mighty natural disaster—a great deluge.

And the ancient Egyptians were not the only peoples who held such a tradition. Vyse quotes Sprenger once more as saying:

The idea of a resuscitation of the world after a certain period, appear to have been alluded to by the Hindoos in their mythology, and also by the Parsees; and Herodotus states, that this was also the belief of the antient Egyptians.[7]

---

*There is a caveat to this that will be discussed in chapter 6.

Of course, with any narrative that has been orally passed down for hundreds or even thousands of years and which is then translated from one language into another and then another, the integrity of some elements of the original content will inevitably become compromised; parts become conflated and embellished while entirely new elements can sometimes be added, usually for political or religious reasons. But what we must keep in mind here is that these Coptic oral narratives were *not* mere whimsical stories but would have formed a vital part of the cultural heritage and identity of the Coptic-Egyptian people, whose written history was mostly expunged and denied them by their many oppressors. As such, it would have been vital to them—just as it was to the Australian Aborigines—to ensure the key elements of their history were kept as accurate as they possibly could be, resisting other cultural influences on its core narrative. Failing to keep the narrative alive and true could have placed their history in danger of being lost forever and put their very existence as a distinct culture in Egypt in peril.

In reading the full Arabic translation of the Coptic-Egyptian oral narrative, we find that it contains elements that are self-evidently true. There are three main pyramids at Giza, two large ones and a smaller pyramid. The largest is to the east of the plateau, while the smallest to the south of the plateau is partly colored with red granite in its lower section. The bracing together of the stones is described as accomplished with the use of chiseled notches in the blocks into which would be poured molten metal, and we find evidence of such a binding method on some of the stone blocks at Giza. The narrative further informs us that the pyramids have various chambers and passages both above and below ground: again, this is perfectly true. The narrative tells us that some of the blocks were brought from Aswan, some 540 miles from Giza: again, all true. The king who built the structure is said to have been Surīd, a name that is believed to be a corruption of the name Suphis, that is, the Khufu of ancient Egypt that Egyptologists believe was the builder of the Great Pyramid.[8]

Fodor writes, "Manetho names the second ruler of the IVth Dynasty Σοῦφις [Sufis], and he is in fact Kheops . . . the name Σοῦφις could easily have been misread by the translator or copyist as Σοῦριδ, thus furnishing the base for the Arabic form Sūrīd."[9] If so, then, once again, the Coptic-Egyptian oral tradition gets it right.

There are, however, elements in the narrative that do seem quite fantastical, such as, for example, the moving of the blocks from the quarry to the pyramid with the use of paper that caused the stones to somehow rise to the pyramid like an arrow being shot through the air. While such a story may sound bizarre and barely credible to our modern thinking, there may actually be an underlying truth to such a strange statement; the problem may simply be that the manner by which the stones were raised is being described using "analogous language" without any mention of the underlying lifting mechanism, that is, the *science* that might have permitted stone blocks to move through the air in such a fashion. What this fanciful language of the narrative may, in fact, be alluding to is an ancient understanding and use of thermodynamics, the use of a tethered hot air balloon made of paper (and perhaps also linen, just like the first Montgolfier balloons) to lift the blocks from the quarry, up into the air, all the way to the pyramid.*

Just like the orally transmitted Homeric epic poems, the *Iliad* and the *Odyssey,* we will likely never know for sure just how old the Coptic-Egyptian oral narrative truly is. It seems likely, though, that core elements of the Sūrīd legend predate the Jewish, Christian, and Muslim embellishments, having been passed down by the Coptic-Egyptian oral tradition from generation to generation for hundreds or even many thousands of years. In this regard, Fodor, having extensively studied the Sūrīd legend, informs us:

> It seems logical to look for the origin of the elements of the [Sūrīd] legend in the Egypt of the Hellenistic and the Pharonic Age. . . .
>
> The frame-story, containing the dreams, merges Egyptian elements with motifs taken from Jewish and Christian apocalyptic literature. The prophecy uses the general topoi of the Hermetic Asclepius but in the Sūrīd legend, since they are closely associated

---

*You can find a detailed explanation of this concept in my earlier book *The Secret Chamber of Osiris: Lost Knowledge of the Sixteen Pyramids,* 182–98.

with a definite king and definite events, they gain a more concrete meaning. The Christian influence transferred the emphasis to the Biblical Flood; the Flood of the Sūrīd legend, however, takes place not in a dark, mythical age, but in a chronologically determined period of Egyptian national history. . . .

The exact time of the birth of the Sūrīd legend is impossible to establish. . . .

The Christian influence manifest in the story indicates that it cannot have gained its final form earlier than the second half of the 3rd century. The development of the legend must have taken a longer time, so that only its final shape can be the work of a Christian. Naturally, the story was not handed down in an unchanged form by the Copts and the Arabs, but with minor changes and additions.[10]

While it is clear from his extended paper that Fodor views this Coptic-Egyptian account of Sūrīd as being mostly legendary in nature—a fable—he does, however, concede that there are elements to it that are clearly ancient Egyptian in origin, that these particular elements could possibly stretch as far back as the "Pharonic Age," and that the story comes from "a chronologically determined period of Egyptian national history." This is to say that Fodor appears to accept that some Egyptian elements of the Sūrīd story may actually be *historical* in nature and that it is *not* entirely a fable. It seems then that—as the old saying goes—at the heart of every legend there really is a grain of truth.

Given Fodor's comments on the Sūrīd "legend," then it surely becomes entirely possible that the legend's grain of truth, the construction of the pyramids as a means for Sūrīd's kingdom to be reborn after a devastating deluge, might not be of a legendary or mythical nature at all. Rather, at its heart, there are actual facts based on a true historical account (however distorted the account is made out to be through its use of analogous language and later by other cultural additions, conflations, and embellishments).

As briefly outlined earlier in this chapter, many of the claims in this ancient Coptic-Egyptian oral tradition can be shown to be factually correct and true, including, it seems, the very name of the builder of the

Great Pyramid. But what about other, more contentious and seemingly outlandish aspects of the narrative, such as the stars wandering from their normal course or, indeed, the deluge itself? What evidence, if any, is there to support these controversial aspects of the ancient Coptic-Egyptian oral tradition?

3

Wandering Stars

The Coptic-Egyptian oral tradition tells us that "the stars wandered confusedly from their courses." The first thing to observe here, of course, is that stars wandering from their normal courses across the heavens can only occur with a disturbance of some kind to the regular geodynamics of the Earth. Such a disturbance would, to an Earth-based observer, give the *appearance* that the stars (and other celestial bodies) are moving from their normal path across the sky, when, in fact, it is the Earth that is deviating from *its* normal course via a rapid pole shift. While modern science dismisses the possibility of such a calamitous event, it is perhaps worth remembering that there are many eyewitness accounts from numerous sources all over the world that speak to us of just such a calamity having occurred in our ancient past.

> And Noah saw that the Earth had tilted and that its destruction was near.[1]

> Behold, the Lord maketh the earth empty, and maketh it waste, and turneth it upside down. . . . The earth shall reel to and fro like a drunkard . . . and it shall fall, and not rise again.[2]

> And it shall come to pass in that day, saith the Lord God, that I will cause the sun to go down at noon, and I will darken the earth in the clear day.[3]

The pillars of heaven were broken and the corners of the earth gave way. Hereupon Nu Kua melted stones of the five colours to repair the heavens, and cut off the feet of the tortoise to set upright the four extremities of the earth. Gathering the ashes of reeds she stopped the flooding waters and thus rescued the land of Chi.[4]

The earth shook to its foundations. The sky sank lower towards the north. The sun, moon and stars changed their motions. The earth fell to pieces and the waters in its bosom uprushed with violence and overflowed . . . the system of the universe was totally disordered.[5]

Now this has the form of a myth, but really signifies a declination of the bodies moving in the heavens around the earth, and a great conflagration of things upon the earth, which recurs after long intervals.[6]

This time he ordered the Twins, Poquanghoya and Palongawhoya, to leave their stations at the North and South poles and let the world be destroyed. . . . After the Twins left their stations, the world's stability was removed and so it flipped end over end and everything on it was destroyed by ice.[7]

In his controversial book *Worlds in Collision* (1950), the Russian scholar Immanuel Velikovsky proposed that in remote antiquity the Earth suffered a series of catastrophes as a result of a reorientation of its terrestrial axis and cited many additional ancient sources that testify to this cataclysmic event.

In the second book of his history, Herodotus relates his conversations with Egyptian priests on his visit to Egypt. . . . The priests asserted that within historical ages and since Egypt became a kingdom, four times in this period (so they told me) the sun rose contrary to his wont; twice he rose where he now sets, and twice he set where he now rises.

Velikovsky goes on to present a wealth of other documentary evidence from Egypt and much farther afield, all testifying to the veracity of an ancient pole shift event:

> Pomponius Mela, a Latin author of the first century, wrote: "the course of the stars has changed direction four times, and that the sun has set twice in that part of the sky where it rises today."
>
> The Magical Papyrus Harris speaks of a cosmic upheaval of fire and water when "the south becomes north, and the Earth turns over."
>
> In the Papyrus Ipuwer it is similarly stated that "the land turns round [over] as does a potter's wheel" and the "Earth turned upside down."
>
> In the Ermitage Papyrus (Leningrad, 1116b recto) also, reference is made to a catastrophe that turned the "land upside down."
>
> Harakhte is the Egyptian name for the western sun. . . . The inscriptions do not leave any room for misunderstanding: "Harakhte, he riseth in the west."
>
> The texts found in the pyramids say that the luminary [the sun] "ceased to live in the occident [the west], and shines, a new one, in the orient [the east]."
>
> Plato wrote in his dialogue, "The Statesman" (*Politicus*) "I mean the change in the rising and setting of the sun and the other heavenly bodies, how in those times they used to set in the quarter where they now rise, and used to rise where they now set. . . . At certain periods the universe has its present circular motion, and at other periods it revolves in the reverse direction."
>
> According to a short fragment of a historical drama by Sophocles (Atreus), the sun rises in the east is only since its course was reversed. "Zeus . . . changed the course of the sun, causing it to rise in the east and not in the west."
>
> Caius Julius Solinus, a Latin author of the third century of the present era, wrote of the people living on the southern borders of Egypt: "The inhabitants of this country say that they have it from their ancestors that the sun now sets where it formerly rose."
>
> "The Chinese say that it is only since a new order of things has come

about that the stars move from east to west. . . . The signs of the Chinese zodiac have the strange peculiarity of proceeding in a retrograde direction, that is, against the course of the sun."

The Eskimos of Greenland told missionaries that in an ancient time the earth turned over and the people who lived then became antipodes.

In Tractate Sanhedrin of the Talmud it is said: "Seven days before the deluge, the Holy One changed the primeval order and the sun rose in the west and set in the east."

The Egyptian papyrus known as Papyrus Anastasi IV contains a complaint about gloom and the absence of solar light; it says also: "The winter is come as (instead of) summer, the months are reversed, and the hours disordered."[8]

Given the prevalence of so many eyewitness accounts from antiquity testifying to the reality of such a calamitous event, can our modern scientists really be so certain that rapid geographic pole shifts/Earth inversions are as impossible as they claim? Are we to believe that all of these ancient eyewitness accounts of the sky falling, of the Earth tumbling, of the stars changing direction, of the sun rising in the west and setting in the east, of the seasons reversing are but mere legends, the vivid imaginings of primitive people? Or is there truth in what they say, and are we arrogantly dismissing their message at our peril?

Proceeding on the basis that there may well be an element of truth to these ancient accounts, if the stars in the heavens had moved from their regular course at some time in our ancient past, then what might have been interpreted as a sign from the heavens would not bode well and, naturally, would be viewed by many (even today) as an ill omen. As such, it is perfectly understandable that Sūrīd's astronomer-priests, by observing this apparent turmoil in the heavens, would have predicted dire consequences for their kingdom, one of which was the foretelling of a great deluge some centuries in their future. And it is worth emphasizing this point: the Coptic-Egyptian legend tells us that the stars wandered from their regular path across the heavens (in other words, a pole shift event was seemingly *already in progress*) and that only after observing this ominous portent unfolding in the heavens did the king order the construction of the pyramid recovery vaults in an effort to secure the kingdom's future after the deluge. While the ongoing pole shift event itself would almost certainly have brought with it untold disaster and misfortune to many parts of the world, the Coptic-Egyptian tradition appears to suggest that its worst effect, a great deluge that would drown the entire kingdom, was anticipated to take place a few centuries *after* the pole shift itself had begun.

In consideration of such a future calamity, the first and most natural desire would be to try to find a means to survive and recover from the disaster. The second would be to find a means of recording *what* happened and *when* it happened. Finally, were it understood by Sūrīd's astronomer-priests that this cataclysm was of a cyclical nature, it would seem expedient to also find a means of informing their descendants of the *periodicity* of these catastrophes—the duration between these events—to allow future generations to learn when the *next* event was due to occur.

We do not have to look very far to find the record of this cataclysmic event because it appears the builders recorded it within the very architecture of their pyramid recovery vaults. Through an analysis of these architectural clues, we can begin to re-create the world the ancient builders knew, the geophysical nature of the Earth before, during, and after this calamitous pole shift event occurred. However, before we consider this record, it might help us to first understand a little of the nature of pole shift events and how they might be triggered.

TYPES OF POLE SHIFTS

There are three possible scenarios by which the Earth's geographic pole can (theoretically) be changed:

1. Earth inversion (with axial inversion),
2. Earth inversion (without axial inversion), and
3. Axial wander (often called true polar wander or geographic pole shift/crustal displacement). Earth inversions may occur independently of axial wander, or they can occur simultaneously.

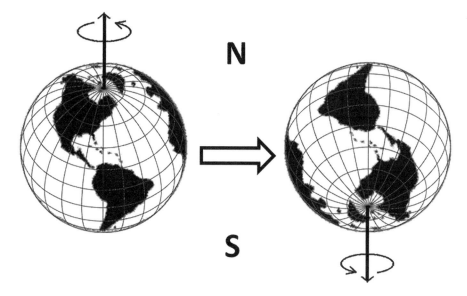

Figure 3.1. Earth before (left) *and after* (right) *an inversion (with axial inversion). The Earth's poles and equator remain in the same geographic locations, and all points on the Earth remain the same distance and orientation from the poles. The sun will continue to rise and set in the same places as before a tilt of this type.*

Earth Inversion (with Axial Inversion)

In this scenario, the Earth tumbles over in space *along with* its rotational axis, which means the sun will continue to rise in the east and set in the west. The North and South Poles (though now inverted) remain in the same geographic locations, as does the Earth's equator (fig. 3.1). With a pole shift of this nature, any monuments built anywhere on Earth, such as the Great Pyramid or the Sphinx, would keep the very same orientation toward the cardinal directions.

Earth Inversion (without Axial Inversion)

With this inversion of the Earth, its rotational axis remains in place (relative to the fixed stars) and does *not* tumble with the planet. Such a scenario may seem counterintuitive, but as shown by physicist Peter Warlow, a spinning object can, in fact, be "decoupled" from its rotational axis. Warlow demonstrated the principle of this by spinning a simple tippe-top.* Shortly after the top begins its spin, it will perform a 180° inversion while its rotational axis remains *unaffected* (the axis does not tumble with the top). As a result of this, the top continues to spin in the *same direction* after its 180° flip, and in this scenario, we find that north and south exchange positions but so *also* do sunrise and sunset; the sun would now rise in the west and set in the east with such an inversion.

> The rotation and the rotational axis are left alone and basically all that happens is that the geographic poles are displaced away from the rotation poles. The displacement of the geographic poles is, of course, a well-known and much discussed phenomenon amongst catastrophists of all schools. The uniqueness of my tippe-top thesis is that it points out a fact that everyone failed to recognise, namely that, if the displacement of the geographic poles is taken to an extreme, the result is not only an effective north-south inversion but also an effective east-west reversal as far as the motion of the Sun and stars across the sky is concerned.[9]

Warlow also extends his theory to explain the Earth's geomagnetic flips, of which there have been many in our ancient past, the magnetic orientations of which have been recorded in rocks that were once ancient lava flows. Conventional wisdom maintains that it is the Earth's magnetic field that flips while the Earth remains stable and upright, whereas Warlow contends that it is the Earth itself that flips while the magnetic field remains in place. During his research, Warlow calculated that a complete inversion of the Earth could, in theory, occur in as little as fourteen days. While all locations across the Earth would maintain the same distance to the inverted poles and the equator, the *climate* in most locations across the planet could change dramatically, depending

---

*Wikipedia defines a tippe-top as "a kind of top that, when spun, will spontaneously invert itself to spin on its narrow stem." They were invented in 1950 by the Danish engineer Werner Ostberg.

on how much the tilt angle of the Earth's rotational axis changed (if at all) during any inversion event.

Axial Wander (True Polar Wander or Geographic Pole Shift/Crustal Displacement)

The term "axial wander" or "polar wander" is something of a misnomer here since it is not actually the rotational axis itself that migrates but rather the Earth around it: the rotational axis remains in place (relative to the fixed stars). Because the Earth is not a rigid body but has a fluid and semifluid interior, this allows for the redistribution of mass within the planet's core to occur. Such a redistribution of mass may, on occasion, result in an imbalance that can change the planet's moment of inertia and, ultimately, may induce a reorientation of the planet itself (around its fixed axial rotation). We would then see that, while the rotational axis itself remained fixed, the Earth's surface would precess in a spiral fashion (thereby conserving angular momentum) around and through the fixed rotating axis; a spiraling "path of the pole" would bring other parts of the Earth into the polar regions (in essence, around the poles) while moving the former polar regions *away* from the poles into more temperate zones, a factor that (as previously stated) would

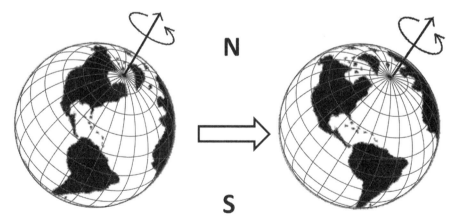

Figure 3.2. Earth before (left) and after (right) an axial wander from the Arctic Sea to the southeast of Greenland. All latitudes on Earth would change as would the location of the poles, the equator, and (with a full inversion of this type) the sunrise and sunset would also swap places.

also be influenced by any change to the obliquity (tilt angle) of the planet's axis, which may simultaneously occur as a result of the geographic shift event. In this type of pole shift event, all points across the Earth would change their relative position to the poles, the equator, and all cardinal directions, and upon a full inversion and with the rotational axis the same as before, the sun would then appear to rise in the west and set in the east (fig. 3.2).

While mainstream science mostly rejects the possibility of rapid, massive pole shift events, it does, nevertheless, accept that the Earth's surface can wander far from its rotational axis and refers to this motion as true polar wander. The view of science, however, is that this type of motion occurs very, very slowly, typically around 0.2° every million years or so. Science further insists that there is no physical evidence of any significant pole shift event having occurred in recent geological epochs. This view, however, may be a shortsighted one.

> In his dismissal of theories of ancient civilizations, Brass (2002) states that there is no paleomagnetic evidence for Earth crustal displacements having occurred. As noted earlier, Kirschvink et al. (1997) concluded from paleomagnetic data collected in Australia and North America that a massive crustal shift did occur between 534 million and 505 million years ago. Paleomagnetic dating methods are intended to measure geological processes that occur over timescales of millions of years. Although it is beyond the scope of the present article to elaborate on this point, the absence of paleomagnetic evidence of Hapgood pole shifts may not be evidence of absence but could be due to the inability of paleomagnetic dating methods to temporally resolve and thus detect climate-induced events occurring over timescales that are two or more orders of magnitude faster than tectonic processes.[10]

Slow, gradual true polar wander may well be the natural and normal state of our planet's polar wander cycle, occurring as part of the long, uniform fluctuations in the geodynamics of the Earth. However, what our ancient texts seem to be speaking of is a catastrophic event that occurred in the prehistoric era that punctuated the otherwise gradual and regular motions of the Earth, a time when an *abnormal* polar wander event occurred suddenly and rapidly, giving birth to a new age of the sun and a very different world.

POSSIBLE MECHANISMS

Modern scientists tell us that the only means by which there could be sufficient external force to bring about a reorientation of the Earth's poles would be a direct collision of the Earth with a planet-sized object. There is simply no mechanism, they insist, that could bring about such a rapid migration of the Earth's geographic poles without, at the same time, vaporizing every living organism on the planet.

More recently, however, a number of scientists (such as the previously referenced Peter Warlow) have brought that long-held view into question and have formulated various alternative pole shift mechanisms whereby a life-extinction collision of the Earth with another planet-sized object is not, in fact, required to bring about a complete inversion of the Earth.

These other proposed mechanisms generally fall under the following categories: asteroid or comet impacts (on land or sea), instability of the Earth's ice caps, grand planetary alignments, massive deluges or tsunamis, sunspots, galactic core explosions, coronal mass ejections, tidal forces from the close transit to the Earth of a planetary-sized object on a highly eccentric orbit, deep-Earth nuclear explosions, the Dzhanibekov effect, and a variety of other, more exotic, possibilities.

Some of the more credible modern theories are backed by considerable scientific research and mathematical modeling. We should keep in mind, however, that it may not have been a single mechanism that brought about the onset of a geographic pole shift event in our ancient past but rather a combination of particular conditions. For example, the close passing of a Mars-sized object may have induced colossal tidal forces on and within our planet, resulting in a sudden and rapid redistribution of mass when oceans and ice caps were "dislocated." Such massive upheaval could then have caused an imbalance on or within the

Earth, which, in turn, may have triggered the tumbling motion known as the Dzhanibekov effect.

Although the mathematics describing this peculiar motion have been known since the early nineteenth century, the phenomenon itself had gone wholly unnoticed until 1985, when the cosmonaut Vladimir Dzhanibekov first observed it during a space mission to repair the Russian Salyut-7 space station. Dzhanibekov was unscrewing a wing nut, which he did with a flick of his fingers. As the wing nut spun free from its bolt, it carried on in a straight line, spinning through the station's zero gravity environment. As it spun, Dzhanibekov noticed that, at regular intervals and with no external force being applied, the wing nut flipped a full 180°, back and forth, again and again and again. The Russian government kept Dzhanibekov's observation classified for ten years until they understood its cause, which we now know is the natural consequence of an object spinning around its least stable axis. It is also known as the tennis racket theorem or the intermediate axis theorem. Since the spherical Earth has only one axis of rotation and is gyroscopically stable (due to its equatorial bulge), scientists believe that it is impossible for the Dzhanibekov effect to flip it over. The great unknown, however, is what would happen if a second/intermediate rotational axis was introduced due to a sudden and massive redistribution of mass, either in the Earth's core or on its surface. Might then the Earth (or at least its outer shell) behave more like a tippe-top than a gyroscope?

While it is likely that there is no single mechanism that could trigger the onset of an Earth inversion event, we will now consider here three possible mechanisms that might bring about a redistribution of mass that could potentially induce a reversal of the planet's poles.

Crustal Slippage (Atomic Core Explosion)

One such mechanism that does perhaps deserve particular mention is that formulated by Chan Thomas in the early 1950s. Intrigue surrounded the publication of his theory in his 1993 book *The Adam and Eve Story*, which, for reasons unexplained, the CIA had withdrawn and censored, with only a heavily redacted version of it appearing in pdf format on the CIA website in 2013. Thomas writes:

> Once every few thousand years neutral matter escapes from the 860-mile-radius inner core into the 1300-mile thick molten outer core, and there is a literal atomic explosion inside the Earth. The explosion in the high energy layer of the outer core disrupts completely the electrical and magnetic structure in both the molten outer core and the outer 60-mile thick molten layer. Finally the ice caps are allowed to pull the shell of the earth around the interior, with the shallow molten layer lubricating the shift all the way.
>
> You can see, then, that ice ages are not a matter of advancing and retreating ice; it's simply that different areas of the Earth are in polar regions at different times, for different durations of time, with the changes between positions taking place in a fraction of a day.[11]

To this day, Thomas's work remains censored and redacted on the CIA website. For whatever reason, the CIA has deemed it necessary that the general public does not get to see the full content of this publication, and we can only speculate as to why that would be.

Asteroid Impact (Water)

In an article about the possibility of instantaneous pole shifts, Italian naval engineer Flavio Barbiero writes:

> An object as small as a half-kilometre-wide asteroid, hitting the planet in the right spot and at the right angle, is capable of developing an impulsive torque of the same magnitude of the maximum Earth's reaction torque. In this case the Earth assumes, for a very short instant, a different [second] axis of rotation.
>
> If at the moment of the impact the force of the Sun-Moon gravitational attraction on the equatorial bulge has the same direction as the force developed by the impact, a shift of the poles will inevitably follow. Immediately after the impact, in fact, the torque should go down to zero, and the Earth should recover its previous rotational

axis. But if the torque exerted by the sun-moon attraction has the same direction, the torque cannot be zeroed and therefore the Earth keeps "memory" of the impact and of its direction. This "memory" consists of an extremely small rotational component, with the same direction as that of the impact, in the order of 1 millionth of the normal rotation. . . .

Under the effect of this tiny rotational component, sea water begins to move towards a circle perpendicular to that rotation (the new equator). This is a very small effect, and if it was the only component, the resulting equatorial bulge would be of a few meters only. But as this happens, the value of the rotational component increases, at the expense of the main rotation, therefore increasing the centrifugal force which makes more water move towards the new equator, thus increasing the force and so on. This process starts very slowly, but accelerates progressively, until the centrifugal force developed by this rotational component grows strong enough to induce deformations of the Earth's mantle.

From here on the equatorial bulge is quickly "re-shaped" around the new axis of rotation and Earth will soon be stable again, with a different axis of rotation and different poles.[12]

An Additional Planet (Tidal Forces)

A body in space of around the size of Mars could, during a close passage by the Earth, bring about a reorientation of the planet. This idea was put forward in the 1950s by Immanuel Velikovsky and was followed in the early 1980s by Peter Warlow. More recently, another group of scientists has analyzed this possibility, producing a mathematical model that demonstrates how such a pole shift could actually come about.

Between 3 Myr and 11.5 kyr BP a Mars-sized object existed which moved in a highly eccentric orbit. Originating from this object, gas clouds with a complex dynamics reduced Earth's insolation and caused a drop in the global temperature. In a close encounter, 11.5 kyr ago, tidal forces deformed the Earth. While the shape of the gyroscope Earth relaxed, the North Pole moved geographically from

Greenland to its present position. During this close encounter, the object was torn to pieces, each of which subsequently evaporated or plunged into the sun. These events terminated the Ice Age Epoch.[13]

It does seem, then, that some scientists, contrary to long-held scientific opinion, are now coming to the view that the reorientation of the Earth's poles can be brought about by other, less Earth-shattering mechanisms. It is one thing, however, to theorize as to how these cataclysmic events *could* come about but altogether different trying to prove that they actually did occur and were observed by our ancient ancestors. Let us now consider evidence that suggests the Earth was once oriented very differently from the present.

EARTH'S FORMER POLES

If the Coptic-Egyptian oral tradition is indeed telling us of a pole shift event that occurred in remote antiquity, a time when other texts tell us the sun rose in the west and set in the east, then where exactly were the Earth's poles formerly located? There is a considerable body of evidence from a number of sources that seems to indicate one particular location for the North Pole—southeastern Alaska. In 1958, professor Charles Hapgood proposed that the Earth's past ice ages were actually the result of different temperate zones of the Earth shifting in and out of the planet's polar regions (the great circle around the Earth's fixed axis of rotation) and that these past shift events occured several times in the past twenty thousand years or so. The evidence Hapgood presented in support of his theory was as comprehensive as it was compelling, and in his final book, *The Path of the Pole* (1970), he revised the dating of these ancient pole shift events to much more recent times, writing:

Some of the results of the chronology of the glacial epoch worked out here are surprising. For example, I have found evidence of three different positions of the North Pole in recent time. During the last glaciation in North America the pole appears to have stood in Hudson Bay, approximately in Latitude 60° North and

Longitude 83° West. It seems to have shifted to its present site in the middle of the Arctic Ocean in a gradual motion that began 18,000 or 17,000 years ago and was completed by about 12,000 years ago.[14]

In his earlier book *Earth's Shifting Crust,* Hapgood theorized that Earth's northern pole, before finally settling at its present location in the Arctic Sea, was previously located in a number of geographic locations, including southeastern Alaska, Hudson Bay, southern Greenland, and the Norwegian Sea. More recently other researchers, such as the environmentalist and author Mark H. Gaffney,[15] have also included Baffin Island as a former geographic pole location, while the engineer and author Mark J. Carlotto proposes the Bering Sea and northwestern Greenland as additional former pole locations. Intriguingly, Carlotto identified a curious correlation relating to the former poles theorized by Hapgood. Carlotto writes:

> In a previous study of more than two hundred ancient sites, the alignments of almost half of the sites could not be explained. These sites are distributed throughout the world and include the majority of the Mesoamerican pyramids and temples that are misaligned with respect to true north, megalithic structures at several sites in Peru's Sacred Valley, some pyramids in Lower Egypt, and numerous temples in Upper Egypt. A new model is proposed to account for the alignment of certain unexplained sites based on an application of Charles Hapgood's hypothesis . . . of displacements of the Earth's crust and corresponding shifts of the geographic poles. . . . The alignment of these sites are consistent with the hypothesis that if they were built in alignment with one of these former poles they would be misaligned to north as they are now as the result of subsequent geographic pole shifts.[16]

Another piece of evidence supporting southeastern Alaska as the location of the former pole comes from independent researcher Jim Alison (inspired by the earlier work of researcher and author Jim Bowles). In 2001, Alison published an article on the Graham Hancock online forum that showed that many of the Earth's most ancient sacred sites and monuments, including Giza, could be connected together with a great circle or "horizon ring" going right around the planet. Alison writes:

> The alignment of these sites is easily observable on a globe of the Earth with a horizon ring. If you line up any two of these sites on the horizon ring, all of the sites will be right on the horizon ring. . . . Inspired by Charles Hapgood's Earth crust displacement theory, . . . Bowles observes that the Great Pyramid and the Nazca lines and figures would have been on the equator if the North Pole had been in southeastern Alaska.[17]

We can observe this grand alignment of ancient sites in figure 3.3.

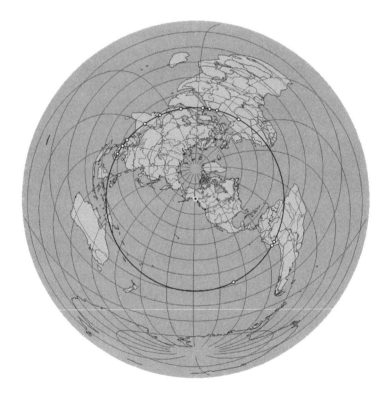

Figure 3.3. A ring of ancient sites may have been constructed along the Earth's former equator at a time when the Earth's North Pole was centered in southeastern Alaska. (Image courtesy of Jim Alison)

And so, with the Earth's North Pole centered in southeastern Alaska (as per Hapgood's original proposal) at a latitude of around 63.5° north, 146° west, this would have placed Giza within a few degrees or so from the horizon ring of this ancient equator and around 26.5° from its present latitude of just under 30° north. And so, with this data, we are perhaps seeing our first glimpse that a pole shift event may indeed have occurred in ancient times, just as many ancient traditions tell us.

But what about the Coptic-Egyptian tradition that tells us the Great Pyramid was built during this calamitous period when the stars wandered from their normal courses? What, if anything, does this monument have to say about this former Alaskan pole and how it was replaced by the Arctic Sea as the new geographic pole?

A RECORD IN STONE

Almost no one disputes that the Great Pyramid possesses a number of astronomical features built into its very architecture. We find, for example, that it is one of the most accurately aligned man-made structures in the world, with just a tiny fraction of an error in its alignment to the cardinal directions. To achieve this level of accuracy in alignment requires the use of astronomical techniques. The pyramid's inward-sloping concavities are believed by some to be equinox markers because the shadow effect they produce is most easily observed (from ground level) during the spring and autumn equinoxes. It is also believed by many Egyptologists that the monument's slopes are symbolic of the sun's rays—another astronomical association. And then we have what Egyptologists call the pyramid's star shafts, four shafts that run through the superstructure of the pyramid from the north and south sides of the King's and Queen's Chambers. It is believed by Egyptologists that these narrow shafts served to guide the king's soul to various stars in the northern and southern skies, though why the king's soul supposedly went to four different stellar destinations is never adequately explained.

Here then we have a number of architectural aspects of the Great Pyramid that Egyptologists readily accept are of an astronomical nature.

This raises the obvious question: If these aspects of the Great Pyramid are accepted as such, then is it not likely that *other* features within the structure might also be of an astronomical nature, perhaps presenting to us data about the Earth's former astronomical and geophysical status? It is entirely likely and, in fact, quite probable. Let us see.

Earth's Former Solstice and Equinox Points

A study of the Queen's Chamber and its curious niche (a narrow recess built into the chamber's east wall) may reveal additional astronomical clues of our planet's former geophysical properties (fig. 3.4). Egyptologists believe that this corbelled recess was designed to contain a statue of Khufu. However, there's another, more radical interpretation of this feature.

Since the east wall in this chamber is aligned almost perfectly due east, then a vertical line from the apex of the chamber's gabled roof to the floor, dividing the wall into two equal parts, would essentially represent the *equinoctial point,* that is, due east. The angle from the apex of the roof to the chamber's side walls (at floor level) may then also indicate the angular limits of the summer and winter solstice points at around 23° north and south of due east (fig. 3.5).

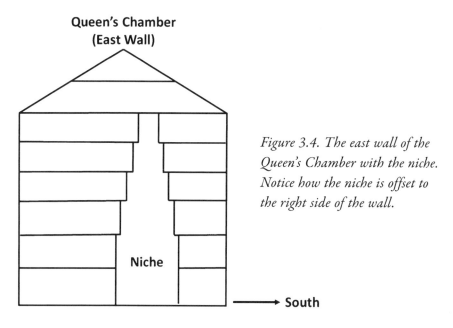

**Queen's Chamber
(East Wall)**

Niche

⟶ **South**

Figure 3.4. The east wall of the Queen's Chamber with the niche. Notice how the niche is offset to the right side of the wall.

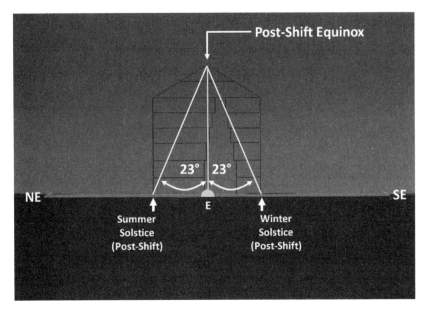

Figure 3.5. A vertical line from the apex of the roof to the floor of the east wall of the Queen's Chamber may represent the post–pole shift equinoctial position of the sun on the eastern horizon, while the angle from the apex to the side walls may represent the angular limit between the summer and winter solstice points.

But how does this help explain the purpose of the niche? There is an optical illusion known as the "moon illusion," a phenomenon that also happens with the sun. When the sun is close to the horizon (rising or setting), it can appear much larger than when it is high up in the sky. If we now consider the curious and unique feature of the niche within the east wall of the Queen's Chamber (fig. 3.4), we find that it is wider at the bottom and gradually narrows as it rises in height, just like the rising sun illusion can often appear. And so, accepting that the center of this chamber's east wall represents the post–pole shift equinoctial point (due east; fig. 3.5), then it may be that the offset position of the niche represents the pre–pole shift equinoctial position of the *rising* sun some 6° to the south of east (fig. 3.6), with its side walls perhaps also representing the angular distance between the former solstice points (fig. 3.7) in the pre–pole shift world.

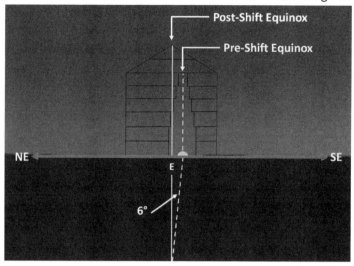

Figure 3.6. The corbelled design and offset position of the niche may have been designed to represent the pre–pole shift equinoctial point of the rising sun at 6° south of east. (Note: post-shift the sun will now set on the eastern horizon.)

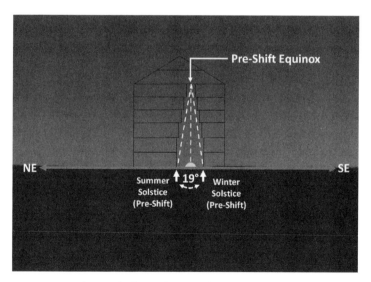

Figure 3.7. The angle from the top of the niche to the side walls may represent the pre–pole shift angular limit between the summer and winter solstice points. Such a narrow angular distance between the solstices suggests that Giza, at this time, was much closer to the equator and that the Earth's axial tilt was different.

Two Motions

One of the most curious aspects of the Great Pyramid is the prevalence in its internal design of two particular angles—6° and 26.5° (fig. 3.8). We find the 26.5° angle in the slope of the Ascending Passage, with a mirrored angle branching into the Descending Passage, as well as in the incline of the Grand Gallery. Likewise, the angle of 6°, as we have already seen with the 6° offset position of the niche, is also found in several other key features of this monument. That we find these two angles being repeatedly used in different aspects of the pyramid's architecture suggests that (*a*) they were purposely encoded into the monument, and (*b*) they must serve a particular function, most likely of an astronomical or geophysical nature.

And it's not just within the pyramid that these angles appear. In addition to his observation of the former Alaskan pole and Giza being close to the horizon ring, Bowles also observed a peculiarity in the orientation of the Sphinx at Giza. He writes, "Interestingly, this

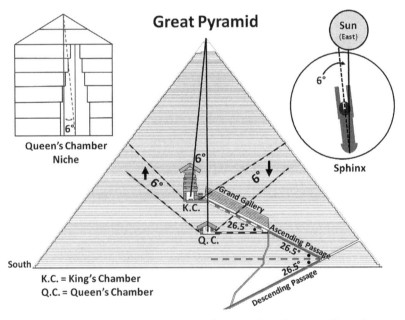

Figure 3.8. The angles of 26.5° and 6° are found repeatedly in key architectural features of the Great Pyramid and possibly also the Sphinx. Note the mirroring effect of the 26.5° angle between the Ascending and Descending Passages.

[Alaskan pole] equator passed through Giza, Egypt at 5° north of east, and the spine of the Sphinx (itself laying 5° north of east) follows this ancient equator with precise accuracy."[18]

Assuming that the 5° Sphinx misalignment from due east observed by Bowles is actually nearer to 6°, then it too would fit into the pattern observed within the various features of the Great Pyramid. Assuming further that these two values, 6° and 26.5°, are indeed astronomical in nature, then what is it that they are telling us? How do they fit together into a cohesive, astronomical picture? If Hapgood, Bowles, and Alison are right that the Earth's North Pole was once located in southeastern Alaska, thereby placing Giza much closer to the equator, then we may, in fact, already have the answer to this particular question, for if we relocate the Earth's North Pole from its present location in the Arctic Sea and move it to southeastern Alaska (where it was once theoretically located), then something rather remarkable occurs (fig. 3.9).

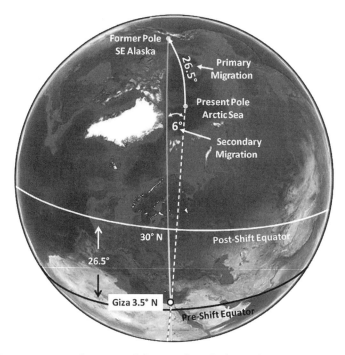

Figure 3.9. A relocation of the North Pole from the Arctic Sea to southeastern Alaska produces the two key angles of 26.5° and 6° that we observe in the Great Pyramid.

As we can see in figure 3.9, for the Arctic Sea to replace southeastern Alaska as the new geographic pole, then the planet would need to pivot, simultaneously, in two directions: a larger vertical (primary) pivot of 26.5° with a smaller horizontal (secondary) pivot of around 6°—the very same two angles we find repeated again and again within the key features of the Great Pyramid (fig. 3.8). In reality, these two motions would occur in a single, curving action on the Earth's sphere, but they would each present different observable astronomical effects that would require different architectural features within the pyramid to convey.

The Primary Motion (26.5°)

If we accept that Giza was formerly located at a latitude of around 3.5° north, then clearly to have it at its present latitude of around 30° north, Giza had to have shifted a further 26.5° from the equator. And this may be the astronomical data that the Grand Gallery within the Great Pyramid, inclined at 26.5°, is conveying to us (fig. 3.10): that Giza was shifted by 26.5° from a former latitude of 3.5° north to a new latitude of just under 30° north. Of course, if Giza was raised by 26.5°, then it would have been observed that the sun must, conversely, have fallen in the sky by the same figure (a phenomenon described by some of our ancient eyewitness accounts).

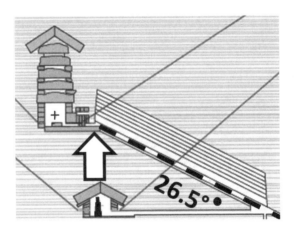

Figure 3.10. The 26.5° slope of the Grand Gallery
may be conveying that Giza was raised by 26.5°, from
3.5° north to its present latitude of around 30° north.

The Secondary Motion (6°)

We saw that during the pole shift event when the Arctic Sea moved toward the Earth's northern rotational axis to become the new geographic pole (fig. 3.9), that it did so in a curved movement consisting of a primary motion of 26.5° and a smaller secondary motion of 6°, each of which would have presented different astronomical effects to a ground-based observer. While the primary motion apparently raised Giza's latitude by some 26.5° (thereby lowering the sun by 26.5°), it seems that, simultaneously, the smaller secondary motion actually raised the southern stars (including Orion's Belt) some 6° *higher* in altitude (fig. 3.11), a counterintuitive and somewhat paradoxical motion of the heavens that the builders appear to have built into the pyramid's four star shafts.

A quick analysis of these four shafts shows that the angular difference of each pair, just like the Queen's Chamber's niche and the Sphinx, is offset by around 6° and that the trajectories of the two north shafts present a crossover point while the south shafts do not.

What this configuration seems to suggest is not four static points in the sky, targeting four different fixed stellar destinations for the king's soul, as Egyptologists believe, but rather just *two* points in the sky that were in *motion;* two starting points each at an altitude of around

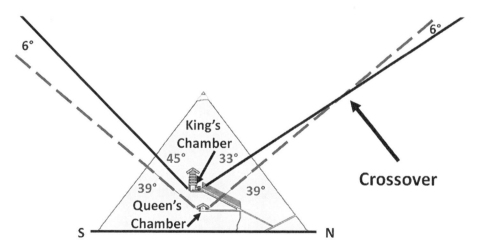

Figure 3.11. The Great Pyramid's four star shafts, showing an angular difference of around 6° between each set of shafts. Note also the crossover of the north shafts' trajectories.

39° (one in the southern sky and a mirror point in the northern sky) that moved from one position in the sky to a different position. As the southern point increases in altitude by 6° from around 39° to 45°, so its mirror point in the northern sky will correspondingly *fall* by 6° from around 39° to 33°. With one set of shafts from one chamber (the Queen's) marking the start positions and the second set of shafts in the second chamber (the King's) marking the end positions of the shift, you will inevitably end up with a crossing over of one or other set of shafts, the particular crossover set dependent on the rotational direction of the shift (clockwise or counterclockwise).

Had these shafts been built as conduits to guide the pharaoh's soul to particular afterlife destinations among the stars, as Egyptologists believe, then the shafts could just as easily have targeted the same stellar destinations without any crossover of the shaft trajectories (fig. 3.12). In this sense, the crossover seems to be indicative of something much more profound; it screams at us of the heavens in motion since its presence in the north shafts is, quite simply, the natural outcome of observing two points (stars) at opposing locations in the heavens, rotating rapidly and equidistantly around the sky from one position to another, stars wandering from their normal courses just as the ancient Coptic-Egyptian tradition tells us.

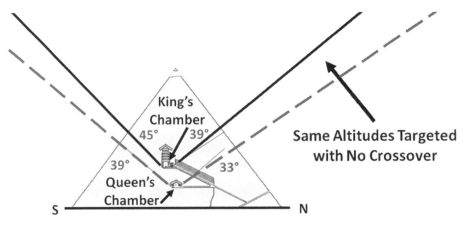

Figure 3.12. Had the pyramid's north shafts targeted destinations for the pharaoh's soul, they could have targeted these stellar destinations without any need for the crossover.

The opposing effect of the smaller secondary motion would be to lower Giza in latitude by 6° (while it was, simultaneously, rising in latitude via the larger primary motion). However, if the net outcome saw Giza raised from 3.5° north to 30° north (a net latitudinal gain of 26.5°), then the overall latitudinal shift must actually have been around 33.5°, whereby the opposing smaller secondary motion of 6° effectively cancelled out 6° of the larger primary motion, ostensibly reducing the primary motion from 33.5° to just 26.5°. Another observable astronomical effect of the smaller secondary motion would be that the cardinal directions would have shifted around the horizon also by 6°, a fact that, as noted above, may have been recorded in the positioning of the niche within the Queen's Chamber (fig. 3.6) and also in the misalignment of the Sphinx.

THE INVERSION AND THE MISALIGNED MONUMENTS

While all of the foregoing may be suggestive of a pole shift event of around 26.5°, such a shift would not have seen the world turned upside down or the sun rising and setting on the opposite horizons, as some of our ancient traditions tell us. What evidence is there, then, to tell us that in addition to Giza migrating 26.5° from the equator, the Earth also fully inverted 180° at the same time? In order to help us answer such a question, we would need to find and compare two cardinally aligned monuments, one that was built pre–pole shift and one that was built post–pole shift. Since the cardinal directions at Giza appear to have been shifted by around 6°, then we should see this disparity when comparing the alignment of the pre–pole shift monument with the post–pole shift monument. So do we have any such misaligned monuments?

The Sphinx and the Niche
We have already seen how Bowles observed that the body of the Sphinx at Giza is now aligned some 5° (possibly 6°) north of the sun's present equinoctial point while the head of the monument gazes

directly due east (having possibly been recarved from the head of a lion to the head of a pharaoh much later in dynastic Egypt). Likewise, we observed earlier that the niche in the Queen's Chamber has been aligned 6° south of our present due east. This, of course, raises the obvious question: Why is the Sphinx's body (not its head) aligned 5° (or thereabouts) north of east while the niche is aligned 6° south of east? If a pole shift event had occurred, then surely we should find that either both features are misaligned in the same direction or that one of them is misaligned from due east and the other is perfectly aligned to due east. However, with the Sphinx and the niche, we find that they are both misaligned from due east by almost the same amounts but in entirely *opposite* directions. How can this mismatch in these two features be explained?

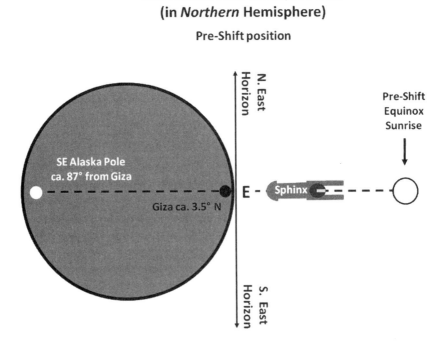

Figure 3.13. With the North Pole located in southeastern Alaska, the Sphinx (head and body) would have fully gazed due east at the equinoctial rising sun.

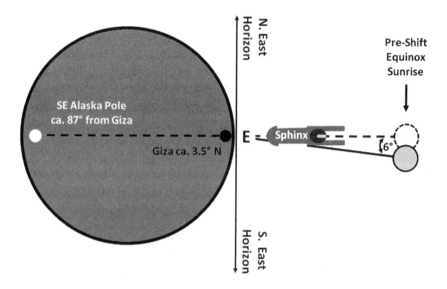

SE Alaskan Pole ca. 10,000 BCE
(in *Northern* Hemisphere)

After 6° Geographic Migration

Figure 3.14. As the geographic pole shift commences, the effect of the secondary motion would have been to shift the equinoctial point 6° to the south of east, resulting in the Sphinx becoming misaligned and now gazing around 6° north of east.

There is but one explanation, and it is one that entirely accords with what our ancient traditions tell us occurred in our ancient past: a complete inversion of the Earth whereby the sun rose in the west and set in the east (figs. 3.13–3.15). It is worth noting here that the smaller shifts of 6° and 26.5° would occur together with, and as a consequence of, the much greater 180° inversion event. In effect, the total latitudinal change amounts to 206.5° (26.5° migration + 180° inversion). Keep in mind also that the inversion event is not a simple flipping or tumbling of the planet. The Earth's rotational axis (its poles) remain in place (relative to the fixed stars) while the planet itself passes through it in a great spiraling motion (thereby conserving angular momentum).

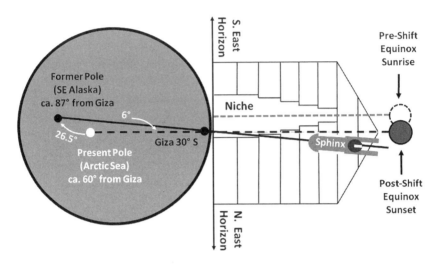

Figure 3.15. As the Earth completes its 180° inversion, this results in the Arctic Sea being relocated to the planet's polar axis and Giza rising in latitude by 26.5° but now situated at 30° south of the equator. From the perspective of the Southern Hemisphere, the sun now sets 6° to the left of the Sphinx (and rises in the west). The niche in the Queen's Chamber may have been constructed at this post–pole shift time to mark the former (pre–pole shift) rising position of the sun.

The Subterranean Chamber and the Ascending and Descending Passages

Just like the King's Chamber, the niche, and the star shafts, the Subterranean Chamber also presents the same 6° offset from the pyramid's central axis (fig. 3.16). If we consider that these three chambers are symbolic of Giza's changing latitude, then what we also observe is a mirroring (or inversion) of the Ascending and Descending Passages, perhaps indicating a 180° inversion of Giza itself. As Giza migrated in latitude by 26.5° (indicated by the Grand Gallery), it would reach its final position of 30° north of the equator. However, as the 180° Earth inver-

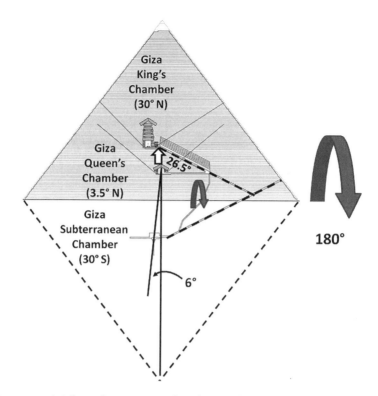

Figure 3.16. The Subterranean Chamber is also offset from the pyramid's central axis by 6°. The mirrored angles of the Ascending and Descending Passages of the Great Pyramid seem to hint also at a 180° inversion event whereby Giza, having migrated northward by 26.5°, also flipped its position from north to south of the equator.

sion progressed (perhaps indicated by the mirroring of the Ascending and Descending Passages), Giza would finally end up at 30° *south* of the equator.

After the shift was completed, the sun would now rise in the west and set in the east. Such an inversion could have occurred via a rapid true polar-wander event or via the tippe-top inversion method proposed by Peter Warlow. However the inversion actually came about, the end result would have placed Antarctica in the Northern Hemisphere while the Arctic Sea, as a result of its additional 26.5° migration, would have replaced south-eastern Alaska as the new (Southern Hemisphere) pole (fig. 3.17).

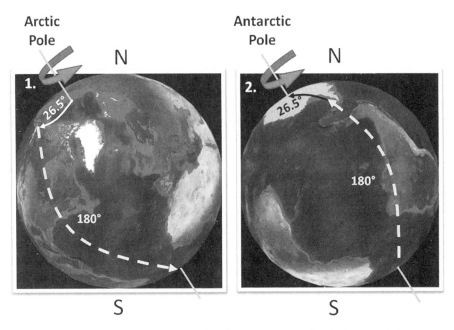

Figure 3.17. With the Arctic Sea having migrated 26.5° toward the Earth's axial rotation and as a consequence of the Earth's 180° inversion, this region will now become the new Southern Hemisphere pole with Antarctica becoming the Northern Hemisphere pole.

Facing the Dawn

With the Sphinx having originally been built to face the dawn on the eastern horizon, it seems that the ancient Egyptians must have held a great reverence for this particular cardinal direction, perhaps seeing it as the "place of rebirth," symbolized by the daily rising of the sun. However, a very curious feature of the Dream Stele, an epigraphic stone tablet that has stood for thousands of years between the paws of the Sphinx, is that it depicts the monument facing in two (opposite) directions (fig. 3.18).

Since sunrise is to the east, why does the Dream Stele also show us the Sphinx facing in the opposite direction, west? Some believe this may indicate that a second sphinx is buried somewhere in the sands to the west of the present monument but, alas, no such discovery has ever been made. There is, however, another possible interpretation as to what this

Figure 3.18. Drawing of detail from the Dream Stele that stands between the paws of the Sphinx at Giza. The stele depicts the Sphinx facing the rising sun on two opposite horizons. (Image based upon original drawing by Karl Richard Lepsius, 1842.)

dual Sphinx image on the Dream Stele is depicting. If we look just above the head of each of these Sphinx drawings on the stele we notice the *akhet* hieroglyphic sign (in the dashed box) which Egyptologists believe represents the sun rising on the horizon. So here we have the Sphinx, observing the sunrise, in the east *and* in the west. This may also explain why the Sphinx carries the ancient epithet of *Horemakhet* or "Horus of the two horizons."

Ancient Egyptians abhorred death and spent much of their life guarding against it, preparing instead not for their death but their afterlife. Accepting that the eastern horizon was regarded by them as the "place of rebirth," one might reasonably wonder why they built their pyramids on the west bank of the Nile, the west being the "land of the dead" and where the sun dies each day. Surely the east bank of the Nile, where the sun is reborn each day, would have been a more appropriate setting for monuments constructed to bring about the afterlife (be it that of the king or the kingdom).

Likewise, we might further wonder why in the so-called burial chamber of these pyramids, the sarcophagus was usually placed in the western end of the chamber, which, in our modern cosmology, is toward the setting sun. If the ancient Egyptians regarded these chambers not as burial chambers but rather as "chambers of rebirth," would it not then have been more appropriate for the so-called sarcophagus to have been placed in the eastern end of the chamber where the sun is reborn each day?

This idea of the eastern horizon as the revered "place of rebirth" is further supported by the evidence of the large numbers of mummies that have been discovered in Egpyt with their faces turned toward this particular horizon. But if, as the ancient Egyptians tell us, the sun once rose in the west, would we then not also find many burials with mummies facing toward this long-forgotten rising sun of the western horizon? In this regard, Egyptologist Kathryn A. Bard, writes:

> Brunton excavated about 750 Badarian burials, most of which were contracted ones in shallow oval pits. Most burials were placed on the left side, facing west with the head to the south. . . .
>
> Orientation of many burials was random, but the later burials in the Wadi Digla were contracted ones, placed on the right side and oriented with the head to the south facing east, unlike those recorded at Naqada, which had the head to the south facing west.[19]

Of course, the orientation of a dead body within its grave would most likely be influenced by the customs and beliefs of the particular culture involved. All that is being said here is that a reverence of the rising sun seems to have been a widespread and predominant practice throughout the entire corpus of known ancient Egyptian history and that this reverence was linked to the deeply spiritual concept of the sunrise symbolizing rebirth and the afterlife. As such, it may then be possible that the numerous west-facing burials that have been found in Egypt (most of which appear to be older burials) actually *were* buried facing the sunrise when the Earth was once upturned long ago and the sun rose in the west; it perhaps wasn't the burial custom of these different groups of ancient Egyptians that had changed but rather the direction of the dawn.

What all of this implies, of course, is that a second pole shift event (a 180° inversion with no geographic migration) must have occurred thousands of years later to reverse this geophysical configuration and to bring Giza to 30° north of the equator, the latitude it sits at today, so that the sun would rise in the east as it had before. We will see, shortly, some evidence that suggests that such a second event may indeed have occurred in (relatively) more recent times.

With everything having now been tilted another 180° (with no geographic migration occurring during this second pole shift event), we would find that the body of the Sphinx ends up aligned some five or six degrees north of due east, while the niche is now misaligned some 6° south of due east (fig. 3.19), the difference between them being around 12° as a result of the Sphinx having been aligned to due east (in the Northern Hemisphere) before the first pole shift event and the niche being aligned

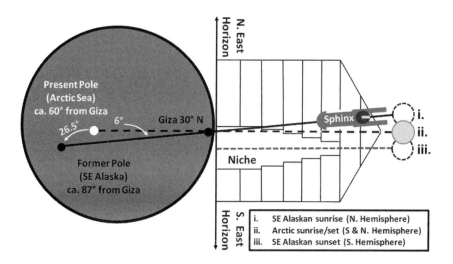

Figure 3.19. A second pole shift event reverses everything again. The sun once again rises in the east and sets in the west. The body of the Sphinx is now 6° or so misaligned toward the northeast, although its head would now have been reworked into that of the pharaoh to be facing due east toward the new equinoctial point. The niche also ends up misaligned by 6°, but to the southeast.

after that pole shift event (to mark the former position of the rising sun in the Northern Hemisphere). This same effect, of course, caused the same 12° difference between the King's Chamber's south shaft at an inclination of 45° and its north shaft at just 33°. And finally, as stated above, the burials that once faced the dawn on the western horizon would now face the sunset (the "land of the dead"), while the more recent burials would now face the dawn on the eastern horizon.

THE PATH OF THE POLE

Hapgood's original hypothesis regarding an Alaskan pole was probably quite correct, but with the caveat that all of the different locations that he had identified in the geological record for the Earth's former pole positions may actually have been part of one contiguous event, a single continuous spiral inversion, occurring over a much shorter and more recent period of time (figs. 3.20 and 3.21).

Figure 3.20. Hapgood's various locations for the Earth's former geographic pole, along with that of Gaffney (Baffin Island) and Carlotto (Bering Sea and northwestern Greenland), can be joined with a spiral.

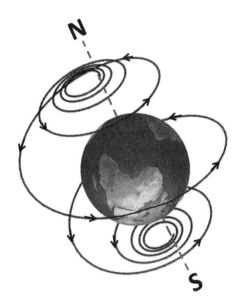

Figure 3.21. The Earth inversion occurs in a spiral motion, thereby conserving angular momentum. As the Earth inverts, its rotational axis remains fixed in stellar space; the axis does not invert with the Earth, which continues to rotate in its usual direction, resulting in the sun rising in the west and setting in the east.

If what the ancient texts are telling us is true and the foregoing astronomical interpretation of the Giza monuments is correct, then it seems that Giza was once located at around 3.5° north of the equator. In this pre-shift world, the Sphinx would likely have long existed, though probably with the body and head of a lion, and would have faced the equinoctial rising sun, due east. At just 3.5° north of the equator, Giza and the Sphinx would have been located in the Earth's equatorial region, with its heavy daily rainfalls, which might help explain the severe water erosion we find today on the Sphinx and its enclosure walls. This equatorial location of Giza, with its high rainfall, might also help explain some ancient maps that show the north-flowing Nile River with a major fork running westward from the main river toward the Sahara Desert and may further explain the "Green Sahara" or "African Humid Period," when the desert we see in this part of the world today was also much wetter and greener around 14,500 years ago.

After the tumultuous inversion event the Earth remained relatively stable for many thousands of years until around the twenty-fourth century BCE, when, as the Australian astronomer George F. Dodwell's research shows, it seems that the Earth was visited by a second pole shift event, possibly as a part of our planet's regular geophysical mechanics. This second event, however, appears to have been an inversion-only event of around 180° without any geographic migration (thus latitudes would have flipped but the cardinal directions would have remained the same, and thus the pyramids would have remained perfectly oriented to them). For the Earth to regain its easterly sunrise, the rotational axis must, once again, have remained in place (relative to the fixed stars) during this most recent shift event. And so, with this second inversion, Giza was inverted from 30° south to its present latitude of 30° north, and the sun, once more, would rise in the east and set in the west. The body of the Sphinx, however, would now be misaligned north of due east by five or six degrees, although its lion's head would probably have been reworked at this time into the head of the pharaoh to align with the new equinoctial eastern sunrise.

The Earth would undergo its most recent pole shift event around 2345 BCE, as observed by Dodwell (discussed below), a time that coincided with the demise of Egypt's Old Kingdom and other ancient contemporary cultures.

POLE SHIFTS: THE EVIDENCE

Other than the ancient texts that tell us of the stars wandering from their regular course and the Earth turning over, there is also the evidence presented by Charles Hapgood and other researchers of ancient pole shifts. Setting this aside along with the peculiar design features within the Great Pyramid that may be suggestive of such an event, what additional evidence might there be to support the view that these sudden and rapid geographic shifts of the Earth really did occur in remote antiquity?

The Dodwell Event

In the early twentieth century, an Australian astronomer, George F. Dodwell (fig. 3.22), presented scientific data to suggest that the Earth's geodynamic status was very different in ancient times. Commencing in 1934, Dodwell spent several decades doing intense research into the astronomical alignments of structures from all over the ancient world, and in

Figure 3.22. The research of Australian astronomer George F. Dodwell showed that a disturbance of the Earth's rotational axis occurred circa 2345 BCE. (Photo courtesy of Barry J. Setterfield and the Dodwell family. Dodwell's original manuscript can be read at barrysetterfield.org.)

1963 he controversially concluded in the manuscript for his unpublished book that a sudden disturbance, a tilt of the Earth's polar axis, had occurred as recently as 2345 BCE, less than five thousand years ago.* Dodwell demonstrated the proof of his controversial conclusion with the presentation of a logarithmic sine curve of ancient measurements that demonstrated a recovery of the Earth's polar axis from a major "disturbance."

> The date of verticality of the curve, 2345 B.C. . . . coincided with an "irregularity," this being a large and sudden change in the inclination of the earth's axis. . . . The curve is therefore a certain and sure mathematical demonstration that in the year 2345 B.C., the earth's axis was suddenly displaced by a major impact. . . . It is a curve of recovery, with restoration to equilibrium after a disturbance; and it shows with certainty that a disturbance of the earth's axis occurred at the date 2345 . . . it seems probable that the earth's rotational axis was suddenly changed by the force of impact in 2345 B.C., from an original inclination of about 5°, by an amount of about 21.5° to a new inclination of about 26.5°.[20]

Dodwell's research was detailed and extensive. While he mentions only the recovery from a major disturbance of the Earth's axial tilt, this

---

*For more on Dodwell's research, see my earlier book *The Giza Prophecy*, 186–89.

is not to dismiss the possibility that this axial disturbance was but the legacy or signature of a much greater and perhaps more recent inversion event. After such a major inversion, our planet would, undoubtedly, have gone through many centuries of geophysical "convulsions" of the type observed by Dodwell.

Of particular interest in Dodwell's findings is that his date of 2345 BCE for this disturbance of the Earth's axis coincides with the rapid decline of the ancient Egyptian civilization into a so-called dark age known as the First Intermediate Period. This date would also coincide with the demise of a number of other contemporary early Bronze Age cultures such as the Akkadian empire, and, curiously, it is also within a few years of the date the biblical scholar James Usher gave for the Flood of Noah, circa 2349 BCE.[21] Could it be that these major flooding events of the Earth are somehow linked to the Earth tipping over? The general dating of Dodwell's axial tilt disturbance is supported also by the earlier research of Georges Cuvier, who, writing in 1812, states, "I agree, therefore, with MM. DeLue and Dolmieu, in thinking, that if any thing in geology be established, it is, that the surface of our globe has undergone a great and sudden revolution, the date of which cannot be referred to a much earlier period five or six thousand years ago; that this revolution overwhelmed and caused to disappear the countries which were previously inhabited by man."[22]

Now if, as Egyptologists insist, the Great Pyramid was constructed around 4,500 years ago (ca. 2550 BCE), then the geophysical data that appears to be encoded into the monument cannot relate to Dodwell's shift of around 2345 BCE (since this event had yet to happen). What the Dodwell findings further suggest is that these great upheavals of the Earth are not at all an impossible or, indeed, abnormal occurrence in the geodynamics of the planet but, on the contrary, would seem to be an inherent feature of it, occurring by some natural but as yet unknown mechanism every so often in its geophysical life cycle.

The Orion Paradox

Another indication that a pole shift event occurred in remote antiquity also comes to us—albeit indirectly—from the research of American astronomer Virginia Trimble and Egyptian-born bestselling author Robert Bauval, each of whom was independently trying to find ways of dating the Giza pyramids using the science of archaeoastronomy.

In 1963, Trimble made an intriguing observation that she believed might assist in helping to date the Great Pyramid (and, by extension, its contemporaries). She calculated that circa 2550 BCE the 45° inclined angle of the shaft that runs from the south side of the pyramid's King's Chamber would have precisely aligned with the star Al Nilam, the center star of Orion's Belt (fig. 3.23).

This discovery was welcomed by Egyptologists as confirmation of the pyramid's age and, since he is believed to have ruled Egypt at this time, circumstantial evidence that the Great Pyramid had been built as the tomb and recovery instrument of the Fourth Dynasty pharaoh Khufu and that this particular shaft had been crafted within the pyramid's superstructure in order to direct the king's soul toward the Orion

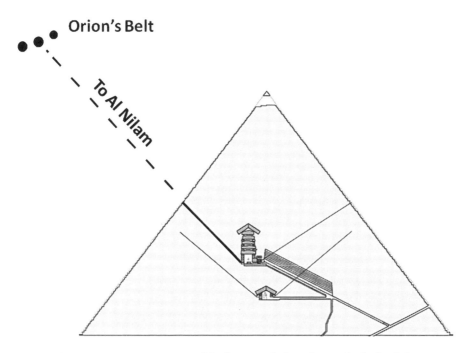

Figure 3.23. Virginia Trimble discovered that the south shaft of the King's Chamber, which is inclined at an angle of 45°, would have aligned with Al Nilam, the center star of Orion's Belt, around 2550 BCE.

constellation, which the ancient Egyptians believed to be the stellar personification of Osiris, their god of rebirth and regeneration. In their acceptance of Trimble's stellar altitude-alignment theory for these shafts, Egyptologists essentially were—perhaps unwittingly—acknowledging the idea that the star shafts of the Great Pyramid could (in theory) be used to date the monuments via stellar alignments. And they may not be wrong in this belief because, as we may recall, the Coptic-Egyptian legend of Surīd tells us, "The king, also, deposited the instruments, and the thuribula, with which his forefathers had sacrificed to the stars, and also their writings; likewise, the positions of the stars, and their circles; together with the history and chronicles of time past, of that, which is to come, and of every future event, which would take place in Egypt."[23]

Some thirty years later, however, matters took something of a dramatic twist when, in 1994, Bauval and coauthor Adrian Gilbert published their international bestselling book *The Orion Mystery,* in which Trimble's star-shaft altitude-alignment dating theory was essentially challenged when Bauval presented his Orion correlation theory as an alternative means of using the Orion Belt stars to date the Giza pyramids. Bauval realized that not only do the belt stars change their altitude in the sky by moving up and down like an elevator when observed due south over a long period of time (as a result of the Earth's slow precessional motion), but that the line of three belt stars also tilts or pivots back and forth, creating a different angle in the heavens as the stars slide up and down the southern meridian over this lengthy precessional year (which lasts around twenty-six thousand calendar years and is sometimes referred to as the Platonic Year or Great Year).

Bauval realized that if the three main pyramids at Giza represented the three stars of Orion's Belt, then the builders may have placed the pyramids on the ground with the same pivot angle that the belt stars possessed on the southern meridian at the time the monuments had been planned, thereby effectively encoding into them a date stamp for their construction (or at least, in Bauval's view, a date stamp for their design).

And so, with this idea in mind, Bauval set about measuring the angle of the line through the apexes of the two largest Giza pyramids

(G1/Khufu*–G2/Khafre), and he found the angle of this line (from the north) to be around 43.20°. He then fired up his star-mapping software (Skyglobe 3.5)† to find when the angle of a line through the two counterpart stars in Orion's Belt (Al Nitak and Al Nilam) had been pivoted on the southern meridian (due south) with the same 43.20° angle, thereby matching their terrestrial pyramid counterparts. Bauval probably expected his belt-pivot dating method to match the circa 2550 BCE date that Trimble had previously obtained using her star-shaft altitude-dating method. However, the Egyptian researcher was in for something of a shock. After he entered the various parameters into his star-mapping software, the program instantly gave Bauval the extraordinary, puzzling, and somewhat contradictory result for his belt pivot alignment method—circa 10,500 BCE‡ (fig. 3.24).

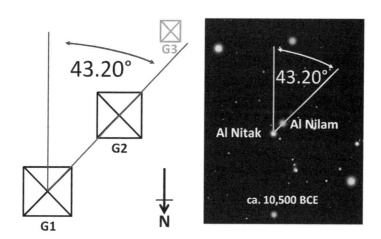

Figure 3.24. Bauval's astronomy software showed that the G1–G2 pyramid angle of 43.20° matched the same pivot angle in the equivalent belt stars (due south) circa 10,500 BCE.

---

*Pyramid G1 is sometimes also referred to as GI, G2 as GII, and G3 as GIII.

†Skyglobe 3.5 has since been found to have some critical flaws, such as a failure to account for the proper motion of stars and a failure to account for such issues as nutation, aberration, and refraction, all of which compromised its ability to give highly accurate star mappings and dates.

‡Bauval would later modify this date to circa 11,000 BCE, although, using more recent software, the G1–G2 alignment becomes more accurate nearer to 11,800 BCE.

And so, while the south shaft of the King's Chamber aligned with the belt star Al Nilam circa 2550 BCE (using Trimble's star-altitude dating method), oddly, Bauval's dating method using the pivot angle of the belt stars at 43.20° (matching the pivot angle of the pyramids) indicated a much greater age of circa 10,500 BCE, making the monuments around eight thousand years older than the conventional pyramid construction date of circa 2500 BCE. Even Bauval struggled to adequately explain his controversial and somewhat perplexing finding since he himself had always accepted the orthodox pyramid chronology.

But in this alignment discrepancy between the different dating techniques of Trimble and Bauval, we may, in fact, be observing a dichotomy that presents to us a more profound hidden truth, a finding that may offer support to the controversial claim in the Coptic-Egyptian oral tradition that the stars wandered from their regular paths across the heavens.

What must be observed and stressed here is that—theoretically, at least—the two different stellar dating techniques used by Trimble and

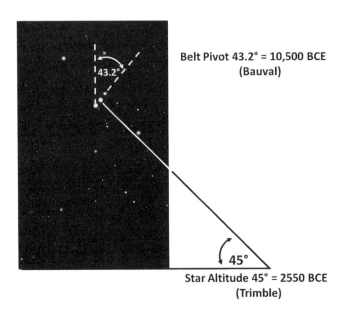

Figure 3.25. Both the altitude of the selected belt star (Al Nilam) at 45° and the belt-pivot angle at 43.2° could easily have been recorded by the builders during the very same stellar observation and this data then encoded into the Giza monuments.

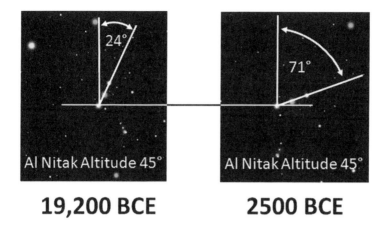

19,200 BCE   2500 BCE

*Figure 3.26. The belt star Al Nitak reaches an altitude of 45° on
the southern meridian on two occasions within one full precessional cycle.
Previously these occurred circa 19,200 BCE and then again
circa 2500 BCE. Only by including the belt pivot, which is different
on each of these two dates, in conjunction with the altitude angle, can the two
possible dates be differentiated and a unique and precise date marker set.*

Bauval should have arrived at the *same* date since the builders would almost certainly have observed and encoded both of these alignments from a single observation of the belt stars (fig. 3.25).

Indeed, encoding *both* alignments into the monuments from the very same observation would actually have been *essential* because only then is it possible to generate a unique stellar date stamp from within the full 26,000 year precessional cycle (fig. 3.26).

Without being overly technical, this unique astronomical date marker arises because the relative rate of change between the altitude and pivot of the belt stars occurs at slightly different speeds, meaning the two alignments can only ever converge on just one occasion per full precessional cycle (or longer). As such, when we find the date for one of the two alignments, we should, automatically, arrive at the very same date for the second alignment since, as stated, both alignment observations would almost certainly have been made (and encoded) from the very same observation. Instead, however, what we find with the Trimble and Bauval alignment observations at Giza is a paradox, an inexplicable mismatch between the two alignments of some eight thousand or so years that is truly puzzling. Realistically, this time gap simply should not exist.

The first question to ask here, of course, is whether there was ever a time in our remote past when the two different alignments observed by Trimble and Bauval *could* have been observed in the belt stars at the very same moment (i.e., a time when these two alignments converged on the same date). If so, then how far back must we turn the heavens for these two alignments we find encoded into the Giza monuments to simultaneously match their stellar counterpart alignments in Orion's Belt? And, of course, if such a condition could be found, then how old might this make the Giza monuments?

LOST IN TIME

In consideration of this question, an analysis of the historical precessional motion of the belt stars over one hundred thousand years (that is, four full precessional cycles) was made using star-mapping software (Stellarium v.0.19.1), and strangely, no date was found in all that time when these two alignment conditions between sky and ground converged on a single date. Certainly over this lengthy period we can obtain a number of dates when each of the three belt stars took a turn at reaching an altitude of 45° on the southern meridian. And yes, we can also find several dates when Orion's Belt was pivoted at 43.20° due south. However, all instances of pivot date and altitude date are separated from each other by many thousands of years, with no convergence of the two ever occurring. There are three possible means to explain this failure to find a convergence date:

1. One or both of the stellar alignments presented by Trimble and Bauval do not actually exist in reality; that is, the builders did not create any deliberate stellar alignments using the belt stars at all, and Bauval's pyramid angle (G1 apex–G2 apex) and the various angles of the star shafts are perhaps merely arbitrary or served some otherwise unknown symbolic function.

2. The convergence date of the Bauval-Trimble dual alignment is so ancient that it goes beyond the one-hundred-thousand-year limitation of the currently available, commercial star-mapping software.

3. If the star shafts do represent a shift of the stars in ancient times (perhaps indicating a pole shift event), then since the time the Bauval-Trimble alignments were first created, a subsequent pole shift event has occurred (as Dodwell's research appears to show) that has effectively overwritten or wiped clean the Earth's former geodynamic parameters (which were encoded into the pyramids), thereby giving the Earth a new (different) set of precessional parameters from those it had before. These new properties of our Earth and cosmos are, naturally, coded into our modern star-mapping software but not into the Giza monuments, which were set in a pre–pole shift world that possessed different geodynamic properties. In short, we may be trying to reconcile the Bauval-Trimble stellar alignments using Earth's present geodynamic properties, which simply did not exist at the time of the pyramids' construction; it's a bit like trying to turn a lock using the wrong key. This further proves, conversely, that the Great Pyramid could not have been built after Dodwell's circa 2345 BCE axial shift event because, were that the case, then the Bauval-Trimble alignments *would* reflect the Earth's present orbital mechanics and we would then have been able to reconcile them to a single date.

   Put simply, that we *cannot* reconcile these two alignments to a single convergence date suggests that two pole shift events occurred in our ancient past, the second (most recent) event erasing the geodynamics of the Earth that had prevailed beween the first and second shift events.

While it is certainly possible that these alignments observed by Trimble and Bauval may have no stellar significance and could be purely symbolic or arbitrary in nature, it is hard to see that this is the case; even most Egyptologists accept that the shafts of the Great Pyramid likely have a stellar function of some kind, albeit one related to the ancient Egyptians' religious beliefs. Could the pyramids be more than one hundred thousand years old? Two points suggest not:

1. Manual calculations beyond the one-hundred-thousand-year limitation of current star-mapping software show that, as we move ever further back in time, the belt stars lose their familiar "dogleg" pattern, and the close correlation we observe today between stars and pyramids completely breaks down.

2. The ancient Egyptians themselves dated the origins of their civilization only to as far back as thirty-nine thousand years ago. (This great age is, of course, contested by Egyptologists, who consider it merely as mythological.)

And so, if we cannot find the Bauval-Trimble convergence date in our star-mapping software within the last one hundred thousand years (or beyond), then all we are left with to explain its absence is a more recent pole shift event—an event that Dodwell's calculations tell us occurred circa 2345 BCE.

What we may be witnessing with these two different alignment dates presented by Bauval and Trimble is actually the end result, the net effect, and the effective proof of a more recent pole shift event that effectively decoupled the builder's original single alignment date, splitting it into the two separate alignment dates that Bauval and Trimble independently observed in the monuments today. As a result of the more recent inversion event (i.e., the Dodwell event of circa 2345 BCE), the alignments simply cannot now converge on a single alignment date within our current precessional cycle.

Turning Giza on Its 'Ed

One of the very earliest criticisms of Bauval's Orion correlation theory (outlined above) was that the relative positions of the pyramids on the ground at Giza did not correspond to the belt stars' relative positions in the sky. The most vocal critic in this regard was Ed C. Krupp of the Griffith Observatory in Los Angeles. In October 2001, Krupp wrote the following critique of the Orion correlation theory:

> In *The Orion Mystery,* Robert Bauval and Adrian Gilbert identified the three main pyramids at Giza as a symbolic representation of the three stars in the Belt of Orion. They fortified this conclusion by pairing an aerial photograph of the three pyramids, which appear as a diagonal line across the page, with a telescopic photograph of Orion's Belt. Those stars follow a similar diagonal across the page. In pondering the two photographs, I realized the image of Giza is presented with south at the top of the page. In the picture of Orion's Belt, north is at the top of the page. Because Bauval and Gilbert treated Giza as a map of the sky, the matching of north in the sky with south on the ground seemed odd. . . .
>
> To map the sky on the ground in a way that matches the pattern of stars we see in the sky (and so preserves the geometry), it is necessary to invert north in the sky with respect to north on the ground. In a sense, this can be accomplished by "sliding" Orion down the meridian to the southern horizon and pulling it north, feet first (south) across the ground. This procedure is, in fact, what Robert Bauval, Graham Hancock, and Dr. Roy do when they say "Just look south" to make Orion's Belt look like the plan of Giza. This is why the two photographs in *The Orion Mystery* put north on opposite sides of the pages.
>
> You can, then, match Orion to Giza by looking south, but you invert the cardinal directions of one map or the other to do it. In this kind of mapping (just face south), the angle of the "Belt" of pyramids is okay, but north in the sky is mapped to the south on the ground. This is equivalent to turning Egypt upside down, and that is what I have said in publications, correspondence, lectures, and on television.[24]

While Krupp is technically correct here, Bauval (and Hancock) invoke artistic license to the correlation by imagining the belt stars of the southern sky being pulled down from the sky to the southern horizon and then, like a roller blind, pulled northward over the ground. It works

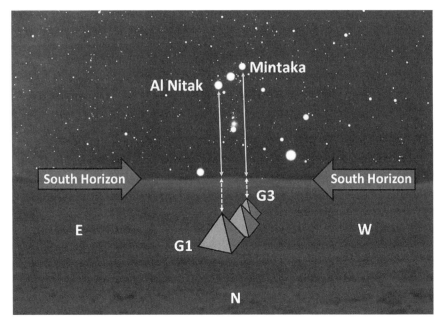

Figure 3.27. Ed Krupp noted that Robert Bauval's Orion correlation theory inverts the positions of the pyramids on the ground relative to the positions of the belt stars. The star Al Nitak, for example, is closest to the southern horizon, but its stellar counterpart, the Great Pyramid, is farthest away from this horizon (or farthest north).

and is arguably the most intuitive way of representing the belt stars on the ground, but as Krupp pointed out, it does, nevertheless, invert the directionality of the belt stars, whereby Al Nitak is observed nearest (lowest) to the southern horizon, but its terrestrial counterpart on the ground at Giza, the Great Pyramid, is positioned farthest away from this horizon (relative to the other two main pyramids). The star Mintaka, on the other hand, being the highest of the belt stars, is farthest away from (or farthest above) the southern horizon, yet its terrestrial counterpart, the pyramid of Menkaure, is nearest to that horizon (fig. 3.27).

Had the pyramids been positioned on the Giza plateau in accordance with a strict observance of each star's relative astronomical position above the southern horizon, then we might expect to see the arrangement of the Giza pyramids on the ground with the Great

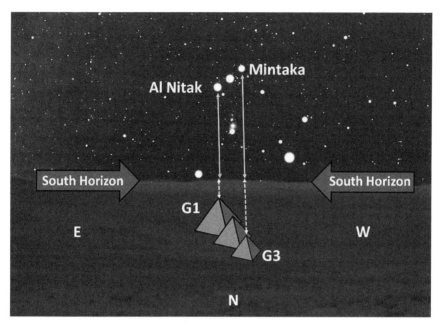

Figure 3.28. The pyramids of Giza as they might have looked had the builders more accurately represented the relative distance of each of the belt stars from the southern horizon.

Pyramid (G1) placed nearest to the southern horizon and G3 farthest away from it (fig. 3.28).

But there is a rather obvious solution to this criticism of Krupp: we simply accept what the ancient texts tell us and invoke an Earth inversion in which Giza quite literally is turned on its head, just as Krupp said would be needed to make the correlation between the stars and the pyramids properly work (from a strictly astronomical perspective).

If we assume that the Earth circa 10,000 BCE had been fully inverted in the manner outlined earlier in this chapter (and there's more on this in chapter 7), then this would have thrust Giza to a latitude of 30° south. As a result of this, the belt stars would appear much, much higher in the night sky. Indeed, these stars would actually then be best viewed not by looking south (or north) but by looking up! The belt stars in this scenario would be found high above your head, close to the zenith (the center of the celestial dome) of the sky at an altitude of

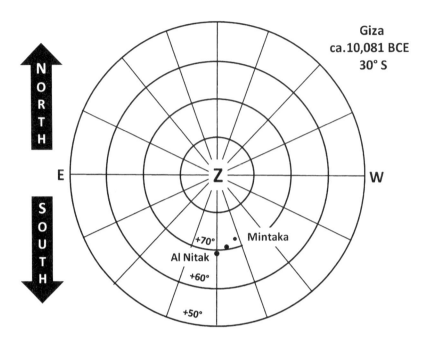

Figure 3.29. The celestial dome of the sky circa 10,000 BCE, with Giza at a latitude of 30° south, shows Orion's Belt overhead at an altitude of 69° (Al Nitak). Note that Al Nitak is nearest the south and farthest east on the celestial sphere while Mintaka is farthest north and west. (The reversed east and west cardinal directions shown here are simply a consequence of looking up at the sky grid with north to your back. If we made a rubber stamp of this sky grid image and then impressed it onto a sheet of paper, the impression becomes the reverse image of the master).

69° (fig. 3.29). Ordinarily, looking up at the zenith of the sky and with north behind your back, you would then have west to your right and east to your left.

We can then project or mirror this sky grid onto the ground at Giza (fig. 3.30), being careful to map each star correctly to the cardinal directions (by keeping Al Nitak farthest south and east and Mintaka the farthest north and west). With the stars properly mapped onto the ground, this then becomes the plan on which to place and build the pyramids.

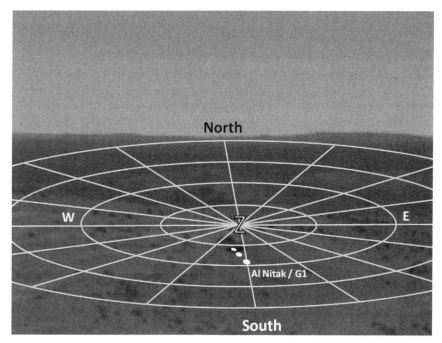

Figure 3.30. Mapping the sky grid onto the ground at Giza will place Mintaka farthest north and west while Al Nitak is placed farthest south and east.

If we now build pyramids according to our Orion's Belt ground plan (fig. 3.31, next page), we find that the Great Pyramid (G1) is placed farthest south and east of the other two pyramids, reflecting the relative position of Al Nitak (G1's stellar counterpart) in this upside-down world, while Menkaure's pyramid (G3) is farthest north and west, reflecting the relative position of Mintaka. This positioning of the pyramids is, of course, a mirror of what we find at Giza today and is essentially what Krupp argued in favor of with his criticism of Bauval's Orion correlation theory.

When the last (and most recent) inversion event occurred, then the Earth (and Giza) inverted, Dzhanibekov style, back another 180° (or thereabouts), giving us the configuration we see at Giza today, with its contradictory Sphinx alignment, star-shaft alignments, niche alignment, and, of course, the peculiar Giza/Orion pyramid alignment. All

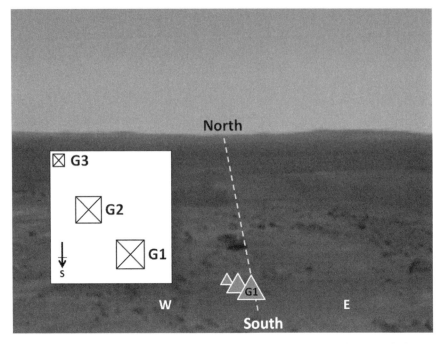

Figure 3.31. Building pyramids according to the Orion's Belt ground plan (from the southern hemisphere perspective) places the Great Pyramid the farthest south and farthest east of the other pyramids, the inverse of what we find today at Giza and what Krupp argued would make a more accurate astronomical correlation between sky and ground.

of these alignment contradictions completely vanish when we simply imagine that the Sphinx was built prior to the first Earth inversion event, the pyramids shortly after this event, and then, thousands of years later, everything turned over again with a second 180° inversion to give us what we see at Giza today (fig. 3.32).

There is, of course, something of a deep irony to all of this. Krupp, in his criticism of Bauval's Giza-Orion correlation, may actually have unwittingly provided the master key to unlocking the entire Giza-Orion mystery, with its many associated alignment contradictions and paradoxes. His comment about having to turn Giza on its head to make the Orion correlation properly work may have been said by him in mocking jest, but in truth, if the pyramids were indeed correlated with Orion's Belt (as

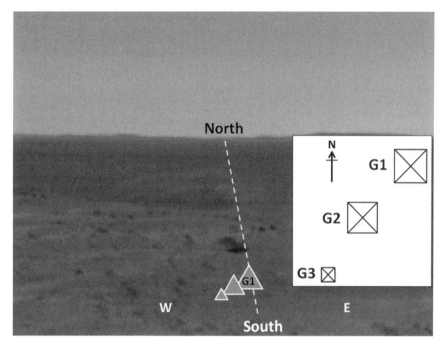

Figure 3.32. A second inversion event would have turned the Earth a farther 180° to give us the configuration we see at Giza today, with all of its alignment contradictions.

seems likely), then the inverted positioning of them we find at Giza today could, in fact, constitute actual physical evidence that the Earth, just as many of our ancient traditions tell us, was indeed inverted long, long ago and that this inversion occurred, not once, but (at least) twice.

The Senemut Astronomical Ceiling

Our final piece of physical evidence pointing to a pole shift event having occurred in remote antiquity comes to us from the curiously oriented astronomical ceiling in the tomb of Senemut (fig. 3.33, p. 80), the architect of Queen Hatshepsut, who ruled Egypt circa 1500 BCE.

This astronomical ceiling is curious for a number of reasons. Of the five planets observable with the naked eye (Mercury, Venus, Mars, Jupiter, and Saturn), all are present in the ceiling's upper (south) panel with the exception of Mars. It is an omission that has caused debate and

South Panel

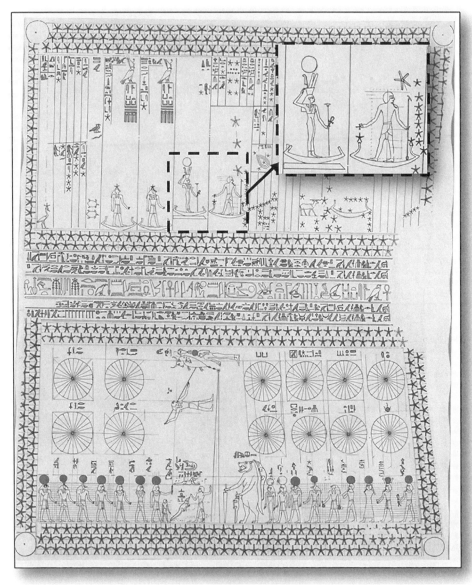

North Panel

Figure 3.33. The Senemut astronomical ceiling consists of two panels depicting the constellations of the northern (lower panel) *and southern* (upper panel) *skies. Sirius* (left) *and Orion* (right) *can be seen in the dashed box.*

speculation even to this very day. However, the most curious aspect of the ceiling is its apparent inverted orientation, which was first noted in the 1930s by the astronomer and classical scholar Alexander Pogo, who writes:

> A characteristic feature of the Senmut ceiling is the astronomically objectionable orientation of the southern panel; it has to be inspected, like the rest of the ceiling, by a person facing north, so that Orion appears east of Sirius. . . .
>
> With the reversed orientation of the southern panel, Orion, the most conspicuous constellation of the southern sky, appeared to be moving eastward, i.e., in the wrong direction.[25]

The seeming reverse motion of the stars on this ceiling is highly peculiar indeed, and one might immediately consider it as some sort of ancient aberration, were it not for the fact that the perceived reverse motion of the stars here appears to be reinforced with the image of the demon/goddess Taweret (the expectant hippopotamus with the crocodile on her back) in the ceiling's lower panel. Typically, Taweret, in astronomical depictions, usually faces eastward (to the right), but in the Senemut ceiling, we find her facing westward (to the left).[26]

After extensive studies of the Senemut ceiling, the scientist and author Michael G. Reade observed further curious anomalies in the ceiling's astronomical layout, writing:

> Sirius towers above Orion on the southern panel; this is only possible when the world is upside-down (except in so far as a modern visitor to Antarctica could see something very similar). . . .
>
> At Thebes . . . Scorpius currently reaches a maximum altitude of about 20–40° above the southern horizon (the range of values is due to the considerable vertical spread of Scorpius when it is on the meridian); should the world turn upside-down, however, it would pass almost exactly overhead and Scorpius is actually found at the extreme top centre of the north panel of the Senmut ceiling, exactly where it should be if the world were upside-down. . . .

Thirdly, given this upside-down situation, the ecliptic would pass slightly below Orion. (It passes above Orion for a northern hemisphere observer in a right-side-up world). The planets always appear to move along the ecliptic, and on the Senmut ceiling (southern panel) they are distinctly shown as floating along at a level slightly below that of Orion, exactly where they should be if the world were upside down.[27]

And finally, even Velikovsky was not without a view on this ancient astronomical artifact, concluding:

> The real meaning of "the irrational orientation of the southern panel" and the "reversed position of Orion" appears to be this: the southern panel shows the sky of Egypt as it was before the celestial sphere interchanged north and south, east and west. . . . The reversal of east and west, if combined with the reversal of north and south, would turn the constellations of the north into constellations of the south, and show them in reversed order, as in the chart of the southern sky on the ceiling of Senmut's tomb. The stars of the north would become stars of the south.[28]

This west-to-east motion of the stars that seems to be depicted in the Senemut astronomical ceiling is precisely what we would come to expect with a north-to-south Earth inversion (thereby allowing Orion to appear east of and lower in the sky than Sirius).

Almost everywhere we look at Giza, it seems, there is evidence pointing to the reality of these ancient pole shift events, just as the ancient Coptic-Egyptian Sūrīd legend implies. Given this evidence, it rather seems to this writer that science has been a little too hasty in its dismissal of the possibility of rapid pole shift or inversion events and should, perhaps, be much more circumspect in its consideration of the considerable evidence suggesting that such events do, in fact, occur at regular intervals and as some natural characteristic of our planet's geophysical properties. It may well be that our Earth, far from being a dependable and steady gyroscope that cannot easily topple over (as most scientists believe), might, in fact, behave more like a tippe-top, which, with sufficient redistribution of mass within its core or on its surface, then becomes sufficiently unstable and susceptible to the Dzhanibekov effect. In short, it seems that Earth inversions do happen: we just have to figure out why, how, and when.

Let us now turn our attention to another aspect of the Coptic-Egyptian oral tradition of Sūrīd that is believed by Egyptologists (and by scientists in general) to be nothing more than a mythical tale—the Deluge. Is there any evidence to support that this supposed mythical event might really have occurred in remote antiquity, as Sūrīd's astronomer-priests had predicted?

4

The Deluge

It is one thing, of course, that the ancient Egyptians may have believed that a future deluge would destroy their civilization, but what evidence is there to show that such a devastating calamity ever actually occurred in Egypt? In one respect, this question would seem somewhat moot. That the ancient Egyptians believed this catastrophic deluge would happen is what actually matters here because it was this belief that seems to have been the motivation for them to construct their pyramid arks, their great recovery vaults. They could very well have constructed the monuments purely on this belief, only to discover, many centuries later, that no deluge ever came, that the predictions of King Sūrīd's astronomer-priests were wrong.

We know from our history books that many ancient civilizations and cultures possessed a catastrophic flood myth similar to that of the biblical Noah. The oldest of these catastrophic flood myths is the Sumerian *Epic of Gilgamesh,* although this flood story may have had its origins in an earlier version passed on to the Sumerians by the preceding Ubaid culture, which dominated Mesopotamia for almost three millennia from circa 6500 BCE.* These regional flood events were extensively investigated and documented in 1929 by the Assyriologist Sir Leonard Woolley, who discovered several ancient alluvial flood deposits deep

---

*The flood myths from this period coincide with the 8.2 kiloyear event, a dramatic cooling of the Earth believed to have been caused by a large meltwater pulse from the final collapse of the great Laurentide Ice Sheet, which caused global sea levels to rise by up to thirteen feet.

underground in the royal cemetery of the ancient city of Ur. There is also the Zoroastrian flood myth of Yima and Ahura Mazda, as well as the Akkadian deluge epic of Atrahasis, while the ancient Greeks possessed their own flood myths of Deucalion and Pyrrha and also Philemon and Baucis. It is often said by Egyptologists that the ancient Egyptians, unlike other contemporary cultures, did not possess a flood myth. There is much, however, to suggest otherwise.

In the Temple of Horus at Edfu, far to the south of Egypt, we find inscribed into the many pillars, walls, and pylons there, hieroglyphics that speak of a far, distant time when the Egyptian gods and sages lived on an island paradise far to the west. This island "home of the primeval ones" had succumbed to a great deluge and was destroyed in a single day and night of calamity. The survivors, so these Edfu building texts tell us, headed east and reconstituted their civilization along the banks of the Nile. This flood story is, of course, very reminiscent of Plato's famous account of the destruction of Atlantis.

Other evidence that a great deluge did engulf Egypt at some time in remote antiquity comes to us from the ancient Egyptian *Book of the Dead,* which tells us:

> Then Thoth, being the tongue of the Great God declares that, acting for the Lord Tem, he is going to make a Flood. He says: "I am going to blot out everything that I have made. This Earth shall enter into (be absorbed in) the watery abyss of Nu (or Nunu) by means of a raging flood, and will become even as it was in primeval times . . . one day the Nile will rise and cover all Egypt with water, and drown the whole country; then, as in the beginning, there will be nothing to be seen except water."[1]

This flood event described by the god Thoth was clearly not a mere annual flooding of the Nile to which most Egyptologists attribute these mythical flood accounts. This was to be a flood that would "drown the whole country" whereby "there will be nothing to be seen except water." Such a flood, were it ever to have occurred, truly would have been a catastrophic, civilization-ending event.

PHYSICAL EVIDENCE OF
AN EGYPTIAN FLOOD

Further sources from some medieval accounts inform us that such a catastrophic flood did indeed occur in Egypt and that evidence of its former presence, a tidal line, could apparently be observed on the sides of the Giza pyramids before they lost their casing stones during an earthquake in medieval times. In *The Chronology of Ancient Nations,* C. Edward Sachau writes, "People are of opinion, that the traces of the water of the Deluge, and the effects of the waves are still visible on these two pyramids half-way up, above which the water did not rise."[2]

According to one modern researcher, Sherif El Morsy, the effects of the waves of this deluge event can still be observed today on various monuments around Giza, particularly the southwest corner of the second pyramid, the mortuary temple of the third pyramid, and within the two giant boat pits to the east of the Great Pyramid. Morsy writes:

I have found that the extensive erosion patterns at the lower elevations of the plateau are different to the erosion patterns found at higher elevations. These erosion patterns are due to the Necropolis's inundation by water. The inundation of water reaches a maximum of 75 meters over our current sea level creating a shoreline at the Khafra enclosure that spans all the way across to the Menkara temple. This shoreline is a 2 meter high intertidal range showing pitting and tidal notches due to seawater, wave mechanics, and tidal ebbing. At the lower levels such as at the Sphinx, the Sphinx temple, the first 20 courses of the Great pyramid including the boat pits; we see erosion due to deeper water saturation, where the stone blocks and wall linings have absorbed sea water. As the waters receded and a dry sunny windy climate took place, these megalithic stone blocks started weathering, creating tafoni erosions which are due to the salt chemically reacting and flaking the limestone with pitting formations. During a catastrophic sea surge and the forthcoming water regression, we clearly observe at certain areas such as corners, outlets, and trenches . . . horizontal indentures due to water force gushing and turbulence. On the top temple blocks we have sediment and alluvium deposits that have collected on the flat surfaces such as seen in shallow sea beds and lagoons, creating an oozing spongy effect due to the water regression that left these deposits. . . .

To my surprise the bulge on the top surface of the block that nearly made me trip was a petrified exoskeleton of what seems to be an Echinoid (sea urchin), which is a shallow sea marine creature. The coincidence to discover a petrified shallow marine creature laying on a top surface of a temple block that sits right under the ancient intertidal range, is a blessing. This is probably the most absolute proof that the Giza Necropolis was inundated by a sea surge. The petrified Echinoid and the dilapidated temple block stand together creating for us such a solid picture of an ancient lagoon that once existed at the Menkara temple during a high sea that inundated the Necropolis. . . .

Geologists and archeologists are debunking this discovery believing that this petrified marine creature has eroded out of the limestone block. I disagree due to these forthcoming points; first, this petrified marine creature's exoskeleton is in pristine condition with minute details of the shell perforation showing clearly, therefore it must have been existing from a much later date such as the Pleistocene or early Holocene periods. Second, this petrified creature is laying gravitational flat in its natural sitting position on the surface of this temple block. Third, it is living in its natural environment which is in the intertidal range in a shallow lagoon with sea bed sediments. Fourth, it is not a miniscule fragment like most shells that make the limestone formation, but a large entire specimen.[3]

In addition to Morsy's research, others have reported considerable silt sediments around the base of the Great Pyramid, as well as salt incrustations within its walls. The cultural anthropologist Martin Gray writes:

Silt sediments rising to fourteen feet around the base of the pyramid contain many seashells and fossils that have been radiocarbon-dated to be nearly twelve thousand years old. These sediments could have been deposited in such great quantities only by major sea flooding, an event the dynastic Egyptians could never have recorded because they were not living in the area until eight thousand years after the flood. This evidence alone suggests that the three main Giza pyramids are at least twelve thousand years old. In support of this ancient flood scenario, mysterious legends and records tell of watermarks that were clearly visible on the limestone casing stones of the Great Pyramid before those stones were removed by the Arabs. These watermarks were halfway up the sides of the pyramid, or about 400 feet above the present level of the Nile River.

Further, when the Great Pyramid was first opened, incrustations of salt an inch thick were found inside. While much of this salt is known to be natural exudation from the stones of the pyramid, chemical analysis has shown that some of the salt has a mineral content consistent with salt from the sea. These salt incrustations, found at a height corresponding to the water level marks left on the exterior, are further evidence that at some time in the distant past the pyramid was submerged halfway up its height.[4]

And the independent researcher into Earth science, John M. Jensen Jr. writes:

There are 3 different salt lines. . . . That is, the water rose to its highest point about 254' up the side of the Great Pyramid, and remained at that level for some short period of time, because the salt line residue was relatively thin. Then, following that level stasis, the waters receded to the level of the Queen's Chamber, and remained there for a long enough period of time, so that the interior salt line grew much thicker. Then the water fell to the lagoon level of 14'–18' as demonstrated by the sediment around its base. Most of the area, as we will document later shows what appears to be a shallow lagoon in terms of stone pitting and turbulence.[5]

Of course, the impact of such a devastating deluge would not be confined solely to ancient Egypt but would, naturally, have been felt all over the world as an event so devastating that it would etch itself on the collective memory of mankind for countless generations to come. In their book *Cataclysm! Compelling Evidence of a Cosmic Catastrophe in 9500 B.C.,* D. S. Allan and J. B. Delair write, "The collective and unavoidable message of these and other innumerable details is that, at some stage, colossal masses of water played a very important (although not the only) role in effecting these changes. This again suggests that the many surviving accounts of a worldwide Deluge long ago may yet be found to rest on a substratum of now dimly-remembered fact."[6]

THE ANCIENT EGYPTIAN CREATION MYTH

But even from the very beginning, as we learn from the ancient Egyptian creation myth found in the world's oldest religious writings, the pyramid texts, a great inundation of water (the primordial ocean) and the primeval mound (the archetypal pyramid) were central elements to this oldest of world-creation stories. Though there were a number of slightly different versions of this myth circulating in different parts of the ancient country, all of them spoke of the world being created out of an endless, lifeless sea of water (Nu or Nun), which, receding slowly, eventually revealed the first mound of land (the pyramid-shaped Benben). From within this primeval mound, all things came forth, including the sun, the Earth, the stars, the moon, and all animals and plants—everything in creation. Egyptologists believe that this creation story came about when the ancient Egyptians observed the annual Nile flood creating small mounds of alluvium as the flood levels of the river rose up and receded again. These mud silts would then be used by the ancient Egyptians to plant their crops.

However, in their translations of the pyramid texts, Egyptologists can only ever circumscribe a general sense of their meaning, and they will, unsurprisingly, miss subtle but potentially important nuances, clues to the true meaning of a particular hieroglyphic sign or piece of script. If we accept that the ancient Coptic-Egyptian oral tradition of an impending deluge has some basis in truth, then it may be that the Egyptian creation myth itself actually derives from this truly cataclysmic flood in a past, forgotten age, a deluge that totally over-whelmed the entire kingdom in the time of the Zep Tepi (the First Time of Creation). However, through its people having built their great pyramid arks, their recovery vaults, the kingdom was able to be born again as the pyramids, with their life-sustaining contents (seeds, tools, knowledge, and other vital items) gradually emerged again from the subsiding floodwaters. This is to say that the pyramids and the foretold deluge may themselves have been the true origins of the ancient Egyptian creation myth, bringing forth everything needed to restart the kingdom.

THE PYRAMID AS RECOVERY VAULT

Whenever Egyptologists come across the pyramid sign in hieroglyphics (fig. 4.1), they invariably simply interpret this sign as meaning "tomb." But the Egyptologists know from reading many other ancient Egyptian texts that the pyramid was much more than a mere final resting place for the deceased king. They understand from these ancient writings that the pyramid was also some kind of "cosmic engine" that would bring about the magical revivification of the king and, by extension, the kingdom. Its purpose, the Egyptologists believe, was to assist in defeating *isfet* (chaos) and preserving the cosmic order, which the ancient Egyptians called *ma'at*.

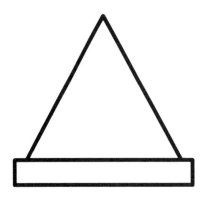

Figure 4.1. The hieroglyphic sign for "pyramid." Egyptologists interpret this sign as meaning "tomb."

It is, however, the contention of this work that the original function of the first pyramids was—as the Coptic-Egyptian oral tradition tells us—to bring about the revivification, the rebirth of the *kingdom* (not the king) after a devastating flood, and as such, Egyptologists have incorrectly labeled these structures as tombs when they should, in fact, be described more accurately as recovery vaults or simply as arks. Kings may well have appropriated and repurposed these pyramids as tombs in later dynasties, but this does not seem to have been their original function. All of which raises an interesting question: If the pyramids were conceived by the ancient Egyptians as recovery vaults or arks to help bring about the revivification of the kingdom, then it surely stands to reason that there would be a distinct hieroglyphic sign that symbolizes the pyramid as a recovery vault built to withstand the Deluge. But does such a hieroglyphic sign actually exist in the archaeological record?

There's a very good possibility that it does.

Given that the pyramid recovery vaults were about the recovery of the earth, the kingdom, after a devastating deluge, they would, naturally, have been packed with many different seed types, agricultural tools, and many other important items.* When we consider ancient Egyptian hieroglyphic signs for buildings that possess an agricultural function, such as an ancient Egyptian granary, we find that they are usually depicted with a "furrowed trench" sign (fig. 4.2) just below the building structure sign.

Figure 4.2. The hieroglyphic sign for "mud floor"
(read: a furrowed trench), usually used to denote
an agricultural context.

---

*For more on these recovery items, see *The Secret Chamber of Osiris: Lost Knowledge of the Sixteen Pyramids,* 147–52.

Figure 4.3. The "mud floor" ("furrow") sign can be observed in this agricultural scene. Gosse, Civilization of the Ancient Egyptians, *29.*

This "furrow" sign can actually be observed in ancient Egyptian agricultural scenes (fig. 4.3).

In figure 4.4, what are believed to be the hieroglyphic signs for ancient Egyptian granaries can be observed. As we can see, all of these signs are presented with the furrow sign below it, indicating that the building structure above possesses an agricultural context or function. Also of note is that these traditional granary buildings all possess the distinctive barrel roof.

In the British Egyptologist Sir Alan Gardiner's standard classification of hieroglyphic signs for building structures (such as a granary), we find that each begins with the letter *O*, followed by a number. While the pyramid recovery vault has some functional similarities with the traditional Egyptian granary, it should not be equated with such and

Ancient Egyptian Granary Signs

Figure 4.4. The hieroglyphic sign for a "granary" (and its variants). The alphanumeric labels below each hieroglyphic sign correspond to the standard classification of hieroglyphic signs by the British Egyptologist Sir Alan Gardiner.

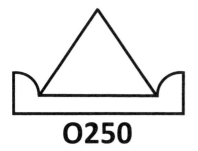

Figure 4.5. Gardiner's O250 hieroglyphic. As an O classification (building structure), this sign may be the hieroglyphic sign depicting the pyramid as a recovery vault, a pyramid structure having a function related to the earth and agriculture (for example, for the storage of seeds, etc.).

would likely have its very own hieroglyphic sign, one different from the traditional barrel-roofed granary structure—a pyramid structure set in an agricultural context (i.e., a pyramid resting on a furrowed base). And indeed, with a further search of Gardiner's hieroglyphic sign list, we find just such a hieroglyphic sign (fig. 4.5).

Critics, however, consider that this pyramid recovery vault sign merely depicts a mound of grain (on a mud floor). What goes against such an interpretation, however, is that scholars have clearly identified and classified this sign as an O sign (denoting a building or structure of some sort). Such a classification would not have been an arbitrary decision and would only have come about after extensive scholarly research showing this sign was indeed representative of a building or structure of some kind and *not* a mound of grain on a mud floor, as critics have suggested. In any case, the ancient Egyptians already have a quite separate and distinct sign to represent a mound of grain, which Gardiner has classified under *M* signs (plants and trees; fig. 4.6).

In short, scholars, having read many ancient Egyptian texts and having considered and understood the context in which the sign O250 has appeared within those texts, concluded that this sign should be classified as a building structure. And given that this pyramid

Figure 4.6. Gardiner's M35 hieroglyphic represents a mound of grain.

building sign rests on the furrow sign, indicating an earth and agricultural connection, then it is entirely possible that this particular hieroglyphic sign represents the pyramid as a recovery vault to bring about the recovery of the Earth after a global cataclysm.

ISIS AND OSIRIS

The ancient Egyptian creation myth may also be connected to another of their myths from the pyramid texts (and other later texts): the myth of Isis and Osiris. While this myth is not actually regarded as a flood myth by Egyptologists, an argument can be made that this is precisely how this myth, this allegorical tale, should actually be understood. This is because the ancient Egyptian god Osiris is closely connected to the ancient Egyptian term *duat*. Egyptologists typically interpret the duat to be some otherworldly realm, the underworld that Osiris ruled in his role as god of the afterlife; it was also said to be the place where human souls would go for final judgment. But Egyptologists remain uncertain exactly how to describe the duat or even where it existed, somewhere between the heavens and the earth; the ancient Egyptian cosmogony does not make the duat easy to identify or understand. But the clues to a proper understanding of what the word *duat* actually means are right there in the ancient texts, albeit in allegorical form.

One of the key elements of the Osiris myth is that his body was placed into a coffin by his jealous brother, Seth, who then cast it into the Nile, whereupon Osiris drowned. Along with other ancient sources, the Shabaka Stone states, strangely, that Osiris "drowned in his own waters." Later in the story, the drowned body of Osiris is recovered by Isis, his wife and consort. Hearing of this, Seth then cuts the drowned body of Osiris into fourteen parts (some versions of the myth say sixteen parts) and has these body parts scattered across the kingdom.

One of the most important aspects of this story from the pyramid texts is that the ancient Egyptians perceived that the construction of the pyramids literally *was* the construction of the "body" of Osiris. These first pyramids consisted of eight large pyramids, six small Queens Pyramids at Giza, and two smaller satellite or "cult" pyramids also at

Giza. (There were also three large incomplete pyramids at other locations along the Nile). And so, not counting the incomplete ones, we have a total of sixteen completed pyramids during this period. Given that Osiris is regarded in the pyramid texts as the literal pyramid, could it be that these first sixteen completed pyramids actually represent the allegorical sixteen body parts of Osiris that Seth "scattered" across the ancient land?*

Even more intriguing is that when we plot the location of these first sixteen pyramids onto a map of Egypt, they present to us a stick figure outline of the classic, archetypal figure of Osiris (fig. 4.7).

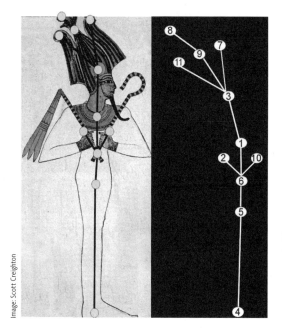

1. Djoser (Saqqara)
2. Sekhemkhet (Saqqara, unfinished)
3. Khaba (Zawiyet al-Aryan, unfinished)
4. Sneferu (Meidum, farthest south)
5. Sneferu (Dahshur, the Bent Pyramid)
6. Sneferu (Dahshur, the Red Pyramid)
7. Khufu (Giza, with four satellite pyramids)
8. Djedefre (Abu Roash, farthest north)
9. Khafre (Giza, with one satellite pyramid)
10. Nebka (Zawiyet al-Aryan, unfinished)
11. Menkaure (Giza, with three satellite pyramids)

Image: Scott Creighton

Figure 4.7. Drawing lines between the primary pyramids along the Nile creates a stick figure outline of the classic Osiris figurine. Note: this number includes the three incomplete pyramids and excludes the six small Giza satellite pyramids.

---

*An inscription on the famous Inventory Stela, refers to Isis as being the "Mistress of the Pyramids." If the pyramids represented the allegorical Osiris, then, as the wife/consort (and sister) of Osiris, this appellation makes perfect sense: The Mistress of the Pyramids was the Mistress of Osiris (the Pyramids).

What this myth may then be alluding to is the pyramids (the body of Osiris) being drowned (flooded) by Seth (the ancient Egyptian god of chaos) and then slowly emerging again from the waters of the Deluge. Thus a connection is made with the ancient Egyptian creation myth. Just as we are told in the creation myth that the primeval mound brought forth everything in creation when the floodwaters of Nun subsided, so too did the pyramids (the body of Osiris) bring forth everything in creation when the floodwaters of the Deluge (the duat) subsided. In essence, then, these two myths may actually be different aspects of the same story, the same ancient flood event, with the creation myth evolving into the myth of Osiris over time and being passed on orally through the generations as an allegorical tale of the Deluge.*

In summary then, in the ancient Egyptian creation myth everything came forth from the pyramid body of Osiris—the sun, the moon, the stars, the seas, the animals and plants and, yes, the life-giving Nile, too. It *all* came from the body of Osiris—the pyramid arks or recovery vaults. This may then explain why, in the Shabaka Stone, we read that Osiris drowned in his waters, because if everything in creation comes from (the pyramid body of) Osiris (including the Deluge), then he will have drowned in waters that he himself had brought forth into creation. Thus, his allegorical body, the sixteen pyramids scattered along the banks of the Nile, was drowned in the duat (the duat here being interpreted as the waters of the Deluge). In this regard, the independent researcher and author, the late Alan F. Alford, tells us of the duat, "The duat is a watery place. It is traversed by boat, and it contains a 'lake of the duat' (sh dati) . . . in addition, the word duat is twice determined in the Pyramid Texts by the hieroglyph of a lake. The duat is a dark place. In the Pyramid Texts, it is identified with ament, 'the hidden land.'"[7]

And here's the thing. Whenever we see the pyramid written in hieroglyphic form, it is almost always presented as a pyramid shape sitting on top of a rectangle shape (fig. 4.8). Egyptologists typically inter-

---

*The number of body parts of Osiris increased over time. This is to be expected, of course, as over time more and more pyramids would have been built by succeeding pharaohs.

pret the lower rectangle shape beneath the pyramid sign simply as a perimeter or enclosure wall around the base of the pyramid. But there's another perfectly plausible (and more nuanced) explanation as to what we may really, in fact, be observing here.

The pyramid standing on top of the rectangle may not, in fact, be just one hieroglyphic sign but two signs! And, intriguingly, in ancient Egyptian hieroglyphics, the rectangle sign actually represents a pool or lake of water—the duat (fig. 4.9).

It is possible, then, that this composite hieroglyphic pyramid sign may, in fact, be depicting the pyramid surrounded by water, the flood-waters rising to submerge the pyramid (allegorically, the pyramid body of Osiris drowning). Or, of course, it could be depicting the pyramid body of Osiris *emerging* from the floodwaters, the duat. Further evidence that the pyramid's "perimeter wall" may, in fact, represent a body of water is presented to us in the actual perimeter wall of the

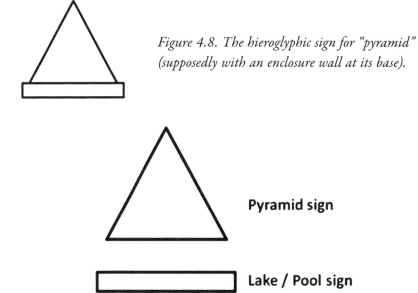

Figure 4.8. The hieroglyphic sign for "pyramid" (supposedly with an enclosure wall at its base).

Pyramid sign

Lake / Pool sign

Figure 4.9. The hieroglyphic sign for "pyramid" may actually be a composite of two separate signs, one for "pyramid" and one for "pool" or "lake," depicting the pyramid emerging from the floodwaters of the Deluge (duat).

Figure 4.10. The wavy perimeter wall of the South Pyramid at Saqqara. (Image: Jean-Pierre Jéquier [1852–1946])

Figure 4.11. The ancient Egyptian hieroglyphic sign representing water.

South Pyramid at Saqqara, which is uniquely shaped like a wave or ripple of water (fig. 4.10), a feature not dissimilar to the ancient Egyptian hieroglyph for water (fig. 4.11).

Thus we have two signs depicting the pyramid recovery vault: one with the pyramid standing on earth and the other with it standing in a pool or lake of water (figs. 4.12 and 4.13).

Naturally, the former land where people once lived their daily lives

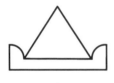

Figure 4.12. The pyramid recovery vault standing on earth (pre-Deluge).

Figure 4.13. The pyramid recovery vault standing in water (post-Deluge).

Figure 4.14. The pyramid body of Osiris emerges from the duat (the Deluge).

would (as the Deluge overwhelmed it) end up entirely underwater, becoming "a dark place . . . the hidden land." And as the waters of the Deluge/duat slowly subsided, the pyramid texts tell us further, "The duat gives birth to Osiris . . . he emerges from the duat."

Which, if we consider the watery duat as being the anticipated Deluge and the first sixteen pyramids as being the body of Osiris, then as the floodwaters receded, the sixteen pyramids (the body of Osiris) would gradually emerge from the floodwaters: the duat gives birth to Osiris—Osiris emerges from the duat.

The pyramid texts further tell us that the body of Osiris is located in a secret chamber in the uttermost depths of the duat (that part of the pyramid that yet remains underwater) and that Osiris is the *akhet* from which the god Re (or Ra) emerges (that part of the pyramid that sits above the floodwaters).

The ancient Egyptian word *akhet* has a number of meanings and associations. It is the name of the first season of the ancient Egyptian year, when mounds of fertile black silt, ready for the planting of crops, would gradually emerge from the Nile floodwaters. It is associated with the king (as Horus) and the gods Osiris and Re. It is also regarded as the "womb of Nut," the ancient Egyptian sky goddess.

Akhet is probably all of these things, but what seems clear is that today we are merely circumscribing its true meaning. It is also translated by Egyptologists to mean "horizon." Indeed, the name given to the Great Pyramid itself is Akhet-Khufu, which Egyptologists believe means the "Horizon of Khufu." The Great Pyramid should not be regarded as the horizon, per se, but like the eastern horizon where the sun is reborn each day, the pyramid seems to have been regarded by the ancients as a place where rebirth would also occur. And this is what Egyptologists have partly correct: that the function of the pyramid was to serve as an instrument of regeneration, of reawakening/revivification, of rebirth, the means by which the cosmic order, ma'at, could be reestablished. However, according to the Coptic-Egyptian oral tradition, originally this revivification or rebirth concerned itself with the kingdom, not with Khufu himself. However, as the theology of the later dynastic Egyptians evolved into the Osirian doctrine, this revivification (brought about through the agency of Osiris; i.e., the sixteen pyramids) would, over time, become a rite for the king himself after death.

As the waters of the deluge subsided, the topmost part of the pyramid would gradually emerge above the floodwaters while the main body of the pyramid remained below, the pyramid apexes appearing as small islands or mounds emerging from the floodwaters just as the mounds of black Nile silt would gradually emerge from the waters of the annual inundation, ready to receive the seeds of life, just as the pyramids held within them the seed of all life, of reawakening, of rebirth: beacons of light amidst a sea of chaos and darkness.

Finally, the pyramid texts tell us that the sun god, Re, is reborn in a mystical union with Osiris and that Re's passage each night is a journey through the duat (the flooded realm of the underworld/the land flooded by the deluge) to emerge from the akhet (that part of the pyramid body of Osiris that has emerged from the floodwaters to be reborn again). Hence, if we consider the first sixteen pyramids as being the symbolic body of Osiris, then each day we are presented with this mystical union between the regeneration god, Osiris (his pyramid body), and the sun god, Re, emerging from the akhet (fig. 4.15).

We have seen in chapter 3 that the claim within the Coptic-Egyptian oral tradition of the stars wandering from their normal course does have some good evidence to show that such an event does seem to have occurred (at least twice) in our remote past. Were the Earth's axis to have changed, then that event would have altered the climate, in different ways, all over the world. One of these changes might have been a

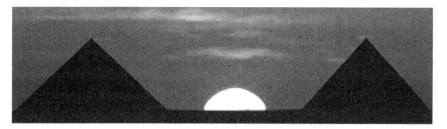

Figure 4.15. The mystical union of (the pyramid body of) the regeneration god, Osiris, and the sun god, Re, emerging from the akhet (that part of Osiris that has emerged from the duat/Deluge).

rapid melting of the former polar ice caps into massive glacial lakes such as Lake Agassiz and Lake Missoula. Over time, as the ice dam gradually thinned and the volume of water being held back increased, the pressure on the thinning ice dams would have become overwhelming, resulting in a catastrophic collapse of the dams, whereby an unimaginable volume of water would have flooded the land and raised sea levels by several feet almost overnight, not to mention the catastrophic tsunamis that would undoubtedly have ravaged coastlines all over the world. This sudden and rapid shift of such a massive body of water from one point on the Earth's surface to another may even have caused sufficient instability in the Earth's rotational axis to induce the Dzhanibekov effect, as discussed in chapter 3.

And so, once again, a deeper analysis of the Coptic-Egyptian oral tradition suggests that the deluge that King Sūrīd's astronomer-priests had anticipated may well have some merit. The stars wandering from their regular course (a shift of the Earth's axis) would have been followed some centuries later by a devastating flood. As Plato recounted in his *Timeaus*:

> That story, as it is told, has the fashion of a legend, but the truth of it lies in the occurrence of a shifting of the bodies in the heavens which move round the earth, and a destruction of the things on the earth by fierce fire, which recurs at long intervals. At such times all they that dwell on the mountains and in high and dry places suffer

destruction more than those who dwell near to rivers or the sea; and in our case the Nile, our Saviour in other ways, saves us also at such times from this calamity by rising high. And when, on the other hand, the Gods purge the earth with a flood of waters, all the herdsmen and shepherds that are in the mountains are saved, but those in the cities of your land are swept into the sea by the streams. . . . And if any event has occurred that is noble or great or in any way conspicuous, whether it be in your country or in ours or in some other place of which we know by report, all such events are recorded from of old and preserved here in our temples; whereas your people and the others are but newly equipped, every time, with letters and all such arts as civilized States require and when, after the usual interval of years, like a plague, the flood from heaven comes sweeping down afresh upon your people, it leaves none of you but the unlettered and uncultured, so that you become young as ever, with no knowledge of all that happened in old times in this land or in your own. Certainly the genealogies which you related just now, Solon, concerning the people of your country, are little better than children's tales; for, in the first place, you remember but one deluge, though many had occurred previously.[8]

If we are to accept the Coptic-Egyptian oral tradition as a true account, then we must accept what it says, and it tells us that these great monuments were not conceived or built as the tomb of just one king but rather as the womb of the entire kingdom, that the ancient Egyptians built their recovery vaults believing that a deluge would occur and that this grand scheme was their best means of survival. Within these pyramids they would place everything that was essential to ensure this hoped-for rebirth of the kingdom could come about, and thus this cache would include, inter alia, all manner of seed types, books, tools, and so on.

But the most vital element of Sūrīd's great recovery device would be placed within a hidden, inaccessible chamber high up in the pyramid's superstructure—within the Big Void, I believe. Without this vital component, its "engine," Sūrīd's great recovery device could simply never work. And this engine remains within the Great Pyramid's Big Void to this very day, awaiting discovery (see chapter 6).

Notwithstanding that there is much to support the Coptic-Egyptian oral tradition, this does not seem to shake Egyptologists from their belief that these pyramids were each built as a tomb for a solitary king. In particular, it is their belief that the Great Pyramid was conceived and constructed as the tomb and recovery instrument for one Fourth Dynasty pharaoh, Suphis, also known as Khufu.

Let us now consider the key evidence that convinces Egyptologists that this monument was built not as a recovery vault for the kingdom, but rather as the personal tomb of just one king—Suphis/Khufu. This king may well have built the Great Pyramid, but does the extant evidence prove that Khufu built the monument as his personal tomb? As we shall now see, the available evidence clearly does no such thing.

5

Distorting the Picture

If you ask most Egyptologists why the giant pyramids of the Third and Fourth Dynasties of ancient Egypt were built, you will hear nothing of a grand recovery system for the kingdom (as the Coptic-Egyptian texts inform us). Instead, they will tell you that these first pyramids (and all the pyramids that came thereafter) were built as the eternal tomb and instrument of revivification for the ruling pharaoh of the time. When you ask for proof of this claim, that's when things become a little trickier. And that is because no mummified remains of any ancient Egyptian king have ever been found in situ within any pyramid.* No burial equipment of any king has ever been found in these pyramids, either; no grave goods and no official inscriptions have been found bearing any king's name anywhere inside these particular monuments, not even within the so-called burial chamber or on the so-called sarcophagus. This situation is all the more remarkable given that mastaba tombs (including many burial chambers) from before, during, and after this period were often copiously decorated and also had inscriptions of the deceased's name and titles inscribed into their sarcophagi. But in the first pyramids, there is none of this. Only much later, at the end of the Fifth Dynasty with the pyramid of Unas, do we begin to see official inscriptions (the pyramid texts) being placed on the chamber walls of the pyramid.

---

*Tutankhamen is the only undisturbed burial of an ancient Egyptian king thus far discovered (not in a pyramid but in an underground tomb in the Valley of the Kings).

Looking specifically now at the Great Pyramid, the Coptic-Egyptian priest Manetho (ca. 300 BCE) tells us that it was built by Suphis. However, as we learned earlier, the Coptic-Egyptian oral tradition informs us that it was King Sūrīd (an Arabic name) who built the Great Pyramid. Now, if the name Sūrīd is an Arabic corruption of Manetho's Suphis (as first suggested by Sándor Fodor), a name that the Italian scholar Ippolito Rosellini later identified as belonging to the cartouche of Khufu (whom Herodotus names Cheops), then it may very well be that this ancient Egyptian king Sūrīd did indeed build the Great Pyramid. But none of these proclamations from these historical sources can be considered as solid proof of Sūrīd/Suphis/Khufu's hand in constructing this monument. It is suggestive, certainly, but it is far from definitive.

NAMES OF THE PYRAMID BUILDER BY HISTORIAN				
Historian	Herodotus	Manetho	al-Masudi	Rosellini
Name of Builder	Cheops	Suphis	Sūrīd	Khufu

As matters presently stand, for the definitive proof of their belief that Khufu built the Great Pyramid as his eternal tomb, Egyptologists point to the only empirical evidence that they believe directly connects this king (and *only* this king) to the monument. This consists of some crudely painted hieroglyphic marks* bearing this king's various names that were supposedly discovered within a series of four sealed compartments of the Great Pyramid. As mentioned at the beginning of this book, the presence of these hidden compartments was detected in 1837 by the British antiquarian and pyramid explorer Colonel Richard William Howard Vyse (fig. 5.1) who blasted his way into them with gunpowder. The claimed discovery of this king's various names within these chambers by Vyse was highly significant because this was the very same ancient Egyptian king that Herodotus tells us in his *Histories* was the builder of the Great Pyramid.

---

*These painted markings are technically defined by Egyptologists as cursive old hieratic or linear hieroglyphic script.

Figure 5.1. Colonel Richard William Howard Vyse.

And so, with the various ancient Egyptian names of this king* having been found on the wall and roof blocks of these hidden chambers deep within the Great Pyramid, Egyptologists insisted that they now had irrefutable proof that the structure had been built by Khufu and for Khufu as the eternal resting place of this king and only this king. And since Khufu is believed to have ruled Egypt in the early Fourth Dynasty, which Egyptologists have fixed at around 4,500 years ago, this then became the de facto age for the pyramid itself. With this evidence, it seemed like the pyramid-as-tomb (of Khufu) theory had, finally, been proven.

Or had it?

EGYPTOLOGY'S HOLY GRAIL

Similar painted marks, including royal cartouches bearing the names of various ancient kings, are evident elsewhere at Giza: on some of the exterior stones of the Great Pyramid itself, on some of the stone blocks that, until relatively recently, sealed the southern boat pits, on the walls of the boat pits themselves, on some stone blocks around Menkaure's mortuary temple, and in a number of the mastaba tombs on the Giza plateau. However, with all of these particular inscriptions

---

*An ancient Egyptian king could have as many as five different names or titles.

being *external* to the Great Pyramid, that means it is entirely possible that these painted marks could have been placed in these other locations at any time after the Great Pyramid's original construction, perhaps during repair works to the pyramid by the Fourth Dynasty (and later) pharaohs, repairs to a monument that was perhaps already ancient even in their time. It is merely an assumption by Egyptologists that the boat pits around the Great Pyramid were sealed with their blocking stones in the Fourth Dynasty, but this could very well have occurred much later.

We know, with a fair degree of certainty, that the Sphinx was repaired by at least two later Egyptian dynasties, so it is not unreasonable to suppose that if the Giza pyramids (and other structures such as the boat pits) were contemporaneous with the Sphinx, then these may also have been part of an ancient reparation program, with the names of the various work gangs (e.g., the Followers of Khufu) from these later periods being the only evidence that now remains of various reparation works from later times. This is to say that the various monuments around Giza may well present us with authentic painted marks on the stonework of these monuments from a number of different periods of Egyptian history. How, then, do we know which painted marks are original and contemporary with the structures and which may have been added to the stonework hundreds (or even thousands) of years later during any reparation work?

This is precisely why the marks within the four sealed Vyse Chambers of the Great Pyramid are so important to Egyptology. Being located within areas that were entirely sealed and inaccessible from the time of the original construction, it follows that the painted marks therein must be contemporaneous with the monument's construction; they could not have been added at any time after these small compartments were first sealed because to do so would have meant having to tunnel one's way into these inaccessible chambers, and there was simply no sign of any such activity ever having occurred before Vyse arrived on the scene. And so, what these particular painted marks in these (hitherto) sealed compartments tell us would, naturally, be crucial to our understanding of this monument—assuming the marks are genuine.

The first of these small, hidden compartments was actually discovered in 1765, not by Vyse but by the British consul to Algiers, Nathaniel Davison. He gained entry to this chamber via a precarious climb using a rickety, improvised ladder at the southern end of the pyramid's Grand Gallery. It seems that the tight passage leading into this previously unknown chamber had actually been accessible since the pyramid's construction. Davison became aware of the presence of this passage only by chance when he noticed some bats flying in and out of it, some twenty-eight feet or so above the floor at the top end of the Grand Gallery.

The compartment Davison discovered was very cramped, being only a few feet in height but of similar length and breadth to the King's Chamber. As Davison explored this area on his hands and knees, he found nothing but a floor covered in bat dung; there was no hidden sarcophagus, no treasure, and just like the rest of the pyramid at that time, there was not a single inscription to be found anywhere. Little did Davison know then, but directly above the chamber that now bears his name, a further four hidden chambers awaited discovery.

THE VYSE CHAMBERS

Seventy-two years after Davison made his discovery, Vyse, following on the intuition of his colleague and business partner at the time, Giovanni Caviglia, blasted his way with gunpowder into four sealed compartments above Davison's Chamber, deep within the pyramid (fig. 5.2). These four Vyse Chambers were approximately the same dimensions as the one discovered by Davison. However, in one very important way, the four Vyse Chambers were quite different, for unlike Davison's Chamber and the pyramid's other main chambers (and passageways), the walls in these chambers were said by Vyse to have been covered with crudely drawn inscriptions in red ochre paint and, significantly, presented the name of the Great Pyramid's supposed builder, Khufu (Sūrīd/Suphis).

As mentioned, the importance of these painted marks to Egyptology simply cannot be overstated, for they represent the only empirical evidence that directly connects this Fourth Dynasty pharaoh to the Great

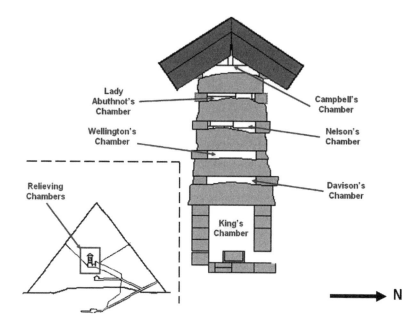

Figure 5.2. Davison's Chamber and the four Vyse Chambers above the King's Chamber.

Pyramid. Vyse's discovery has essentially become Egyptology's holy grail of evidence supporting the entire pyramid-as-tomb-of-Khufu narrative.

Prior to the discovery of these painted inscriptions, the only evidence of Khufu building the pyramid as his tomb that Egyptology could claim was through the writings of Herodotus (writing some two thousand years after the pyramid's supposed construction). But even here, Herodotus does not explicitly state that the pyramid was constructed as Khufu's tomb, only that he was buried on a small island surrounded by water in vaults somewhere beneath the pyramid, a location that has never been found. Egyptologists, however, take the words of Herodotus simply to mean that Khufu was buried in the body of the pyramid rather than in a vault surrounded by water beneath it, as the ancient historian clearly states.*

---

*The ancient Greek historian Diodorus Siculus contests this claim, stating that neither Khufu nor Khafre were buried in their respective pyramids.

But almost from the moment Vyse first presented the painted marks from the four Vyse Chambers to the world, serious questions have surrounded them and, in time, suspicions have grown—particularly that the various names of the king may have been fraudulently placed into these four compartments by two of Vyse's most reliable and dependable assistants, Henry Raven and John Richard Hill (upon Vyse's instructions), and that the colonel perpetrated this great hoax, if not for fortune, then most likely for the prestige, notoriety, and international acclaim that such a major discovery would inevitably have brought. Vyse, by his own account, was a man entirely driven by the desire to make an important, historical discovery, and he expended a sizeable chunk of his own personal fortune (around $1.3 million in today's terms) in pursuit of that very goal. For evidence of Vyse's forgery, turn to the appendices.

BLURRING THE PAST

If we accept that Sūrīd was the likely builder of the pyramid (as the Coptic-Egyptian oral tradition asserts) and we accept that Sūrīd is Suphis and that Suphis is Khufu, ergo, that Khufu built the monument, then do any of Vyse's alleged fraudulent interventions at Giza (to corroborate the monument as belonging to this ancient king) actually matter? Undoubtedly, some will take the view that, ultimately, any nefarious actions by Vyse are irrelevant and that the possibility of these painted marks being the product of fraudulent activity is but a moot point.

Accepting such a view, however, is to entirely miss the insidious and corrupting effect Vyse's alleged actions likely had on the wider study of our ancient history. We simply will never know what unintended consequences may have come about as a result of any fraudulent activity the colonel may have perpetrated within the Great Pyramid. But there are a number of other reasons why Vyse's actions in those chambers in 1837 demand a thorough investigation, and any fraudulent activity therein should be fully exposed.

First of all—and it should really go without saying—frauds and fraudsters should always be investigated and exposed at any level in our society whenever and wherever they are suspected, especially in matters pertaining to our historical and cultural past. That's just good practice. The presence of false evidence serves only to undermine, corrupt, and distort the truth, preventing us from ever seeing the true picture of our past. We do not want our historical understanding to be built on or colored by highly dubious or downright false evidence.

Second, fake evidence proves nothing but can distort much. The fact is, the presence of this highly questionable evidence presented to the world by Vyse effectively permitted Egyptologists to consider that the matter of the Great Pyramid's provenance and purpose had been proven and that any further discussion of the matter was now seen as being without merit and unnecessary. They simply looked no further, dug no deeper because—with Vyse's evidence—the question of the pyramid's builder and its purpose, in their minds, had now been settled beyond question. His actions effectively shaped the thinking of orthodox Egyptology that the Great Pyramid was the tomb and recovery instrument of Khufu and *only* of Khufu. In finding the various names of Khufu (and only this king) in these chambers (there were no other king's or queen's names found), Vyse's "discovery" effectively served to shape and solidify the tomb-of-Khufu narrative and deflected Egyptology from considering other possible purposes for this monument. Like obdurate Clovis-first archaeologists, Egyptologists had the answer they wanted and agreed among themselves that there was no need for further investigation.

The truth, however, is that being dependent on evidence that may very well turn out to have been faked is never a good approach to historical research and is certainly not a scientific one. If anything, Egyptology should have been deeply reticent in accepting the authenticity of these painted marks, the veracity of which rested almost entirely on the reputation and word of one man, Colonel Vyse. Such was the pitiful level of scientific rigor in early Victorian Britain.*

Now let us imagine, for a moment, that forty or fifty different king's and queen's names had been found in these four Vyse Chambers:

---

*See my earlier book *The Great Pyramid Hoax* and the appendices of this book.

Would Egyptology, in such a circumstance, have automatically presumed that this pyramid was merely the tomb of Khufu? Probably not. More than likely, such a discovery would have given them some serious pause for thought. And, equally, what if no king's name had ever been found in any of these four compartments? Given the oral tradition passed down to us from the Coptic-Egyptians, it is quite conceivable in such a circumstance that the tomb-of-Khufu narrative might never have taken root or, at least, might never have become so entrenched, and that an entirely different purpose for these monuments might have arisen as the prevailing view instead.

This is the effect the alleged discovery of these various names of this king presented from these chambers by Vyse has had on Egyptology: it effectively blindsided and stymied its thinking, causing Egyptology to leap to the tomb-of-Khufu conclusion, resulting in the immovable tomb paradigm we find ourselves saddled with today. And the great irony of this, of course, is that Egyptology came to this tomb-of-Khufu conclusion when there already existed another purpose for these structures that the ancients *themselves* spoke of but that Egyptologists simply chose to ignore and dismiss as mere myth and legend. They didn't look any deeper into the superficial painted marks in these chambers. They didn't think they had to. They had their man! That is the legacy of Vyse's potentially fraudulent actions and why we need the chance to reconsider the truth of these monuments. Resetting our minds and relegating the tomb-of-Khufu narrative to the bin where it almost certainly belongs is to get to the real reason why Sūrīd/Suphis/Khufu built the Great Pyramid.

PATTERNS IN CHAOS

When Vyse commenced his operations at Giza in November 1836, the scene that greeted him would have been one of chaos. The base of the Great Pyramid up to its entrance was entirely inaccessible, with a fifty-foot mound of debris—stones and sand—blocking access to the monument. As Vyse worked to have this debris gradually removed, it is conjectured here that, in so doing, he would have stumbled across some limestone blocks recovered from this debris, stone blocks that had painted hieratic signs on them—the names of various ancient quarry gangs with their associated king's names (along with some other sundry markings).

We know from Vyse's writings that he had seen such quarry marks elsewhere outside the pyramid, so any potential discovery of painted marks on any stones among the debris there, while they would likely have been of some interest to academia, could not have conclusively proven the pyramid's association to Khufu. Being found outside the pyramid means that these painted marks could have been painted onto these external stones at any time, perhaps by repair gangs long after the pyramid had been completed.

And so, it may have been while observing the painted marks on these external stones that Vyse had a devilish thought: What if painted marks just like those he was finding on some of the stones outside the pyramid were found within the sealed chambers he was blasting his way into? Such would surely be considered an enormously important discovery since, being found within chambers that had been sealed since the pyramid's construction, then such marks have to be considered contemporaneous with the construction and, as such, would finally corroborate the claim by Herodotus that the Fourth Dynasty king, Suphis/Khufu, had indeed built the Great Pyramid.

With the discovery of these painted marks on the stones in the debris *outside* the pyramid, Vyse could have claimed for himself an academically interesting though somewhat inconclusive discovery, or he could use the painted marks on these external stones in a totally different way in order to claim for himself a highly significant discovery and thus secure for himself a place in the world's history books. And so, given Vyse's near desperation to make an important discovery during his time at Giza, the fame and notoriety of proving Khufu's association with the Great Pyramid may well have been too alluring for the colonel to resist: the painted marks he (hypothetically) discovered outside the pyramid would now be used to much greater effect *within* the monument. In discovering the various names of Suphis/Khufu painted within (hitherto) sealed chambers of the Great Pyramid, a provenance that was, indisputably, contemporaneous with the pyramid's construction, then the colonel would give to Egyptology the holy grail of evidence.

INADMISSIBLE EVIDENCE

As shown in my previous works and in the appendices of this book, considerable doubt can be cast on the veracity of Vyse's claimed discovery of the painted quarry marks within the Great Pyramid at Giza. What we must now do is place his discovery aside, treat it as inadmissible, and take our minds back to a time before it ever existed. Had this evidence never been presented by Vyse, would Egyptologists have been so certain that the Great Pyramid had been built as the tomb of Khufu? Would they have perhaps given more consideration to the Coptic-Egyptian oral tradition that speaks of an entirely different purpose for these monuments?

All that remains for us to do now is to continue our investigation into this ancient monument to see if there is anything within it that might prove the Coptic-Egyptian oral tradition that these pyramids were, in fact, built not as the tomb for an individual king to reach his afterlife but rather as a recovery system for the entire kingdom to be reborn again after an anticipated natural disaster.

This book predicts that the evidence for such a system will be found within the Big Void, for this mysterious, newly discovered space within this monument was the beating heart of the entire recovery system, the engine that, without which, the hoped-for rebirth of the kingdom would have utterly failed. But this engine within the Big Void is not what we might think.

Let us now discover and consider this mysterious new pyramid chamber and the remarkable secret it almost certainly holds within.

6
Into the Void

This book began by presenting the discovery of the Big Void—a potentially massive new chamber within the Great Pyramid—and went on to show how there exists some good evidence to indicate that the Coptic-Egyptian oral tradition that speaks of the purpose of the Great Pyramid as some kind of ark may actually be based more in fact than the myth believed by Egyptology. This Big Void (fig. 6.1) is believed to be almost as big as the Grand Gallery (157 × 28 feet), though at present, scientists remain uncertain as to whether or not the space is horizontal or inclined like the Grand Gallery.

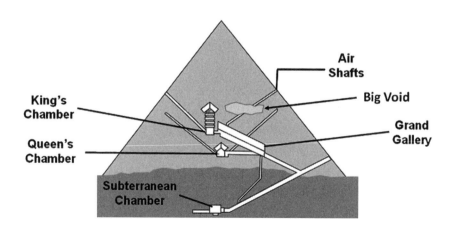

Figure 6.1. The Chambers of the Great Pyramid, showing the Big Void.
(Image: Scott Creighton)

Mainstream Egyptologists are scratching their heads as to why such a massive space should exist within the Great Pyramid at all. While Egyptologists such as Mark Lehner and Zahi Hawass of the ScanPyramids project team advise caution in declaring this space a new chamber, it seems perfectly clear from the data that this massive void is not like many of the much smaller sand- and mortar-filled voids that the Great Pyramid is peppered with. Indeed, this void appears to be something altogether different, and it is highly likely that after further investigation, it will be found to be the fifth major chamber within the Great Pyramid.

One of the reasons why Egyptologists are hesitant to pronounce this void as a new pyramid chamber is that there is no obvious entry to it. No passageways or connecting tunnels have been detected. If it is indeed a purposely built chamber, then it appears to be entirely isolated and apparently without any obvious means of access. Why would Sūrīd/Khufu build his pyramid with a totally inaccessible chamber inside it?

Some have speculated that Khufu may have built this chamber to store his treasure to perhaps take with him to the afterlife.[1] This scenario seems highly unlikely because, in accordance with ancient Egyptian burial rituals, grave goods would be deposited inside the pyramid only after the king's death, by which time this chamber would have been long completed and sealed.[2] How, then, would it have been possible to place Khufu's afterlife goods into a chamber to which there was no access, a chamber that was entirely sealed off as the Pyramid was built upward and over it?

The tomb paradigm, quite simply, cannot adequately explain this anomaly, especially if this void is found to be a purposely built, inaccessible chamber. But while everyone is focused on the Big Void and the modern science that went into discovering it, unsurprisingly, no one is considering what the ancient Egyptians themselves have said with regard to the building of the pyramids and wondering if there is any clue in their ancient texts to shed light on this important discovery.

Vyse quotes what the Coptic-Egyptian texts tell us. This was noted in chapter 2, but now the next important bit of information is given.

The king then directed the astrologers to ascertain by taking the altitude whether the stars foretold any great catastrophe, and the result announced an approaching deluge. The king ordered them to inquire whether or not this calamity would befall Egypt; and they answered, yes, the flood will overwhelm the land, and destroy a large portion of it for some years. . . . Upon which the king ordered the Pyramids to be built, and the predictions of the priests to be Inscribed upon columns, and upon the large stones belonging to them; and he placed within them his treasures, and all his valuable property, *together with the bodies of his ancestors.* (italics added)[3]

And there's the clue: this text suggests that the Big Void within the Great Pyramid is a chamber built specifically to house and protect "the bodies of his [Surīd's] ancestors."

What must be appreciated here is that the ancient Egyptians believed their deceased kings and queens continued to perform a vital role for the living kingdom. In the afterlife, their role was to intercede with the gods in the heavenly realm to assist the living king to ensure the sun would rise, the Nile would flow, and the crops would grow. Indeed, part of the reason why it was essential that the bodies of these kings and queens were preserved and mummified was to protect them against decay, because a decayed body could not fulfill this vital function in the afterlife. It was also the job of the living king to protect the tombs of these long-deceased kings and queens from robbery or desecration and to give prayers and offerings to help nurture them. Indeed, failing to do this could bring dire consequences for the living king and the kingdom. Researcher and author Alan F. Alford explains:

The servicing of the ancestors' tombs by the king generated a virtuous circle of creative energy. By rejuvenating the bodies of the ancestors, the king enables their spirits to make the circuit of the cosmos. . . . He was then able to draw on this power to service the tombs of the ancestors. . . . By supporting each other, across the threshold of death, the [living] Horus-king and the [deceased] Osiris-kings ensured that the repetitions of creation—of the death and rebirth of the world—could be performed in perpetuity."[4]

And so, as a consequence of their religious beliefs, the ancient Egyptians had great reverence for their ancestor kings and queens and would go to quite extraordinary lengths to protect their long-expired bodies, often removing their mummified remains from their original tombs to new, safer tomb locations when it seemed their original tombs were in danger of some kind (usually from tomb raiders). An example of this practice comes to us from the famous tomb DB320 (now referenced as TT320), located in the Theban cliffs of Deir el-Bahri.

When discovered in 1871 (by a tomb robber by the name of Ahmed Abd el-Rassul), the tomb was found to contain the mummified remains of no less than fifty ancient Egyptian kings, queens, and other members of the royal court, placed there at some time during the Twenty-First Dynasty (1069–945 BCE). Included among the kings discovered were the mummies of Amosis, Ramesses I–III, Ramesses IX, Seti I, Tuthmosis I–III, Amenhotep I, and his mother, Queen Ahmose Nefertari. Over the next ten years, the el-Rassul family pillaged this royal cache, selling countless numbers of precious ancient artifacts on the illegal antiquities market. Eventually, the Egyptian authorities became suspicious and soon caught up with the el-Rassul family business.

Émile Brugsch, assistant to the great French Egyptologist Gaston Maspero, described the scene when he became the first person outside the el-Rassul family to enter this tomb.

Soon we came upon cases of porcelain funerary offerings, metal and alabaster vessels, draperies and trinkets, until, reaching the turn in the passage, a cluster of mummy cases came into view in such numbers as to stagger me.

Collecting my senses, I made the best examination of them I could by the light of my torch and at once saw that they contained the mummies of royal personages of both sexes; and yet that was not all. Plunging on ahead of my guide, I came to the [end] chamber . . . , and there standing against the walls or here lying on the floor, I found even a greater number of mummy-cases of stupendous size and weight.

Their gold coverings and their polished surfaces so plainly reflected my own excited visage that it seemed like I was looking into the faces of my own ancestors."[5]

That all of these kings and queens were discovered together in a single tomb was apparently the result of a collapse of the Egyptian state, a collapse that led to a decrease in the protection of sacred sites and a consequential increase in tomb robbery. To protect the kings and queens (and by extension, the kingdom itself) from this danger, the Egyptian priests gathered together the mummified remains from their various original tombs and removed them to what they believed would be a much safer burial location.[6]

But this practice raises an intriguing question: What, then, would you do if you believed your entire civilization was soon to be comprehensively obliterated by a cataclysmic deluge, the waters of which would surge over the entire Earth, washing away all traces of your ancestors and thereby ending forever their ability to maintain the kingdom?

You would build a monumental recovery device consisting of immovable stone mountains that would contain everything required to bring about the recovery or rebirth of the kingdom after the deluge had abated. Yes—seeds, tools, knowledge, and other useful items would be important to place within your recovery device. However, the single most important thing your pyramid recovery device absolutely *must* contain would be the means by which to make the desired recovery actually happen through the agency of the deceased Osiris-kings, the gods.

Were the bodies of the ancestor kings and queens to be destroyed in the coming deluge, then there could be no Osiris-kings to commune with the gods and, therefore, no recovery could ever come about. None. It would be like building a hospital without any medical staff or a car without an engine. These ancestor kings and queens were the key, the *engine,* the *power* that, without which, no recovery could ever even be hoped for. And so the deceased Osiris-kings—Surīd's ancestors—had to be protected from the coming deluge, and this was achieved by relocating them from their original (less protected) tombs and placing them within a great Hall of the Ancestors (that is, the Big Void); a massive, inaccessible chamber built high up in the pyramid recovery device.

In short, the ancient Egyptians' gathering together the mummified bodies of all their ancestor kings and queens from around the country and reburying them in a single massive chamber in the heart of the Great Pyramid was their way of protecting and preserving their ancestors for all time, specifically, from the chaos and destruction, *isfet,* in the foretold deluge and thereby ensuring that the cosmic order, *ma'at,* could be maintained. This reburial was the means of ensuring the preservation and continuation of the eternal union between the Horus and Osirian kings, to bring about the rebirth of the kingdom after its anticipated demise.

It is likely that future, more detailed scans of the Big Void will reveal that there are no access tunnels anywhere leading to this chamber since the bodies of the ancestor kings and queens of Surīd would likely have been lowered into this great Hall of the Ancestors when the roof of this chamber was still open, providing the *only* access to this space. Once all the ancestor kings and queens had been interred therein, the Great Hall would have been completely sealed over as the pyramid was built upward to its completion.

WHY A PYRAMID?

For a number of reasons, the giant pyramids of the early Old Kingdom period were far from the ideal places to bury the ancient Egyptian kings and queens, so choosing such massively visible structures to inter their bodies could only have been made after careful consideration and weighing the pros and cons.* Indeed, it seems that there may have been

---

*This is documented in more detail in my previous book, *The Secret Chamber of Osiris: Lost Knowledge of the Sixteen Pyramids,* 51–81.

a benefit of using the pyramid form for this purpose that outweighed all of the potential drawbacks.

A 2018 headline in the British newspaper the *Independent* read, "Great Pyramid of Giza May Be Able to Focus Electromagnetic Energy through Its Hidden Chambers, Physicists Reveal," and the article itself stated, "The Great Pyramid of Giza may be able to focus electromagnetic radiation into pockets of energy inside its network of internal chambers and underneath its base, a new study has suggested."[7]

Various scientific studies have shown that exposure to electromagnetic fields can reduce or slow the decay rates of bacteria and inhibit bacteria spore formation. The bodies of the ancestor kings and queens had to be preserved at all costs as they were the vital element—the engine—of the entire recovery system. It was absolutely essential to prevent the bodies from decaying or, at least, to much reduce the effects of decay. Embalming the body was one method the ancient Egyptians used, but by then placing the bodies within a structure that itself possessed properties that could further inhibit decay would obviously have been desirable. But what proof is there that the pyramid shape can inhibit the decay of organic matter? Consider the results of the following study:

Six milk samples in glass beakers of 100 ml volume were kept under the test pyramids and one of the samples was kept in open as control. These milk samples were assessed for 2 weeks. The pyramids were kept in a single room and placed 1.5m away from one another. ... The milk specimen placed outside as a control started to deteriorate after 24 hours; while samples placed within the pyramids (test samples) showed delay in deterioration. ... Among wooden pyramids, the octal form was better than the square and small-square pyramids.[8]

Interestingly, in this study it was found that an eight-sided pyramid performed best in reducing deterioration in the milk samples. Perhaps this may explain why the Great Pyramid itself is also an eight-sided structure.

If the true function of the Great Pyramid's Big Void is indeed to be a safe haven for Sūrīd's ancestors, it would then be important to further reduce their mummified bodies to the effects of organic decay (and, of course, from the total destruction of the coming deluge). But how many ancestor kings and queens might we expect to find within it?

While we cannot currently know this with any degree of certainty, there may, in fact, be a big clue to this number hidden in plain sight within the known chambers of the Great Pyramid, specifically the twenty-seven pairs of enigmatic notches or holes cut into the two pavements of the Grand Gallery. In *Pyramid Quest: Secrets of the Great Pyramid and the Dawn of Civilization,* Robert Schoch and Robert McNally note "a series of 27 holes . . . occurring in pairs on either side, and alternating between longer ones of about 23.3 inches and shorter ones of about 20.5 inches. They are about 6¼ inches wide and cut to varying depths, usually 8 to 11 inches. In the walls above these holes are vertically arranged inset stones, each about 18 inches high and 13 inches wide, with a groove cut across each."[9]

In his book *The Mysteries of the Great Pyramids* (1978), the physicist and Egyptology enthusiast André Pochan proposed that these trapezoidal pavement notches and inset holes of the Grand Gallery (fig. 6.2a) were slots into which great statues of Khufu's ancestors were to be inserted (fig. 6.2b)—the larger notches for the larger king statues and the smaller notches for the smaller queen statues. These statues would alternate, king and queen, king and queen on both sides of the gallery, with each king and his queen facing each other.

In support of his hypothesis, Pochan writes:

That the Grand Gallery is simply the gallery of the ancestors is corroborated by two ancient Arab authors. Muhamed ibn Ishaq Ibn al-Nadim, quoted by Ahmad ibn Ali al-Maqrizi, writes . . . "A passage pierces this pavement . . . ; the arch is made of stone and one sees there portraits and statues standing or resting and a quantity of other things, the meaning of which we do not understand." And Ibrahim Wassif Shah writes: . . . "In the eastern pyramid [Great Pyramid], chambers had been built in which the stars and heavens were depicted, and in which was amassed what Sūrīd's forebears had accomplished in the way of statues."

(Undoubtedly, the manuscript's text has been misreported; it should read "in which were amassed the statues that were done of Sūrīd's forebears.")[10]

Figure 6.2a. The trapezoidal notches in the left pavement of the Grand Gallery. The inset holes above each pavement notch have been filled with modern cement. (Image: Scott Creighton)

Figure 6.2b. The Gallery of Ancestors.
(Artist impression based on photo by Keith Adler)

But if the Coptic-Egyptian tradition is right and Sūrīd did gather up and place the actual bodies of his ancestors within an inaccessible chamber high up in the Great Pyramid, why then would the king also have placed statues of his ancestors in the Grand Gallery, as Pochan describes? Why did Sūrīd require the actual bodies of his ancestors in the upper Big Void and also replica statues of them in the lower Grand Gallery?

The answer to this may be that these Grand Gallery statues of the ancestor kings and queens weren't simple profane statues but rather that they served a very specific and highly significant religious function related to the actual mummified bodies in the great Hall of the Ancestors (the Big Void), and that this function was related to the ancient Egyptian religious concept of the *ka,* or "double."

> The ka was a kind of astral double or spiritual duplicate of the deceased that was necessary for existence in the next world. When a person died, the ka continued to dwell in the body, and one reason for mummification was to ensure the ka a dwelling place. In case the mummy was damaged or destroyed, *many Egyptians were buried with a ka statue.* The statue was a portrait of the deceased that the ka could recognize and was meant to be an alternative dwelling for the ka if the mummy was not suitable. (italics added)[11]

If this newly discovered void high above the Grand Gallery is indeed a great Hall of the Ancestors that contains the actual bodies of Sūrīd's ancestors, then this would make sense as each of the ancestor statues believed by Pochan to have once stood in the Grand Gallery would have effectively served as each ancestor's ka double.* It seems that the ancient Egyptians were taking no chances with their great recovery device.

By simply counting the number of these notches in the two pavements of the Grand Gallery, we may have an idea of precisely how many statues (ka doubles) were once in place there and thus the number of

---

*From around the Twelfth Dynasty, this religious concept was extended with the introduction of decorated anthropoid coffins and sarcophagi that served also as the ka double.

ancestor kings and queens that may have been interred by Surīd in the hidden Hall of the Ancestors above: 27 pairs of notches = 54 ka statues = 54 ancestor kings and queens.

It may be no coincidence that from the time of King Menes, the first king of the unified kingdom, through the second king of the Fourth Dynasty, there were indeed a total of twenty-seven ancestor kings of Khufu as shown below.

THE TWENTY-SEVEN ANCESTOR KINGS OF KHUFU

Dynasty One (10 Kings)
Menes (Narmer), Hor-Aha, Djer, Djet, Den, Anedjib, Semerkhet, Snefer-ka, Horus Bird, Qa'a

Dynasty Two (11 Kings)
Hotepsekhemwy, Raneb (Nebra), Nynetjer, Weneg (Ouneg), Sened (Sendj), Peribsen, Sekhemib-Perenmaet, Neferkare, Neferkaseker, Hutchfa (Hudjefa), Khasekhemwy

Dynasty Three (5 Kings)
Djoser, Sekhemkhet, Sanakht (Nebka), Khaba, Huni

Dynasty Four (1 King)
Sneferu (Khufu's father)

Total = 27 kings

Of course, with so many ancient Egyptian kings and queens being reinterred in the great recovery device, it would surely be reasonable to expect some evidence pointing to this process of relocating Khufu's ancestors. As it happens, we may actually have such evidence, the final piece of this historical puzzle.

SHOW ME THE MUMMY

One of the great mysteries of Egyptology is that no original burial of any pharaoh has ever been found within the pyramids. Certainly, bits of human bone, mummy wrappings, and other minor artifacts have been discovered within various pyramids, but none of these have been conclusively proven to have come from an original burial of a king and most, in fact, have been shown to come from much later, intrusive burials.

The stock answer from the Egyptologists to this apparent paradox, this lack of pyramid mummies, is to propose that the pyramid tombs were robbed in antiquity and that every royal mummy was destroyed by the tomb raiders, usually by burning in an attempt to remove the precious amulets that were usually placed in the mummy's bindings during the embalming process. However, even more puzzling is that a number of undisturbed burials have been found with their sarcophagi still fully intact and *sealed*, and yet, when the stone box was opened in modern times, it was found to be empty, entirely devoid of any royal mummy!

One of the most bizarre of these occurrences took place at Giza in 1925 when the archaeological team led by the esteemed Egyptologist George Reisner discovered (by a fluke accident) the hidden, underground shaft tomb of Khufu's mother, Queen Hetepheres I (fig. 6.3a, p. 128), just a short distance to the east of the Great Pyramid. About this, Egyptologist Barbara Mertz writes:

> Distinguished visitors and high government officials were lowered down the shaft in basket chairs and crammed themselves into the little room. The great moment had arrived. The heavy sarcophagus lid was prized up. In a hush of anticipation Reisner stooped to peer inside. Then he straightened and faced the distinguished audience. "Gentlemen," he said wryly, "I regret Queen Hetephres is not receiving. . . ." What puzzled Reisner was why the elaborate care and secrecy had been expended on the burial on an empty sarcophagus. It had been used for burial; certain discolorations on the bottom proved that much. . . .
>
> What disturbs me is the fact that there have been other sarcophagi found in place, unopened—and empty. Two of them date to the Third Dynasty, not so distant in time from the heyday of Hetephres. The cases are not exactly parallel, but yet there remains the incontestable and bewildering common feature of the empty sarcophagi.[12]

This particular empty tomb (designated G7000x by Egyptologists) remains, to this day, one of the greatest mysteries of ancient Egypt. The typical answer by Egyptologists in response to this conundrum is that the royal personage was perhaps lost in battle, or had drowned in the Nile to then be devoured by crocodiles, or was killed by some other calamity that meant the body was otherwise unavailable for burial. These explanations for the absence of the royal mummy are typically given without any evidence to back up the assertion, which, in time, becomes so embedded in the mainstream narrative that it becomes accepted as historical fact rather than seen as the mere speculation that it usually is.

Reisner writes in more detail of the moment the sarcophagus within that small burial chamber was finally opened:

> I never doubted that the mummy was in the coffin. . . . Every eye was fixed on the sarcophagus. The lid started from its place, quite easily breaking the five seals, and came up slowly a line at a time. We saw the inside walls of the sarcophagus gradually coming into view, and moment by moment looked deeper into the interior. It was soon evident that there was no inner case; and finally, after ten minutes, we all realized that the sarcophagus was empty and almost as clean as the day it was made. In my preliminary statement I had mentioned every possibility except the one which lay patent before us. There was no mummy in the coffin. . . . We examined carefully the inside of the coffin. A faint discoloration at one end showed that it had once been used. . . . At last we had found in the tomb part of the mortal remains of the mother of Cheops, probably all that will ever be recovered. These Canopic packages were in a chest which was made of the same stone and clearly by the same craftsmen as the alabaster sarcophagus, and proved that the body which once rested in the coffin had been mummified.[13]

Various artifacts within the burial chamber presented the names of Sneferu and Hetepheres, Khufu's father and mother. Mud seals found among the tomb debris also bore the inscription "embalming

Figure 6.3a. The underground burial chamber (G7000x)
of Khufu's mother, Queen Hetepheres I, at Giza.
(Image: George Reisner, 1925)

Figure 6.3c. The canopic
chest containing the viscera of
Queen Hetepheres I.
(Image: George Reisner, 1927)

Figure 6.3b. When the sarcophagus was
opened, the queen's body was missing.
(Image: George Reisner, 1927)

house of Khufu,"* and as such, Egyptologists concluded that the tomb belonged to Khufu's mother, Queen Hetepheres I.[14] Here then we have a queen, Khufu's mother, the most important queen in Khufu's court, whose body had evidently not been lost to a Nile crocodile or, it would seem, to any other such disaster since the sarcophagus appears to have been used and the queen's internal organs had been removed from the body, embalmed, and placed in a canopic chest in this burial chamber, deep under the bedrock of the Giza plateau.

Many of the queen's grave goods were also found in the chamber, including a number of sheets of gold. The presence of these gold sheets and other items of value ruled out the activity of tomb raiders, who would surely have taken these and, most likely, would have smashed the sarcophagus lid to access the royal mummy and the many precious amulets often placed within the mummy's linen wrappings. Furthermore, it is highly improbable that tomb robbers would have taken the time to replace the heavy lid back onto the sarcophagus after having removed the royal mummy.

Nonetheless, in an attempt to explain this mystery, Reisner goes on to offer his hypothesis as to why the queen's body was missing from the sarcophagus.

> This lady outlived Sneferu and was buried by her son Cheops [Khufu], probably beside her husband's pyramid at Dahshur. The [original] tomb did not remain long undisturbed and the queen's body was destroyed by the robbers who broke into the chamber. A clever prime minister seems to have been able to convince Cheops that little damage had been done. He ordered the lid of the alabaster coffin replaced to hide the absence of the queen's body, and the greater part of the unharmed burial equipment was moved to a secret shaft in front of the Great Pyramid in the new cemetery at Giza. Cheops apparently never discovered the ruse practised upon

---

*This inscription raises an interesting question as to why Khufu would have required an "embalming house" years before his own death. Was this embalming house perhaps a place where the ancestor mummies were sent for checking and possible re-embalming before being placed within the Big Void's Hall of the Ancestors?

him by his minister, for he made an offering to his mother's spirit before the shaft was finally closed.[15]

No one can fault Reisner for his imagination here, but there are simply too many flaws in his hypothesis for it to be anywhere near tenable or even plausible. Indeed, Mark Lehner discounted Reisner's theory, writing:

> The hypothetical original tomb of Hetep-heres I at Dahshur has not been found (the only evidence for this queen's existence comes from G7000x). There is no textual evidence, contemporary with the 4th Dynasty or from later times, for the plundering of this tomb and the transfer of its contents to Giza. Reisner's reconstruction of events is based entirely upon the archaeological evidence gathered from G7000x. Nevertheless, his scenario was passed down in the literature, e.g., *The Cambridge Ancient History* (Smith 1971, 168), as historical fact.[16]

Lehner has his own view that this tomb of Hetepheres I (G7000x) was not a reburial of the queen at all but that this tomb was, in fact, the queen's original tomb, that her body was later transferred by Egyptian officials to the first of Khufu's three so-called Queens' Pyramids (G1-a), and that the lid of the queen's original sarcophagus in G7000x was then reseated and the sarcophagus once again sealed by Khufu's officials. Lehner writes:

> It is possible that . . . the queen mother's body was removed from the tomb [G7000x] before the final blocking of the shaft was effected. Could she have been buried in the first queen's pyramid tomb (GI-a) with a new uncontaminated set of funerary equipment? . . . Even though this opening damaged the sarcophagus slightly, it does not appear the work of thieves who, as said earlier, would have taken the more expeditious approach of smashing the lid entirely. If not thieves, then it must have been officials who opened the sarcophagus.[17]

However, what goes against Lehner's hypothesis is that none of the queen's grave goods were transferred to the new pyramid tomb, G1-a, but appear to have been left behind in their entirety in the original tomb at Giza. Also, there are no inscriptions of any kind in or around pyramid G1-a attributing or in any way connecting this pyramid to Queen Hetepheres I. Finally, pyramid G1-a is believed to actually have been a tomb belonging not to Khufu's mother but rather to one of Khufu's wives, Merytyetes (a daughter of Sneferu and Hetepheres I). Lehner underlines this with the following comment:

> Merytyetes' claim to the first queen's pyramid [G1-a] is thought to be strengthened by the loose principle of familial proximity— that tombs of immediate family members are situated close by one another (Smith 1971, 168). Since the large mastaba directly east of GI-a belongs to Kawab, and if the fragments assigned to his chapel do establish Merytyetes as his mother, the first queen's pyramid could be that of Merytyetes. Smith states this with some certainty: "the position of Kawab's tomb makes it certain that he was the son of Cheops's chief queen buried in the Pyramid GI-a. The above evidence strongly suggests that this chief queen was Merytyetes.[18]

The two other Queens' Pyramids to the south of G1-a are (tentatively) believed to have belonged to Queens Noubet (G1-b) and Henutsen (G1-c). All of which, of course, raises the obvious question: If all of the Queens' Pyramids had been assigned to other queens of Khufu, then where was Queen Hetepheres I, Khufu's mother, interred after being removed from her original underground tomb?

There is, of course, an entirely different narrative by which the circumstances and disappearance of this ancient queen's body can be simply and rationally explained, along with the other Third Dynasty kings' sarcophagi found in similar circumstances.

Lehner is probably correct in suspecting that G7000x at Giza was the original tomb of Khufu's mother, but given the complete absence of a mastaba superstructure over the queen's burial chamber, the haphazard arrangement of her grave goods, and the irregular positioning of the sarcophagus within the burial chamber, we are very much presented with the impression that this shaft tomb was but a *temporary* burial site for this queen. If we suppose that Khufu's mother had died some time before the great Hall of the Ancestors (the Big Void chamber) had been completed or was ready to receive its assembly of mummified ancestor kings and queens, then such a temporary tomb would have been needed for her temporary burial. What would not have been needed in this instance, of course, would have been any mastaba or pyramid super-structure over the tomb—her house of eternity—as her eternal home was to be alongside her husband (and other ancestors) within the great Hall of the Ancestors high up inside the Great Pyramid itself. It is per-haps worth noting here that the Grand Gallery and the Big Void are both oriented north-south and have sloping sides, just like the ancient Egyptian mastaba tombs.

This idea of G7000x being a temporary tomb for Khufu's mother is supported by the Egyptologist Vivienne Gae Callender, who writes:

> As Lehner initially suggested, Khufu may indeed have intended his mother to have pyramid G1a in the Eastern Cemetery; subsequently, during the course of that pyramid's construction, she may have died. After her mummification, there would have been a funeral, com-plete with a procession of goods for the queen's afterlife, but then the need will have arisen for a place to store these things until the completion of the pyramid. A previously abandoned shaft tomb was thus used to hold Hetepheres' body and grave goods until her pyra-mid chamber was made ready (indications of the temporary nature of her interment are the incorrect positioning of the sarcophagus, the non-traditional treatment of the canopic chest, and the evident disorder of the funerary offerings). It must have been intended as a temporary tomb because, at ground level, the very inconvenient proximity of the shaft to the king's mortuary temple and causeway would certainly ensure that this place was never intended to have a superstructure, as it would have been out of place in the final design of the Eastern Cemetery.[19]

The mother of Khufu, according to Egyptologists, was placed in a temporary tomb until her permanent tomb was ready. But this permanent tomb wasn't pyramid G1-a as Egyptologists assume, or any of the other small satellite pyramids beside the Great Pyramid. It was the Great Pyramid itself. Upon completion of the Big Void, Khufu's officials would have reopened tomb G7000x, removed the mummy of Hetepheres I, and transferred her, not to a satellite pyramid as believed by Egyptologists Lehner and Callender (and for which there is no evidence), but to the Hall of the Ancestors in the Big Void, high up within the Great Pyramid, to be placed alongside her husband, Khufu's father, Sneferu, the last in a long line of his ancestor kings and queens to be set inside Khufu's great recovery device, ready to intercede with the gods. The queen's original sarcophagus would have been ritually resealed and her temporary tomb closed up, a process that would likely have occurred with the relocation of all of Khufu's ancestor kings and their queens, leaving behind only their resealed but now empty sarcophagi for modern Egyptologists to puzzle over.

Finally, as with all the other ancestor kings and queens placed within this great Hall of the Ancestors, a ka statue would have been placed for the queen in the Grand Gallery below to serve as a surrogate double for her ka should her mummified body become too decayed.

And so, with the full lineage of Khufu's ancestors now in place, the Big Void's Hall of the Ancestors would then have been sealed as the pyramid was built upward to its completion.

Perhaps the simple truth of the missing body of Khufu's mother and the empty sarcophagi of the Third Dynasty kings is precisely as the Coptic-Egyptian oral tradition tells us: that King Sūrīd/Khufu took the bodies of his ancestors and placed them in a hidden chamber high up within the Great Pyramid to protect them from the foretold deluge.

What is also perhaps significant here is that the examples of sealed and empty sarcophagi that have been found appear only from the period before and up to the construction of the Great Pyramid. This is to say that we find these peculiar empty burials only among Khufu's *ancestor* kings and queens and not among any of those kings or queens that came after Khufu's reign. The empty sarcophagi from these later dynasties are never resealed, and the lids have often been smashed and destroyed by tomb raiders to gain access to the mummified body and the precious amulets within. Had this sealed, empty-sarcophagus phenomenon been a normal practice of the ancient Egyptians of Khufu's time (and thereafter), then we would surely have found examples of such burials from the period *after* the time of Khufu—but we don't. Thus it seems we have evidence of these peculiar reburials only from among Khufu's ancestors—just as the Coptic-Egyptian Sūrīd narrative tells us.

Head Hunters

The ka surrogate statues that once likely stood within the Grand Gallery may also help to explain another of Egypt's strange enigmas—the so-called Reserve Heads. Around thirty-seven of these sculpted limestone heads (male and female) were found in a number of Fourth Dynasty tombs, mostly in the Western Cemetery at Giza and, bizarrely, most seem to bear the scars of deliberate mutilation whereby the ears of each head have been severely damaged or even entirely removed. Many also present a deep vertical gouge running down the back of the head. Egyptologists struggle to adequately explain the seemingly deliberate damage to these heads since acts of this kind occur only rarely in other Egyptian sculpture. If we imagine, however, that each of these heads once belonged to a full ka surrogate statue within the Grand Gallery then we may begin to perceive a better solution to this particular mystery.

Since the only access to the Great Pyramid in ancient times would have been via the very narrow Well Shaft,* it would have been impossible to remove a full ka statue, so robbers merely took the most valuable part, the statue's head. To remove the head would first have required the levering of the statute from its wall and pavement mountings. The most obvious initial point of attack would, naturally, have been each statue's ears since these protrusions would effec-

---

*The Well Shaft is believed by Egyptologists to have been the exit or escape route used by the pyramid builders after they had blocked access to the pyramid's upper chambers by sliding granite blocks believed to have been stored in the Grand Gallery down the Ascending Passage, which by doing so they would have otherwise sealed themselves within the structure.

tively have served as a nub or boss to provide a fulcrum point upon which wood or metal levers could be placed to pry the statue away from the gallery wall. When the ears eventually sheared or crumbled as a result of the applied pressure, the robbers would then place their lever behind the statue's head to apply further pressure to force the statue fully from its mountings and, in so doing, cause the deep gouge observed in the back of each of the affected heads.

With the statue now free from the wall, the head would be cut from the torso, removed from the pyramid (via the Well Shaft) and the torso probably broken up and discarded over the millennia.

KHUFU'S TOMB?

But what of Khufu himself? Would he, after his own death, have had himself placed within the great recovery device he had built? In short, probably not.

The whole point of the great Hall of the Ancestors is that it would be completed and sealed as quickly as possible and that the hall would become entirely inaccessible once completed. The mummified bodies of the ancestors would have been lowered into the chamber when its roof was still open and the chamber accessible. When the pyramid was built upward to its completion, the chamber (the Big Void) would have then become completely sealed and inaccessible, even to Khufu (who was still the living Horus king). Unlike all the other known chambers within the Great Pyramid, there would be no access passages of any kind leading to the Big Void chamber. Indeed, this is its main security feature. If there is no leading passage, then it becomes virtually impossible for any robber to know where to even begin to search and tunnel for such a hidden chamber. And it might even be that the known chambers and passages within the pyramid may actually have been (partially) designed as a decoy system from the very beginning of the project. Khufu, however, could never in his wildest imagination have anticipated the space-age technology that could potentially confound his great plan.

One of the peculiar aspects of the Great Pyramid is that it invites exploration of its internal passages and chambers and has done so right from its very inception.* The Descending Passage, for example, was never filled in and sealed, and it seems to have been accessible from the remotest times. Khufu most assuredly would not have wanted to have been buried within a pyramid with an easily discovered passage system that invited and led tomb robbers more or less straight to the upper chambers of the structure. Granite blocking stones would have been no barrier to determined robbers, men likely well practiced in quarrying heavy stone. And having entered what they believed (and what Egyptologists today believe) to be the king's burial chamber and finding the granite box there filled with nothing more than black Egyptian earth,† then, with no other obvious passageways to examine, they would likely have given up in disgust. In short, if the passageway or entrance shaft to a chamber is difficult to discover (such as that of Hetepheres I), then the chamber at the end of the passageway will likely remain undisturbed for a very long time. And if there is no passageway or shaft whatsoever leading to the chamber, then the chamber and its contents could likely remain hidden, potentially forever.

But if the great Hall of the Ancestors was now sealed (possibly many years before Sūrīd/Khufu's death) and with no passageways leading to this chamber for any later interment, then what became of this king? Where was Khufu buried? While some ancient commentators claim that Khufu was buried within the Great Pyramid, others, such as Diodorus Siculus, question this. He writes:

> And though the two kings built the pyramids to serve as their tombs, in the event neither of them was buried in them; for the multitudes, because of the hardships which they had endured in the building of them and the many cruel and violent acts of these kings, were filled with anger against those who had caused their sufferings and openly threatened to tear their bodies asunder and cast them in despite [sic] out of the tombs. Consequently each ruler when dying enjoined upon his kinsmen to bury his body secretly in an unmarked place.[20]

---

*You can explore this further in *The Secret Chamber of Osiris: Lost Knowledge of the Sixteen Pyramids,* 71–81.

†You can find out more from *The Secret Chamber of Osiris: Lost Knowledge of the Sixteen Pyramids,* 204–11.

So if not inside or beneath the Great Pyramid, then where? The ancient Egypt researcher Ian Onvlee may have the answer. He proposes:

There is a pyramid further south along the Nile that does contain the cartouches of Khufu. This pyramid stands at El-Lisht, near Meidum, and has no associated pharaoh, although some have thought of King Seankhare, Nebtaire, and Amenemhat I. Strangely enough, although this pyramid contains many cartouches of Khufu in the related temple complex, their existence has been interpreted as the result of pillage from the Great Pyramid. . . . Under normal scientific scrutiny such inscriptions would automatically have instead led Egyptologists to assign the El-Lisht pyramid to this pharaoh. The pyramids of Dashur and Meidum have been assigned to Khufu's father Sneferu on much weaker grounds![21]

The pyramid at El-Lisht has been attributed by Egyptologists to the Twelfth Dynasty pharaoh Amenemhet I because his name was found on fragments of reliefs in the foundations of the pyramid's funerary temple. They also believe that, for spiritual reasons, Amenemhet I appropriated stones from other pyramid sites, including Khufu's, to build his own pyramid, thereby perhaps explaining how the name of Khufu (and the names of other ancient Egyptian kings) came to be in this pyramid.

Another possibility for the location of Khufu's actual tomb comes to us from a Japanese team led by the Egyptologist Sakuji Yoshimura. During their exploration of the Western Cemetery of the Giza plateau in 2017, the team reported the discovery of a massive underground chamber complex deep below the Giza bedrock, a location they dubbed Akhet Khufu (the Horizon of Khufu) and which they believe will reveal the true burial site of Khufu. Whether this claim turns out to have any merit remains to be seen.

But Sūrīd/Khufu had achieved his goal: the construction of a monumental recovery device for his kingdom that contained everything, including the regenerative power of the all-important ancestor kings and queens—the Osirian Kings—essential for the kingdom to revive and reawaken after the great deluge had finally abated. And it seems that Khufu may have had himself buried close by, deep underground in the Western Cemetery at Giza. From the pyramid texts, we read,

> This pyramid of the king is Osiris, this construction of his is Osiris; betake yourself to it, do not be far from it in its name of pyramid.

Wherever Khufu is buried, it seems that he will not be far from his Great Pyramid.

NEXT STEPS

If science can devise a nondestructive means to explore the Big Void's Hall of the Ancestors, perhaps using an endoscopic camera, and it finds nothing of significance, then we can simply seal off the small drill hole and leave things be.

However, if the camera finds a whole series of stone boxes (sarcophagi), then we might need to find a way of exploring the chamber more thoroughly. Assuming there is the will to do this, and the stone boxes are opened and Khufu's ancestors are discovered, then this would surely prove to be the discovery of the millennium. If the stone boxes are inscribed with the deceased's name and titles, then we may well find among those the name of Khufu's mother, Queen Hetepheres. Such a discovery would, of course, prove beyond a reasonable doubt that Khufu built the Great Pyramid and that he did so not for his own personal burial but as a recovery device for his kingdom, just as the Coptic-Egyptian oral tradition informs us.

If, on the other hand, no such discovery is found, then the purpose of the Big Void as being the location of Sūrīd/Khufu's ancestors—the central proposition of this book—will have been falsified. This is not to say, of course, that this means the Great Pyramid was built as a tomb for Khufu; the monument may still have been built as part of a recovery system for the kingdom with the ancestor kings and queens having been relocated to some other safe haven.

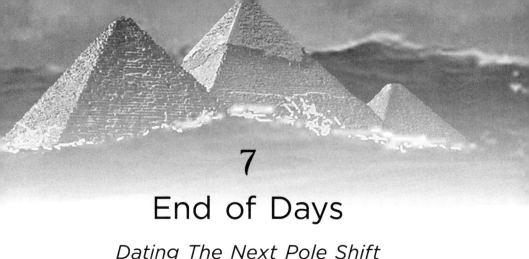

7
End of Days

Dating The Next Pole Shift

In chapter 3, we learned that Australian astronomer George F. Dodwell found compelling evidence that the Earth's polar axis had been disturbed circa 2345 BCE, possibly as the result of a pole shift event. That there may have been two pole shift events in our remote past suggests that these events are not merely randomly occurring calamities but that they are actually an inherent feature of the Earth's natural geodynamic cycle, occurring after a regular interval, many thousands of years apart. But how might we be able to determine these cycles?

Recall what we have learned from the Coptic-Egyptian oral tradition: that King Sūrīd sent his astronomer-priests to study the stars in the heavens. "The king then directed the astrologers to ascertain by taking the altitude whether the stars foretold any great catastrophe, and the result announced an approaching deluge."[1]

In measuring the altitudes of the stars, it's possible that Sūrīd's astronomer-priests made a much more profound discovery—the *periodicity* of this cycle of cataclysm. If so, then the ancient builders of Giza would have been able to predict when the next pole shift event was due to occur (in their future) and perhaps may also have devised a means of recording and passing on this crucial knowledge to future generations. Again, the Coptic-Egyptian texts suggest that this is exactly what they did. Recall this portion of text: "The king, also, deposited the instruments, and the thuribula, with which his forefathers had sacrificed to the stars, and also their writings; likewise, the positions of the stars, and their circles; together with the history and chronicles of time past, of that, which is to come, and of every future event, which would take place in Egypt."[2]

In this passage, we may have an indication that the designers and builders of Giza did, indeed, ascertain the periodicity of this "disturbance of the heavens" (pole shift events) by observing the "positions of the stars, and their circles," and with this knowledge, they were able to determine precisely "that, which is to come," that is, when the next such disturbance would occur. Furthermore, it seems from this passage that this knowledge was somehow "deposited" (that is, encoded) "within" the pyramids. But how might this have been done?

If we accept that the star shafts and the alignments of the main pyramids were designed primarily to encode the date of their construction (perhaps shortly after an initial, more ancient pole shift event was observed), then it stands to reason that it would likely require additional structures to record the moment the next disturbance was likely to occur, as well as the specific periodicity between these events (thereby allowing future generations to calculate when future shifts were likely to occur).

MARKING TIME

In the 1980s, Mark Lehner (working with the late Egyptologist Hans Goedicke) noticed a peculiar alignment of the Giza pyramids, writing: "A great SW-NE diagonal cuts the diagonal of Menkaure's first queen's pyramid, touches the SE corner of his pyramid, cuts the diagonal of his Mortuary Temple, passes the SE corner of the Khafre Pyramid court, cuts the diagonal of the fore-temple of Khafre's Mortuary Temple, touches the SE corner of Khufu's Pyramid, very nearly cuts the diagonal of his first queen's pyramid and ends in a large block of masonry built into the escarpment."[3]

In another instance, Lehner also noted, "These alignments are out by just about the amount that we would expect from methods of

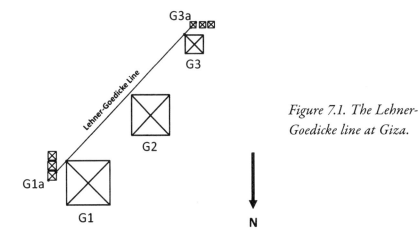

Figure 7.1. The Lehner-Goedicke line at Giza.

sighting and measuring using long cords across a kilometre of sloping plateau."[4]

While most Egyptologists fail to recognize that there is a very specific purpose to this grand alignment (fig. 7.1) and tend to play down its significance, there are some who assert that it was made in order to create an alignment with the ancient city of Heliopolis (Iunu), as explained by the Italian archaeoastronomer Giulio Magli. "It is known that the disposition of the Giza pyramids on the ground is characterized by what is customary called the 'Giza diagonal.' It is an ideal line which connects the south-east corners of the three pyramids with good accuracy. It was observed already many years ago that this 'Giza diagonal' might have had a symbolic meaning, since it points in the direction of the city of Heliopolis, north-east of Giza."[5]

But the alignment isn't quite as perfect as Magli asserts because, for some unknown reason, the middle pyramid (G2)—unlike the two other main pyramids—sits several meters back from the theoretical Lehner-Goedicke line (fig. 7.2, p. 142), a peculiarity that Egyptologists are at a loss to explain other than to assert the notion of a builder's error. However, this slight offset of G2's southeast corner that creates this small gap from the theoretical line was no error. It was likely to have been deliberately created by the builders and for a very specific reason, as we shall shortly see.

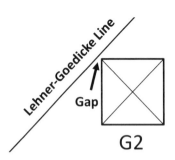

Figure 7.2. The southeast corner of the middle pyramid (G2) sits slightly off the Lehner-Goedicke line.

The key aspect of this Lehner-Goedicke line isn't so much concerned with the three large pyramids (although they do feature) but rather with the two sets of smaller satellite pyramids to the east of the Great Pyramid (G1) and those to the south of Menkaure's pyramid (G3) that are "connected" at the endpoints of this theoretical line (which can be seen in fig. 7.1). These two sets of three satellite pyramids are essentially the larger pyramids in miniature in that they also represent Orion's Belt but at very unique and specific moments in its precessional cycle.

What immediately stands out here is that these two sets of satellite pyramids are aligned at right angles to each other. This arrangement is no accident and serves a very specific purpose: it effectively transforms the simple Lehner-Goedicke line into a stellar time line or "star clock" that the designers used to mark the timing of the next pole shift cataclysm! This is to say that while the main pyramids possess features (such as the pivot angle and star-shaft alignments) that could help us date the first pole shift event when Sūrīd's astronomer-priests observed the stars wandering from their normal course across the heavens,* the placement of the two sets of satellite pyramids appears to have been a design feature to encode and pass down crucial additional knowledge that would enable future generations to determine the periodicity of, and the date when, the *next* pole shift event was likely to occur.

---

*As we saw in chapter 3, determining a precise construction date using the main pyramid alignments and star shafts is no longer possible since the second, more recent, pole shift event would have overwritten much of the Earth's former geodynamic properties that would have been recorded into the architecture of the main pyramids shortly after the first pole shift event.

To understand how this stellar time line functions, we need to understand a little about the precessional motion of the Earth and how this affects our observation of the Orion Belt stars over time. To do that, let us first consider the (apparent) motion of an object much closer to home—the sun.

Imagine that you live near to the equator and that you get up each morning for an entire year and go outside to observe the sun rising on the eastern horizon. Let's say you begin your first observation on the day of the summer solstice (June 21) when the sun is 23.5° north of due east, its maximum northerly position at the equator (an angle governed by the Earth's 23.5° axial tilt). As each day passes, you notice that the sun shifts slightly southward along the eastern horizon toward due east (toward the autumn equinox point), and onward it travels until it reaches the winter solstice point (23.5° south of due east), its farthest southerly extent on the eastern horizon (fig. 7.3, p. 144).

When the sun rises at its winter solstice position (fig. 7.4), it then appears to change direction (due to the Earth being halfway into its orbit around the sun) and begins to move northward along the eastern horizon for the next six months, past the spring equinox point and onward toward the summer solstice point, whereupon, at that moment, it changes direction again—a pendulum cycle that repeats forever.

Now imagine that we wanted to mark a specific date in the year—let's say July 17 (fig. 7.5)—how could this be done?

The placement of two stone obelisks aligned to the sunrise on this date would serve to permanently mark July 17 (fig. 7.6).

An alternative method of marking a specific date would be to place two markers on the ground symbolizing the summer and winter solstice points with a line drawn on the ground connecting these two solstice markers—a solar time line (fig. 7.7, p. 146). Since we know there are 365 days per year (182.5 for the half year) and we know the dates when the solstices occur, by measuring the length of the line between the two solstice markers, the correct relative position can be calculated along the line for the July 17 date (26 days or 14.2% along the line from the summer solstice marker) and an obelisk or some other marker could then be placed at that precise spot along the solar time line, marking that particular date.

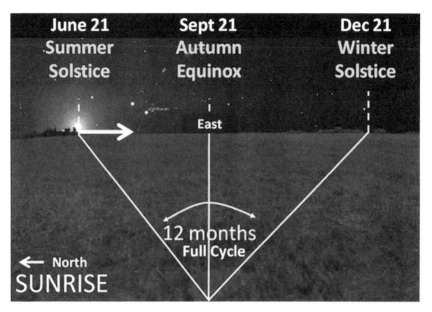

Figure 7.3. The sun rising on the summer solstice.
Each day, the sun rises slightly farther south along the eastern horizon,
past the autumn equinox, toward the winter solstice point.

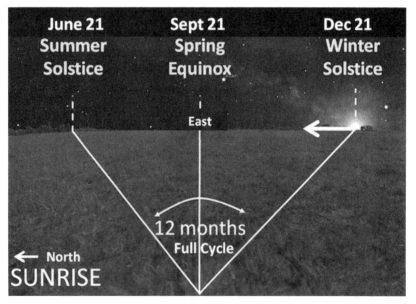

Figure 7.4. At the winter solstice point, the sun (apparently)
changes direction on the horizon and now moves toward the
spring equinox point and onward toward the summer solstice point,
where it will change direction again—like an eternal pendulum swing.

Figure 7.5. Sunrise on July 17.

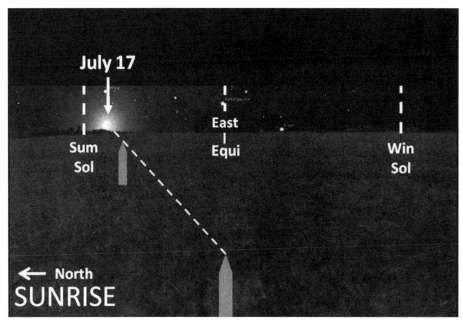

*Figure 7.6. An alignment of two obelisks toward the sunrise
would mark the date of July 17.*

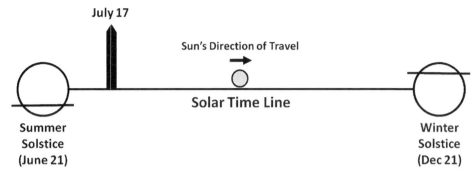

Figure 7.7. A stone marker is placed between the two solstice markers to mark the solar time line with the date July 17. (Note: The part of the circle above the short horizontal line in the solstice symbols indicates the day length. The summer solstice symbol indicates the longest day, while the winter solstice symbol indicates the shortest day.)

However, there's a minor complication with both of these methods. The direction of travel the sun is seen to be making on the eastern horizon (i.e., heading toward the summer solstice or heading toward the winter solstice) will determine the actual date. In the July 17 example, this date can only be July 17 when the direction of travel of the sun is southward toward the winter solstice marker. If the sun was traveling in the opposite direction, northward toward the summer solstice, our date marker would then be indicating the date of May 17 (fig. 7.8).

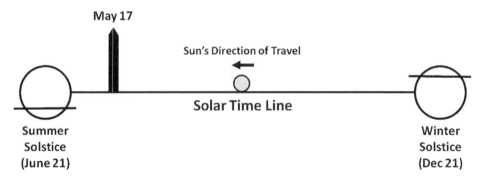

Figure 7.8. The date marker stone at this same position between the two solstice markers can also indicate May 17 if the sun is moving northward toward the summer solstice marker.

And so, because any point along the solar time line can be one of two possible dates (depending on whether the sun is moving toward the summer or winter solstice markers), then we require some additional information (a symbol of some kind) to indicate to us which of the two solstice points the sun was moving toward when this particular alignment was made (that is, when the date marker stone was placed on the solar time line). With this additional information, we can then correctly identify the correct alignment date. The additional marker could be anything, for example, a simple center dot within the solstice symbol to indicate that the sun's direction of travel was toward this particular solstice (fig. 7.9). It's not being said here that the sun has actually reached the marker stone (the solstice point), only that, at this particular moment, the direction of travel is toward this particular marker stone.

Had the sun been heading toward the summer solstice point when the date marker stone was placed on the solar time line, then this would, conversely, indicate the date of May 17 (fig. 7.10, p. 148). Another way of thinking of this issue is to consider the spring and autumn equinoxes. Both equinoxes will, naturally, occur when the sun reaches the midpoint of the solar time line. However, without knowing the direction of travel of the sun, it is impossible to know if a marker stone aligned to the equinox point on the solar time line is

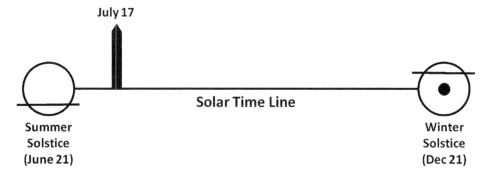

July 17

Solar Time Line

Summer
Solstice
(June 21)

Winter
Solstice
(Dec 21)

Figure 7.9. The additional symbol (center dot) placed within the winter solstice circle indicates the direction of travel of the sun (in this figure, toward the winter solstice) when the date marker stone was placed, giving the date unequivocally as July 17.

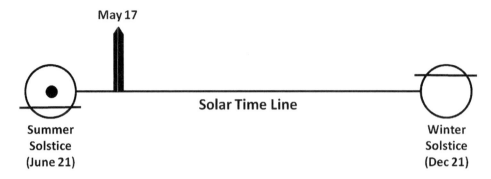

Figure 7.10. With the additional symbol (the center dot) placed within the summer solstice marker, this then indicates the direction of travel of the sun was toward this solstice when the date marker stone was placed, thereby giving the date as May 17 (as opposed to July 17).

marking the spring (March 20) or autumn (September 22) equinox.

Such a dating method is perfectly adequate if we merely wish to mark a specific date within the solar year. Indeed, many of our ancient monuments all over the Earth are aligned to the solstices and also the equinoxes. Such solar alignments would have been created to provide vital information to assist ancient farmers with the planting and harvesting of their crops. However, if we wanted to mark a date beyond a single calendar year, how might we achieve that? Consider, for example, Halley's comet, which passes by the Earth every seventy-five years. How can we mark the date of its next arrival using the solar time line method? The simple fact is that this method would be entirely inadequate in predicting (and marking) the return date of Halley's comet since the solar calendar time line is limited to only 365 days—a single year. To record events on the time line with a periodicity greater than one solar year requires not a solar time line but a *stellar* time line, so we must turn to the stars.

THE GIZA STELLAR TIME LINE

At Giza, we find that our two solstice markers are presented to us, not with two solar solstice markers, as in our example above, but with two stellar markers in the form of the two sets of satellite pyramids,* which represent the two "solstices" of Orion's Belt. These two significant moments of the belt stars aren't referred to as solstices but rather as culminations, and our two belt markers essentially perform the same function as our solstice markers, although they mark a much longer period of time. The duration between these two pivotal moments of Orion's Belt—the two solstice/culmination points—isn't a mere six months (twelve months for the full return cycle) as in the solar time line example above, but has been calculated by modern astronomers to be 12,886 years for the half cycle (25,772 years for the full return cycle)!

Using astronomy software, we can observe that over this long period of time, the belt stars will rise on the eastern horizon vertically at the moment of their maximum culmination (their "summer solstice"), and around 12,886 years later, at the moment of their minimum culmination (their "winter solstice"), they will set horizontally on the southwest horizon (fig. 7.11, p. 150). Just like the two solstice moments of the sun, the two culminations of the belt stars are the moments when they appear to change direction when halfway through their full cycle to return to their point of origin.

Thus, we can observe that the two sets of satellite pyramids at Giza have been carefully positioned (perpendicular to each other) on the plateau to mimic the key transitional moments (the two solstices/culminations) of the precessional motion of the belt stars over this lengthy duration—a stellar time line of 25,772 years as opposed to a solar time line of just a single year (fig. 7.12).

This stellar time line can then be used to mark a specific year (rather than a specific day, as in our solar time line example above), up to a maximum of 25,772 years into the future. But how would the designers have marked or encoded a particular date onto this stellar time line, the

---

*The orthodox view that these satellite pyramids were built as queens' tombs seems highly questionable due to the fact that the pharaoh Khafre had more queens than either Khufu or Menkaure, and yet there are no so-called queens' pyramids alongside pyramid G2 (attributed to the pharaoh Khafre) for any of his five known queens.

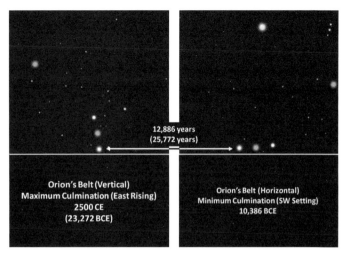

Figure 7.11. The two "solstices" (maximum and minimum culmination) of Orion's Belt, circa 2500 CE and circa 10,386 BCE. Calculated using Stellarium v.0.19.1 star-mapping software, the duration between these two culminations is 12,886 years (25,772 years for the full return cycle). Note: the belt stars are presently moving toward their maximum culmination, which will occur circa 2500 CE.

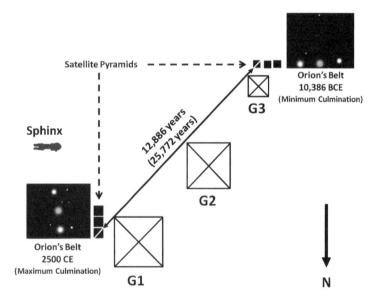

Figure 7.12. The two solstices of Orion's Belt are symbolized on the Giza plateau with the perpendicular arrangement of the two sets of satellite pyramids, which mimic the same perpendicular arrangement of the Orion Belt stars (rising and setting) at the moment of their two culminations.

Lehner-Goedicke line? To help answer this will require the following assumptions:

1. The designers would wish to encode the year of the next pole shift event. Let's call this "Event Z." This would be a single future date for Event Z (from their perspective), which would require a single marker (data point) to be placed somewhere along the Giza stellar time line.

2. The builders would also encode the periodicity, the number of years that will pass between each pole shift event. The periodicity will require a further two markers (data points) to be placed on the Giza stellar time line (one to mark the periodicity count's *starting* point and a second marker to indicate the periodicity count's *ending* point).

3. We must assume that the builders would be consistent in how they marked the Giza stellar time line for each of the three data points and that they would have included a means for us to differentiate the single Event Z data point from the two periodicity data points. If these data points were unclear, then we could end up with incorrect data and thus incorrect dates.

4. Finally, it must also be assumed that the designers of the Giza stellar time line would have understood that the future pole shift date they were encoding into the time line (Event Z) would likely be rendered meaningless after that event had actually come to pass since the Earth would then have had its geodynamic and precessional properties altered by the event itself. In anticipation of this, the designers would likely have built into their stellar time line a means whereby the precessional properties from their time could still be retrieved from the time line because only by retrieving this data can we have the true values and work out the true future (and past) dates encoded into the time line.

This brings us now to two key questions:

1. How exactly did the ancient designers of this stellar time line mark the three data points on the line?

2. Did the ancient designers of Giza mark their stellar time line to predict the date of a future pole shift event; that is, does the stellar time line present the date of the most recent pole shift event (as indicated by the research of George Dodwell) as occurring circa 2345 BCE?

Dating Event Z: Finding the Three Data Points

A close analysis of the Giza monuments in relation to the stellar time line presents some intriguing features. As we learned earlier, the southeast corners of pyramids G1 and G3 sit right on the Giza stellar time line (the Lehner-Goedicke line), while the southeast corner of pyramid G2 does not, being set several meters from it. We *also* find that G1 and G3 are eight-sided monuments,* whereas G2 presents only four sides. As such, we find that we have two quite distinct styles of pyramid; two eight-sided structures (G1 and G3) whose southeast corners connect with the time line and one four-sided structure (G2) whose southeast corner is set back from it. Since we require two data points to encode the periodicity of Event Z, then this may be why we are presented with two similar eight-sided structures, each of which connect directly with the time line (fig. 7.13). And since the date of Event Z will require only one marker, then this may be why we find just one four-sided structure that is set back from the time line. When we know the date for Event Z (i.e., the most recent pole shift event), then by simply adding or subtracting the periodicity count from this date, we can determine future and past dates for Event Z (i.e., past and future pole shift events).

What else might the designers have marked or encoded? How else might they have recorded their predictions for the dates of future calamities in order to ensure the survival of their civilization and, most important of all, how might they have drawn our attention to it?

The "Wow!" Signal

One of the most curious aspects of the Giza monuments arises when we draw a circle around the three outermost points of the Giza pyra-

---

*For more on how and perhaps why these pyramids have eight sides, see *The Giza Prophecy*, 215–16.

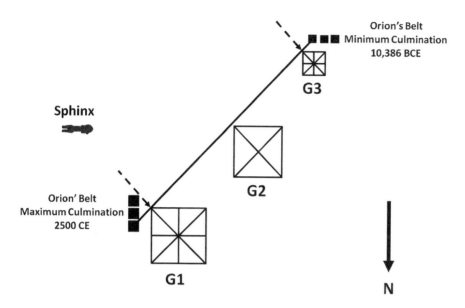

Figure 7.13. The southeast corners of pyramids G1 and G3 sit right on the stellar time line (indicated by the dashed arrows), whereas the southeast corner of G2 is set slightly back from this line. Note also that pyramids G1 and G3 are similar eight-sided structures, whereas G2 is a simple four-sided pyramid. The similarly styled and arranged G1 and G3 may encode the periodicity since this requires two similar data markers, while G2 may encode the date of the most recent pole shift event, which requires only one data marker.

mid field: we find that the Sphinx ends up sitting right on the outside edge of this great circle (fig. 7.14, p. 154). The chances that such an occurrence could have come about as a result of simple happenstance are remote in the extreme and, as such, this suggests that the layout was wholly intentional and that the Sphinx is likely an integral and functional part of the Giza stellar clock.

It may also be that the slight change of G2's position on the plateau (it does not correspond perfectly to the relative position of its stellar counterpart, the belt star Al Nilam) was necessary in order to create a specific angle from the apex of this pyramid to connect with the Sphinx, thereby crossing over and intersecting the stellar time line

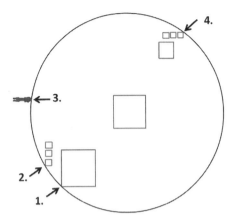

Figure 7.14. With a circle connecting the three outermost corners of the Giza pyramid field, we find that the Sphinx ends up sitting just outside the perimeter of this circle.

at a very specific point/date along its length (fig. 7.15, p. 156).

While this method of placing a data point on the time line seems intuitive and logical, there are, of course, any number of points that could be selected from pyramid G2 to this point at the rear of the Sphinx, all of which would intersect the stellar time line at slightly different points along its length, giving different potential data and thus different (wrong) dates for Event Z. What would be helpful here would be to have some means of corroboration, some kind of beacon that indicates to us that this pyramid-apex-to-Sphinx intersecting method is correct. This is to say that it would make sense for the designers to encode some meaningful or intelligent value (i.e., some kind of "wow!" signal)* into the dating method they used in order that we might recognize this "intelligent signal" and know for certain that we had indeed found the correct method of intersecting and marking the time line at the correct point from the many other possibilities.

Remarkably, it seems that the builders did indeed build such a beacon into their stellar clock to show us the way forward. While I was discussing this intersecting method with my good friend and former coauthor

---

*The "Wow!" signal was a strong narrow-band radio signal received on August 15, 1977, by Ohio State University's Big Ear radio telescope in the United States, which was then used to support the Search for Extraterrestrial Intelligence (SETI) program. The signal appeared to come from the direction of the constellation Sagittarius and bore the expected hallmarks of extraterrestrial origin.

Gary Osborn some years ago, he pointed out to me a quite breathtaking observation. Gary had noticed that the line from the apex of G2 to the Sphinx that I had presented him with intersected the stellar time line and divided it into a ratio of 1 to 1.314285714, the digits after the decimal point presenting, of course, the pi approximation (i.e., pi = 22/7 = 3.14285714)* divided by 10. And so, with the pi digits found within this simple and intuitive division of the time line, we have a clear beacon of intelligent and deliberate design encoded into the intersection line from G2 apex to the Sphinx, our "wow!" signal, and meaningful confirmation that we have, indeed, found the correct method the ancient designers used to encode data into and mark their stellar time line at specific points—a line from the apex of G2 to the Sphinx that intersects the stellar time line precisely at a desired point/date.

It naturally follows, of course, that if a line from the G2 apex to the Sphinx is the method used to intersect the time line to provide the single data point and date of Event Z, then (assuming the rule of consistency) the other two main pyramids would likewise have been used to encode the two other data points (the two values that are needed to obtain the periodicity value), with intersecting lines from the apexes of G1 and G3, respectively, to the rear of the Sphinx, crossing the stellar time line and intersecting it at very specific points (fig. 7.15, p. 156).

If we then take the modern value of 12,886 years as the precessional half cycle and divide this number by 2.3142857 (to obtain the ratio split of 1 to 1.314), this returns the ratio of 5,568 (rounded) : 7,318 (fig. 7.16). This suggests then that the date for Event Z occurred some 5,568 years before the maximum culmination of Orion's Belt. Since we know that Orion's Belt is due to reach its maximum culmination circa 2500 CE, then 5,568 years *before* that culmination event takes us back to the year 3068 BCE (2500 CE − 5,568 years).

We can similarly determine the duration of the periodicity with this method. When we measure the distance between the two intersection points of G1 and G3, it returns a count value of 8,762 years (fig. 7.17).

---

*This implies, of course, that the designers of the stellar time line understood the mathematical constant pi as a decimal fraction.

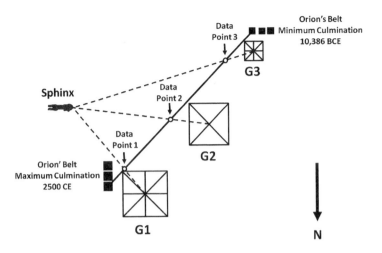

Figure 7.15. Lines from the apexes of the three Giza pyramids to the Sphinx intersect the stellar time line at three specific points. The three data points are differentiated from each other by the pyramid's styles. Since the periodicity requires two values, this would logically be encoded with the two pyramids G1 and G3 because these are pyramids of similar style (being eight-sided and touching the time line), whereas the single date for Event Z would logically be encoded with G2, this being the only four-sided (main) pyramid and the one that doesn't touch the time line.

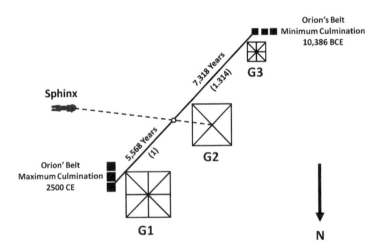

Figure 7.16. Using the time line ratio of 1 to 1.3142857 with the modern precessional half cycle of 12,886 years splits the stellar time line into the ratio of 5,568 : 7,318 years. This suggests that Event Z happened 5,568 years before the maximum culmination of Orion's Belt in 2500 CE, thereby giving us the Event Z date of circa 3068 BCE.

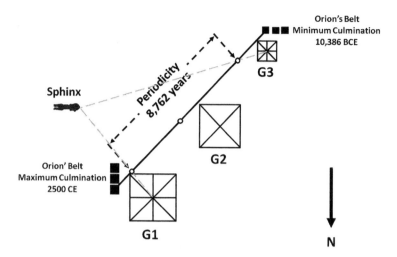

Figure 7.17. Based on our modern precessional half-cycle
duration of 12,886 years, the periodicity count (the distance
between G1 and G3 data points) returns a value of 8,762 years.

On the basis of our present precessional half cycle of 12,886 years, it seems then that Event Z occurred circa 3068 BCE and had a periodicity of 8,762 years, which means the next Event Z won't occur until circa 5694 CE (3068 BCE + 8,762 years' periodicity).

But wait: How can we know that this event is to occur 5,568 years before the maximum culmination of the belt stars and not 7,318 years before their minimum culmination?

Given that the last minimum culmination of the belt stars occurred circa 10,386 BCE (with respect to our present precessional half cycle of 12,886 years), then 7,318 years before this culmination gives us the date of circa 17,704 BCE (10,386 BCE − 7,318) as a second possible date for the last Event Z. So how can we know which of these two possible dates (ca. 3068 BCE or ca. 17,704 BCE) is the correct Event Z date?

Direction of Travel

The reader will recall that in our half-year solar time line example earlier in this chapter, it was explained that it was important to know the direction of travel of the sun in order to definitively determine the actual date of a particular marker placed on the solar time line. For instance, we learned that the July 17 date on the solar time line can only be this date when the direction of travel of the sun (when the alignment was made) is toward the winter solstice. If, however, the direction of travel of the sun was toward the summer solstice (when the alignment was made), then the very same point on the solar time line becomes May 17.

The very same dating issue arises with the Giza stellar time line. Unless we can determine the direction of travel of the Orion Belt stars at the time the three data points were created on the stellar time line, then we cannot know which of the two possible dates is the correct date for Event Z. If the belt stars were moving toward maximum culmination, then the G2 intersection date becomes circa 3068 BCE. If they were moving in the opposite direction, toward minimum culmination, then the G2 intersection date becomes, as stated above, circa 17,704 BCE.

It was also explained in the solar time line example that an additional symbol (or other unique marker of some kind) needed to be placed alongside either the summer or winter solstice markers in order to make known the direction of travel of the sun (recall figs. 7.9 and 7.10, pp. 147 and 148) at the time the alignment was made and thus the intended date. Again, the same principle applies with the Giza stellar time line. Some additional marker is required to tell us the direction of travel the belt stars were making when the three intersection data points were encoded onto the stellar time line. Were they moving toward maximum culmination or toward minimum culmination? One such additional marker presents a very obvious possibility.

Beside G1 (at the maximum culmination end of the Giza stellar time line), there is what Egyptologists call a cult pyramid (shown in fig. 7.18). This cult pyramid is considerably smaller than the other satellite pyramids and stands between the Great Pyramid and its three "Queens' Pyramids." Today, only the foundations of this small pyramid can be seen. There is no similar structure at the opposite end of the stellar time line beside the three satellite pyramids of G3. It may then be that this smallest pyramid functions as the additional marker

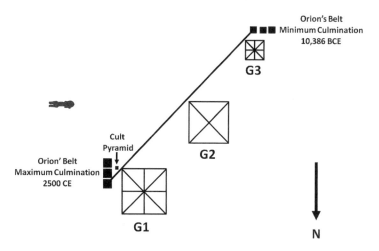

Figure 7.18. The placement of the so-called cult pyramid at the maximum culmination end of the Giza stellar time line may have been done to indicate that the direction of travel of Orion's Belt was toward this end of the time line when the time line was devised.

needed to indicate to us that the direction of travel of the belt stars was toward the G1 satellite pyramids (toward maximum culmination). Had the direction of travel of the belt stars been toward their minimum culmination, then we would likely have found this small pyramid placed beside the G3 satellite pyramids to indicate this.

In summary, this small so-called cult pyramid right beside the three G1 satellite pyramids might have been placed at that location to serve as a marker to indicate to us that the direction of travel of the belt stars when the stellar time line was devised was toward their maximum culmination.

As such, we can then be reasonably sure that the intersection date is indeed circa 3068 BCE and not the 17,704 BCE alternative (a date that requires the belt stars to have been moving in the opposite direction, toward minimum culmination). In short, the monuments at Giza appear to indicate that the G2-Sphinx intersection date on the stellar time line occurred 5,568 years before maximum culmination and not 7,318 years before minimum culmination, which means, as already mentioned, that Event Z, the last pole shift event, according to the Giza stellar time line was scheduled to have occurred circa 3068 BCE. But did it?

Time Slip

The reader will recall that the Australian astronomer George Dodwell calculated from various astronomical observations of ancient monuments around the world that the last pole shift event occurred circa 2345 BCE, a date that is some 723 years adrift from the Event Z date we find encoded in the Giza stellar time line. It seems clear that there is something amiss here. Are Dodwell's calculations wrong? Or did the ancient designers of the Giza stellar time line miscalculate the periodicity of Event Z by 723 years? The answer may, in fact, be neither of these but rather simply the result of something already mentioned at length earlier in this book: this 723 year discrepancy could simply be yet another manifestation of the Bauval-Trimble convergence problem. This is to say that our present rate of precession (12,886 years per half cycle) is likely not the same as it was prior to Dodwell's pole shift event of circa 2345 BCE. And if these precession rates were indeed different, then it means the results we find in our time line calculations above will be in error, including the date for Event Z. The only way we can correct this error and establish the true date for Event Z (the last pole shift event) is by knowing what the rate of precession (i.e., the half-cycle length) was *prior* to the most recent pole shift event and then calibrating this former precessional duration using our present precessional duration.

By way of analogy, imagine you and a work colleague are having a teleconference meeting tomorrow and that you both need to set your alarm clock to be sure you are awake and do not miss the meeting. You both agree the meeting should occur at 9:00 a.m. the following day. To ensure you don't miss your meeting, you both set your alarm clock to awaken you one hour before your meeting. Now imagine that the only clock you have is a novelty "decimal clock" that has only ten hours around its clock face (as opposed to twelve hours in your colleague's clock). What time would you need to set your decimal alarm clock to ensure that your alarm went off one hour before your meeting? This is essentially the same issue we have in calibrating the two stellar time lines, although, unlike the two alarm clocks, we presently only know the duration of one of the time lines (i.e., our present precessional half cycle of 12,886 years). We need to know *both* time line durations before we can calibrate the time lines and establish the true dates encoded within it.

In advancing this idea, we have to presume here that the ancient designers of the Giza stellar time line would have been aware that the precession rate (from *their* frame of reference) would likely be altered by the future pole shift (Event Z) whose date they were attempting to encode into their stellar time line. Were the ancient designers not to account for the likely precessional after-effects of Event Z, then it would be nearly impossible for any future civilization using the time line to determine the past Event Z date and equally impossible to predict any future Event Z date. In short, if the pre-shift rate of precession was altered after Event Z (which it almost certainly would have been), then the precession time line data will be flawed and any dates produced worthless.

However, if we further presume that the designers of Giza would have been aware of this potential problem, then it is reasonable to consider that they would have found a way of encoding into the stellar time line the absolute values of the duration of their own precessional half cycle, thereby giving future generations the necessary information needed to calibrate their own rate of precession with the former rate of precession used by the builders and, by doing so, the ability to determine an accurate Event Z date and also a more accurate periodicity count.

But how could the builders have encoded their precessional half-year duration into the Giza stellar time line in a way that future generations would be able to easily see and extract without the encoded data being corrupted and misread? A possible solution that the builders may have used comes from the pi ratio observation made by my *Giza Prophecy* coauthor Gary Osborn, the builders' "wow" signal encoded into the Giza stellar time line. He was not to know during that early research into this phenomenon just how crucial his observation was to become. He had discovered an important key, but, at that time, neither of us really knew which door it would open or precisely how this "pi key" should be used. Until now.

The Pi Ratio

For any future civilization to be able to extract the numerical value for the duration of the Earth's former (pre–pole shift) precessional half cycle would require that the designers somehow express and lock this key value into the stellar time line in absolute terms. One means of achieving this is, of course, to use a ratio.

Imagine, for example, that you have a line of 20 inches in length and you divide that line into two equal halves. If you measure the line to the division point, you will, naturally, be presented with the value of 10 inches (half the line length). However, if you then measure this same line in centimeters, you will have a half length of 25.4 centimeters, which is a different numerical value from the 10-inch value (although the line length is the same). You obtain these different numerical values because you are using two different measurement scales. However, if you then divide one length of the line (say a half) into the other, you will always get the same value (1), and you will be able to obtain this value regardless of the measuring scale being used (e.g., 10 / 10 = 1 and 25.4 / 25.4 = 1).

Thus, by using ratios, we can always return the same numerical value regardless of the measurement scale being used. This is to say that if we wanted to encode the number 11 into a particular line using ratios, then we simply draw a line with an intersecting point that divides the line precisely midway along its length. Since each part of the line division is two equal halves, we thus have a ratio of 1 to 1 or 1:1 or simply 11. In this example, the 11 is not a numerical value, per se; all that is being said here is that ratios can be used in this manner to hardwire or lock in specific numerical digits that can then be retrieved and interpreted as meaningful within a specific context. And it doesn't matter the length of the line; if it is precisely split at the midway point, it will always return the 1:1 ratio (the digits 1 and 1 to form 11).

If we now extend this idea to the Giza stellar time line, we know that it is split into a ratio of 1 to 1.314 or 1:1.314 or simply 11314. Because of the very specific split in the Giza stellar time line (the "wow" signal observed by Osborn), we will always return the ratio of 1:1.314 regardless of whether the precession duration was subsequently altered (by a later pole shift event). As such, this specific and unalterable ratio value 1:1.314 that we find in the Giza stellar time line may have been used by the builders as a way to hardwire the half-stellar time line with the value of 11,314 years, which would be the half-precession cycle that existed before the most recent Event Z changed the rate of precession to give us our present half-precession cycle of 12,886 years, a precessional half-year difference of 1,572 years and 3,144 years for the full precessional year.

And so, we may then have found the importance of using the pi split in the Giza stellar time line, as it essentially encodes very specific and incorruptible numerical values into the line that can easily be noticed and retrieved. Accepting that this pi ratio (1:1.314) is to be regarded as an absolute value of 11,314 and that it does represent the Earth's former precessional half-cycle length, then how does this impact our modern time line of 12,886 years for the half cycle? How do we calibrate the two time lines to obtain the precise date for the past Event Z and, of course, to determine the calibrated date for the next event?

Calibrating the Giza Stellar Time Line

If we now divide the pre-shift precessional half-cycle value of 11,314 years by 2.3142857 (the Giza time line pi ratio) we find that the lead time, that is, the number of years from the maximum culmination of Orion's Belt (ca. 2500 CE) to the intersection point on the former (pre–pole shift) time line is now 4,888 years (as opposed to the former value of 5,568 years), with a periodicity count now of 7,693 years (as opposed to 8,762 years). If we now calibrate the two time lines (fig. 7.19, next page), we find that the calibrated Event Z date is given as:

$$\text{circa } 2500 \text{ CE} - 4{,}888 \text{ years} = \text{circa } 2388 \text{ BCE}$$

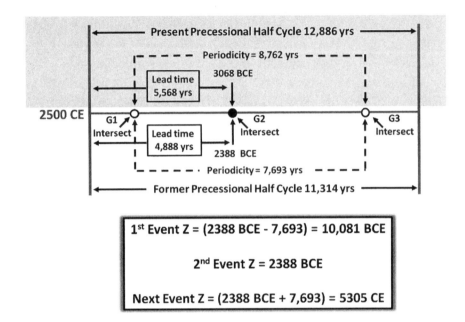

Figure 7.19. The calibrated Giza stellar time line shows that Event Z occurred circa 2388 BCE and that its periodicity is actually 7,693 years, (not the 8,762 years our present precessional duration produces).

This calibrated Event Z date of circa 2388 BCE is now within just 43 years* of Dodwell's 2345 BCE date for the last pole shift event, an accuracy of over 99.8 percent. What is also important here is that the periodicity value given is now considerably lower, at 7,693 years. This is the periodicity value the ancient designers would have calculated. It is an absolute value in solar years calculated during the Earth's former precessional half cycle of 11,314 years and, as such, should remain constant.

As noted earlier, Halley's comet returns to our skies every 75 years. This periodicity for Halley's comet will remain the same regardless of any alterations to the Earth's precessional cycle because the periodicity

---

*This small error may have been introduced by the designers as a consequence of the need to encode into the stellar time line the significant "wow" signal. Had they encoded the actual value of, say, 11,357 years (11314 + 43) then this value would not have stood out as a beacon, and this important data would likely have gone unnoticed; a slight compromise of accuracy to facilitate and improve the chances of discovery.

of this comet is entirely external and independent of anything occurring to the Earth. And so too is the periodicity of Event Z; it will be fixed not at the 8,762 year periodicity given by our present precessional duration but at the 7,693 years of the Earth's former precessional duration, and it should keep this periodicity regardless of any future changes to the Earth's precessional rate.

With this information, we can now determine the date of the first pole shift event (and thus the date when the pyramids would likely have been built) that the calibrated time line gives as:

circa 2388 BCE - 7,693 years (periodicity) = circa 10,081 BCE.

Similarly, the *next* Event Z date can be calculated as:

circa 2388 BCE + 7,693 years (periodicity) = circa 5305 CE.

IS GIZA TWELVE THOUSAND YEARS OLD?

The age of the Great Pyramid (and its contemporaries) is arguably one of the most hotly contested aspects of the Giza monuments, even among some mainstream Egyptologists, who, by and large, insist that they were all built circa 4,500 years ago, give or take a few hundred years. However, with the age of the Sphinx being pushed many thousands of years back in time (as a result of the research of the rebel Egyptologist, the late John Anthony West, along with the evidence presented by geologist Robert Schoch of Boston University), this has brought many to also question the age of the Great Pyramid itself, along with the other contemporary Old Kingdom pyramids in Egypt.

The stock response by Egyptologists to claims of a much greater antiquity for these monuments is probably best epitomized by Mark Lehner, who famously asked, "Show me a single potsherd" of an older civilization with similar capabilities to those of the early dynastic Egyptians. Lehner's comment was made in the early 1990s during a debate with Schoch and, unfortunately, long before the 12,000-year-old megalithic site of Gobekli Tepe had been excavated by the German archaeologist, the late Klaus Schmidt, a site that clearly demonstrates that mankind's ability to construct complex megalithic architecture comparable to that at Giza had been achieved many thousands of years earlier than had previously been thought possible.

It may be, however, that Lehner was actually asking the wrong question. Instead of asking "Show me a single potsherd" of this purported older Egyptian civilization that built the pyramids, Lehner may have been better to consider the possibility that it is not the older civilization of ancient Egypt that has been lost but rather that it is a more *recent* Egyptian society that is lost to history. This is to say that it is a curious and documented fact that we have considerably more evidence of and know more about the preceding Old Kingdom period than we do, for example, of the more recent First Intermediate Period (FIP) of the ancient Egyptian civilization. You might ask why should this matter?

The periods in ancient Egypt we call the Old Kingdom and Middle Kingdom were separated from each other by a transition period that Egyptologists, as stated above, refer to as the First Intermediate Period. This transition period in ancient Egyptian history is often described by Egyptologists as a "dark age" since (comparatively) little is known about this time due to there being very little by way of monumental architecture or documentary records having survived from this period. Orthodox Egyptology believes that this dark age lasted around 150 years, from circa 2181 BCE to 2055 BCE[6] and that it came to a close with the rise of the Twelfth Dynasty. The FIP is typically defined by Egyptology as a time when chaos existed all across Egypt, when the central authority of the pharaoh had utterly collapsed, resulting in numerous local rulers assuming kingship of the various nomes of Egypt for themselves. This chaotic period is described in three Middle Kingdom texts: *The Admonitions of Ipuwer, The Prophecy of Neferti,* and *The Instructions for Merikare.*

However, not everyone agrees that the FIP was a time of chaos at all.

Our perceptions of the First Intermediate Period are heavily colored by later literary texts such as the Admonitions of Ipuwer and the Instructions for Merykare. Almost half a century ago, Gun Björkman showed that the Instructions for Merykare did not match the milieu in which it was set. Stephen Seidlmayer has shown that there is an increase in wealth at the end of the Old Kingdom and into the First Intermediate Period, which does not fit with the narrative of the Middle Kingdom narratives. . . .

Since there is no economic decline in the First Intermediate Period, there is no economic collapse at the end of the Old Kingdom. It is merely a figment of the imagination of the Middle Kingdom propaganda. Without the picture of chaos derived from the Middle Kingdom literary sources there is no collapse at all. This is not to question the existence of a transition between the time periods since a number of differences between the Old Kingdom and the First Intermediate Period indicate that they are indeed distinct eras. Indication of differences include such things as the presence of monumental architecture in the Old Kingdom and its absence in the First Intermediate Period, or multiple concurrent rulers. Instead of trying to explain why the Old Kingdom collapsed, we need to explain why the First Intermediate Period was more prosperous.[7]

Here then we find something of a paradox. The supposed chaos of the FIP seems to have been based entirely on three later Middle Kingdom texts that speak of an earlier time of chaos across the land, but, paradoxically, it seems that this chaotic period could not have belonged to the FIP identified by Egyptologists, which appears, actually, to have been a time of prosperity in the country, albeit with a quite different society from that of the Old Kingdom. Thus, if we accept that these three texts depicting this former chaotic period are indeed speaking of true events (as opposed to being but "a figment of the imagination of the Middle Kingdom"), then, if not during the FIP, when exactly did the chaos described in these texts actually take place? A brief look at another of these Middle Kingdom texts, *The Prophecy of Neferti*, may offer a clue.

The description of the land in chaos and turmoil shows clear primeval overtones. Several phrases can be understood as referring to a time before the creation of the world (*the Sun is obscured and gives no light for the man may see . . . Ra should create again . . . what is done will be what is undone*). The vision of Neferty thus seems to present a metaphor in which the time of trouble is related to a time in which creation has reverted into an original chaos and so the process of creation needs to start again.[8] (italics in original)

The process of creation needing to start again is exactly the reason the Coptic-Egyptian oral tradition gives us for the construction of the first pyramids, so that the kingdom might be revived or could be created again after the coming deluge (*"Ra should create again . . . what is done will be what is undone"*). *The Prophecy of Neferti* (and the other texts from this period) seems to hark back to a time of chaos that prevailed in Egypt at some time after the Old Kingdom (and the construction of the pyramids) but before the FIP—in other words, a *lost period* of ancient Egyptian history and thus lost time. This then raises the question: What if what we're actually looking at with our present understanding of Egyptian history is, in fact, a much compacted or truncated history, a much compressed chronology? What if there is a lost period (lost time) between the Old Kingdom and the FIP, and what if this lost period was many, many thousands of years in duration? How might that affect the chronology of the Old Kingdom pyramids?*

If this were, indeed, the case, then this much longer, intervening lost period between the Old Kingdom and the FIP would have the effect of pushing the chronology of the Old Kingdom (and everything that came before this period), lock, stock, and barrel, back in absolute time by, potentially, thousands of years, and as such, this may help to explain the findings of Schoch with respect to the anomalous weathering of the Sphinx and its enclosure, which he argues could only have occurred as a result of the much higher rainfall that prevailed in ancient Egypt many thousands of years before circa 2550 BCE, when Egyptologists believe the Sphinx was crafted. This is to say that we have not so much lost the ancient civilization that built the

---

*The ancient Egyptians themselves believed that their civilization went far back into antiquity, long before the mortal kings, the sages, and the demigods, 39,000 years back to the Zep Tepi (the First Time of Creation), the time of the gods.

pyramids and the Sphinx but rather that we have lost a much more *recent* incarnation of the Egyptian civilization that existed between the Old Kingdom and the FIP. It seems almost as though after this period of chaos, the entire land of Egypt had gone into a long, deep sleep and that the archaeological evidence we have from the FIP actually represents the reawakening, providing us with the first historical evidence of the Egyptian civilization flourishing again long after the original civilization had been decimated, perhaps many thousands of years earlier.

By way of analogy, it's a bit like having, say, a hundred books on a bookshelf sitting between two bookends, and, unknowingly, someone comes along and removes a number of books from the middle of the shelf. Having removed those books, the person then pushes the two bookends together again, closing the gap between the remaining books, thereby presenting a continuous (though shorter) line of books. A chunk of knowledge has been lost from the shelf, but we don't even realize it's been lost because both bookends remain; we can see the beginning and the end, and we assume that what we have is a continuous, unbroken line, that nothing has been lost.

In short, it is possible that a more recent Egyptian society has been erased from our history because, by compacting the time line between the Old Kingdom and the Middle Kingdom to a mere 150 years (which included the FIP), Egyptology has effectively closed the chronological gap by pulling the Old Kingdom pyramid-building age forward in absolute time, perhaps by many thousands of years, to now sit but a mere 150 years from the start of the Middle Kingdom period. In so doing, this chaotic period of unknown duration—a time that does not seem to belong to the Old Kingdom or the FIP—then becomes erased and becomes mere legend; we do not know that this lost legendary period ever truly existed because we have pulled the bookends of the Egyptian civilization together, closing the chronological gap.

Radiocarbon Dating

Surely, what is then required is a means by which we can measure the ancient Egyptian chronology scientifically in order to obtain absolute date-reference points. In this regard, two radiocarbon dating studies of the Old Kingdom pyramids were conducted in the 1980s and 1990s, and their findings roughly concur with the orthodox age of the structures of around 4,500 years (within a couple of hundred years or so). More recently, in December 2020, it was announced that a small piece of cedar wood that had been discovered inside the sealed southern shaft of the Queen's Chamber by British engineer Waynman Dixon in 1872, and which had subsequently become lost, was rediscovered in the archives of Aberdeen University in Scotland. A sample of the wood was radiocarbon-dated and its calibrated age found to be between 3341 and 3094 BCE, some 500 to 800 years before the time of Khufu.

This age discrepancy is typically explained away by Egyptologists as being the result of the ancient Egyptian builders recycling wood that had been cut down many centuries before, an issue known as the "old wood problem." On the face of it, one might consider that all of this conclusively settles the dating issue. However, the science of radiocarbon dating, while sound in theory, seems not to be without its problems and limitations.

> Since 1947, scientists have reckoned the ages of many old objects by measuring the amounts of radioactive carbon they contain. New research shows, however, that some estimates based on carbon may have erred by thousands of years. . . . The group theorizes that large errors in carbon dating result from fluctuations in the amount of carbon 14 in the air. Changes in the Earth's magnetic field would change the deflection of cosmic-ray particles streaming toward the Earth from the Sun. Carbon 14 is thought to be mainly a product of bombardment of the atmosphere by cosmic rays, so cosmic ray intensity would affect the amount of carbon 14 in the environment at any given time.[9]

In an effort to resolve the issue of these cosmic ray fluctuations in the Earth's past, scientists have developed techniques such as ice-core analysis and dendrochronology (tree-ring dating) to try and smooth out these dating errors, generating a whole series of "calibrating curves" that allow them, in theory, to determine more accurately the age of a particular organic specimen. There are many of these calibration curves, and each depends on a number of additional factors and assumptions such as a particular specimen being from the Northern or Southern Hemisphere, whether it is land-based or water-based, and its proximity to nuclear testing during the 1950s. As time progresses, however, scientists are learning of additional factors that need to be taken into account when determining the radiocarbon calibrating curve and thus the true age of organic material.

Recently, for example, scientists have discovered that the proximity of the Earth to the sun's electromagnetic field can slow down the decay rate of radioactive isotopes, a finding that may have profound implications for the science of radiocarbon dating since it had always been a fundamental cornerstone of radiometric dating techniques that the decay rates of radioactive isotopes were constant and immutable. And it raises the further question: if the pyramid itself can indeed focus electromagnetic fields into its internal chambers as some scientists now claim (see chapter 6), then we must surely ponder just how such a property might also affect the decay rate of radioactive carbon within any organic material stored therein.

Other problematic issues, such as contamination of a specimen, are not so easily resolved. If, for example, a small amount of modern ash had ever come into contact with the cedar wood sample found in the Great Pyramid, then this could result in an artificially young date being returned for this wood. A 2011 article from the *New York Times* serves to highlight this particular problem. "Until now bones from several Neanderthal sites have been dated to as young as 29,000 years ago. . . . But researchers report that tests using an improved method of radiocarbon dating, based on a new way to exclude contaminants, show that most, and maybe all, Neanderthal bones in Europe are or will be found to be at least 39,000 years old."[10]

That contaminents can skew radiocarbon dates by as much as 10,000 years is no small issue, and especially so given that we simply do not know the full provenance or chain of custody of the small piece of cedar found in the Queen's Chamber shaft. Given that modern ash is one of the main culprits for skewing radiocarbon dates and given that this piece of wood was undoubtedly handled by numerous people and then stored in a tobacco tin (of all things) for over seventy years, can we really be certain its dating of between 3341 and 3094 BCE is accurate, or might its true date have been skewed by thousands of years in the same way the Neanderthal bones were found to have been?

As each review of the radiocarbon dating technique is published, we find that scientists are learning of ever more factors that need to be taken into account in order to produce a more accurate date for a particular artifact. And with each new calibration curve that is produced by these reviews, we find that the mean dates of ancient artifacts just seem to be getting pushed ever farther back in time, the old wood becoming ever older and farther away from the believed time of Khufu. We can only ponder here just how long it might be before scientists have finally perfected the radiocarbon dating technique and, of course, just how much older organic artifacts might then be.

In short, radiocarbon dating, though theoretically sound, is an imperfect science that is known to produce flawed results, even after calibration. This may be why radiocarbon dating results are usually cited in academic papers only when the date agrees with other archaeological and historical findings and perhaps also why Zahi Hawass described radiocarbon dating as "useless." In the *Egyptian Independent* online newspaper, Valentina Cattane wrote, "Hawass remains categorical in his rejection of the technique: 'Not even in five thousand years could carbon dating help archeology. We can use other kinds of methods like geoarcheology, which is very important, or DNA, or laser scanning, but carbon dating is useless. This science will never develop. In archeology, we consider carbon dating results imaginary.'"[11]

Earth Changes

Is it merely coincidental that 12,000 or so years ago, around 10,081 BCE, our planet was in the grip of major sea-level rises as the great ice sheets of Europe and North America were in meltdown (fig. 7.20)? Even today, scientists struggle to identify the underlying cause of this (relatively)

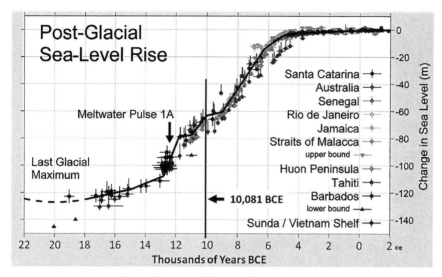

Figure 7.20. The midpoint of the Earth's post–Ice Age sea-level rise occurs circa 10,081 BCE, the date of the first pole shift event and the time when the Giza monuments would likely have been built.

rapid warming of the planet that caused the great ice sheets to collapse and disappear.

If the year 10,081 BCE, cited in figure 7.20, was the time when King Surīd's astronomer-priests observed that the stars had wandered from their normal course across the heavens (when a pole shift event was underway), then is it mere coincidence that this occurred almost midway through the Younger Dryas cooling period (10,900 BCE to 9700 BCE), when the Earth gradually became warmer again, resulting in a further spike in global sea level? Is it perhaps the case that as the oceans gradually rose over the preceding thousands of years, a tipping point was reached circa 10,081 BCE that resulted in the Earth becoming unstable and flipping over, Dzhanibekov style? And could this flip have then shifted the Earth's former great ice sheets into even warmer latitudes, thereby accelerating their meltdown and causing further rapid rises in global sea levels, just as Surīd's astronomer-priests had predicted?

8

A New Landscape

For centuries, mainstream Egyptologists have insisted that the giant pyramids of the early Egyptian dynasties were built as the eternal tomb of just one man, the pharaoh. The function of each pyramid, it seems, according to their interpretation of the ancient Egyptian hieroglyphics, was to serve as some kind of revivification machine that would take two aspects of the king's soul (his *ka* and his *ba*) and, through some mystical alchemy, convert them into *akh,* a light-being that could ascend to the heavenly realm, the afterlife, to intercede with the gods to ensure the continued well-being of Egypt and its people. In the minds of the ancient Egyptians, we are told, the role of the king in death was just as important as his role was in life, if not more so.

But we have to ask: Where did such religious ideas come from? How did they form and evolve? And why were giant pyramids suddenly required to help make this journey to the heavenly realm possible when, for most of Egypt's long history, its kings built no pyramid afterlife machines, each being buried instead in a simple mastaba tomb or in an underground tomb such as those we find today in the Valley of the Kings? Indeed, there are numerous reasons why pyramids would simply *not* have been the most desirable place for the burial of an ancient Egyptian king,* at least not in the conventional sense so embraced by Egyptologists. Could it be, then, that the early, giant pyramids of Egypt were conceived

---

*See *The Secret Chamber of Osiris: Lost Knowledge of the Sixteen Pyramids,* 51–81.

and built to serve some alternative purpose, to fulfill some other important need for the ancient Egyptian people?

It is the contention of this book that this was, indeed, the case. But this alternative purpose is not one imagined or first proposed by the author of this work. Rather it is one that has come down to us from prehistory, from the ancient Egyptians themselves, whose descendants, the Coptic-Egyptians, kept alive their history and cultural traditions, passing them down in oral form, generation after generation, possibly for thousands of years. In time, this oral history would finally be committed to the written form by a number of Arabic scholars in the early Middle Ages.

This Coptic-Egyptian narrative speaks of a time when the stars in the heavens lost their way, wandering from their usual course across the night sky. King Surīd (Suphis/Khufu) asked his astronomer-priests what this portent in the heavens would mean and was told by them that the kingdom would be destroyed by a great deluge some three hundred years in the future. Upon hearing this, Surīd embarked on the construction of sixteen great stone pyramids,* immovable man-made mountains, into which he would place everything the kingdom would require to ensure its revivification after the coming flood had abated. This would also include the construction of a great chamber within the Great Pyramid for twenty-seven of his ancestor kings and queens, without which the hoped for revivification of the kingdom simply could never occur because if their mummified remains were destroyed in the coming deluge, then they could no longer intercede with and seek the benevolence of the gods to bring about the rebirth of the kingdom.

It was crucial, then, that the ancestors were placed in a safe, inaccessible haven as far from the floodwaters as possible, high up in the Great Pyramid's superstructure—the Big Void. It is thus easy to understand how those from ancient times believed the pyramids were tombs of the pharaohs while at the same time believing that the Great Pyramid was also some kind of revivification machine. The Great Pyramid was *all* of

---

*There is more detail about the construction of these sixteen pyramids in my book *The Secret Chamber of Osiris: Lost Knowledge of the Sixteen Pyramids*, 41–48.

these things, although not in the conventional sense; the original function of these pyramids was not so much to serve as the tomb of the king as it was to act as the womb of the kingdom. In later dynasties, as religious ideas evolved around the pyramids, it would not be surprising that the king's own rebirth and afterlife would gradually become inextricably linked with these monuments because there would have been a long memory that they were the means through which death could be defied and rebirth assured. If the pyramids once brought about the rebirth of the kingdom, then they could now serve to bring about the rebirth of the king.

It is, however, unsurprising that these Arabic translations of the ancient Coptic-Egyptian accounts are dismissed by modern scholars and other skeptics as nothing more than myth and legend. After all, according to most modern scientists, there is simply no evidence for a global deluge nor, they believe, is it possible for the Earth to tumble over on its axis—two central claims of the Coptic-Egyptian oral tradition.

And yet, for all the modern skeptics' haughty insistence and scientific claims to the contrary, the ancient testimonies speaking of these calamitous times in remote antiquity continue to persist, leaving the nagging questions forever fermenting in our minds, taunting us: What if this ancient Coptic-Egyptian legend is actually true? What if this calamity, as many other ancient writings also tell us, is indeed part of a great convulsion of the Earth that occurs at regular intervals, over long periods of time, wiping out civilizations and leaving us to begin again as children, with little knowledge of our past?

This book has presented much evidence from ancient sources from all over the world that speak of a time when the Earth tumbled over on its axis. If there were perhaps only a handful of such accounts, then we might easily be able to say, with some confidence, that such stories *were* but mere myth. However, to stand in the presence of so many accounts from ancient times that describe a similar pole shift event surely suggests that there may very well be much more truth to this particular legend than modern science is ever prepared to admit or accept. Did all these ancient witnesses simply imagine the same tumultuous and traumatic event?

We find scientists such as Ed Krupp insisting that in order for the main Giza pyramids to strictly correlate with the Orion Belt stars (as per the theory of Robert Bauval), then Giza needs to be turned upside down. What Krupp is effectively arguing here is that if Bauval's pyramid-star correlation has a basis in fact, then the Giza monuments must have been built when the Earth was once upside down (and that it has since returned to its original upright orientation). Of course, the great irony here with Krupp's throwaway remark is that the Earth probably *was* in just such a condition and that this is precisely why we find the Giza monuments so peculiarly aligned today, having been built after an initial pole-shift event (when the pyramids would have aligned with the belt stars in the Southern Hemisphere) and then having subsequently become misaligned (specifically, turned upside down after a second, more recent, pole shift event).

These pole shift events explain a number of other peculiar anomalies we find within the monuments at Giza and elsewhere in Egypt, such as the misalignment of the Sphinx and the niche in the Queen's Chamber. These two features are misaligned by around the same amount but in two different directions, suggesting that the Sphinx was built before the first-pole shift event when Giza was located close to the equator in the Northern Hemisphere, while the niche was built after this event when Giza was shifted to the Southern Hemisphere. With the pre-shift Sphinx having faced the dawn on the eastern horizon, post-shift it would find the dawn at its rear on the western horizon (perhaps explaining the opposite-facing Sphinx image on the Dream Stele). This new sunrise on the western horizon may also explain why the pyramids were constructed on the west bank of the Nile and the so-called sarcophagus placed in the western end of the King's Chamber; the western horizon would now be regarded as the place of rebirth. This new dawn may further explain why many older burial customs had the head of the deceased facing the western horizon; it perhaps wasn't so much that the burial customs of these ancient people had changed but, rather, that the place where the sun rose had changed.

The most telling physical features of the Great Pyramid's internal architecture that strongly speak to us of an ancient pole shift event are, of course, the four sets of so-called star shafts that seem to point to the stars in motion. In their attempts to date the Giza monuments using archaeoastronomy, Virginia Trimble and Robert Bauval unwittingly found perhaps another indicator of an ancient pole shift event, albeit the most recent event. The two researchers found two different dates encoded into the pyramid's architecture. Trimble's star altitude method gave the date circa 2550 BCE, while Bauval's belt pivot technique returned a date of circa 10,500 BCE. If both methods used by these researchers were originally deployed simultaneously by the ancient designers (and there are good reasons to believe that this *would* have been the case), then there is no reason why we should find a discrepancy of around eight thousand years (equal to around 33° of precessional change) between the two dates. However, that these two researchers failed to find a common convergence date for the pyramid's construction may have little to do with any failure of the specific techniques they each employed in their research but rather has more to do with an ancient pole shift event driving the observed alignments and findings apart. This second, most recent pole shift event would undoubtedly have altered aspects of the Earth's geodynamics, thereby erasing some of the properties we find encoded into the Giza monuments and thus making a convergence of the Bauval-Trimble dates impossible to find in modern star-mapping software since the pre-shift convergence would, almost certainly, no longer exist.

Finally, we have the curious astronomical ceiling of Senemut (the chief architect of Queen Hatshepsut during the Eighteenth Dynasty), which presents several features that can only be made sense of from the perspective of an upturned Earth. North is south and south is north and the stars and planets seem to be depicted moving in the opposite directions.

And just as stories of ancient pole shifts come to us from every corner of the Earth, so too do stories of an ancient, global flood that the Coptic-Egyptian legend also predicted. Scientists typically dismiss these as merely exaggerated tales of localized flooding events from these ancient people because, according to the science, there is no evidence of any cataclysmic global event of the type described in these ancient texts, including the Bible, ever having occurred.

But once again, the evidence—documentary and physical—appears to be at odds with the scientific position. The ancient Egyptians tell us that they anticipated a great flood that would drown the entire country. Indeed, their very creation myths can be interpreted as a catastrophic flood event whereby the pyramids seemingly arose from the duat (a watery realm) to give rebirth to the world. Even the hieroglyphic for the pyramid is shown as arising out of a body of water, the rectangular sign at its base that has been interpreted in the pyramid texts as meaning the duat. This pyramid emerging from water iconography is confirmed with the South Pyramid at Saqqara, where we see the base of the pyramid is surrounded by a wavy wall, the ancient Egyptian symbol for water.

While science generally dismisses notions of a global deluge, it cannot deny that sea levels at the end of the last ice age were around four hundred feet lower than they are today. Something clearly happened to cause the great ice sheets to melt away and the sea levels to rise. Scientists insist, however, that the rise in sea levels occurred very slowly over many thousands of years, which is mostly true. However, this slow, gradual rise in sea levels wasn't always so because, on occasion, it was punctuated by instances such as Meltwater Pulse 1A, circa 12,500 BCE, when sea levels rose instantly and dramatically by several feet all over the world. This rise doesn't sound like very much, but to the mostly coastal communities of the Earth at that time, an instant rise in sea levels, even of just a few feet or so, would have been catastrophic, and its effects would have been burned deep into humanity's collective memory, with the calamitous consequences passed on, generation after generation, in the oral tradition by different cultures all over the world.

But what could have caused the sea levels to rise in the first place when it is known that they had been stable for hundreds of thousands of years? What occurred toward the end of the last ice age, circa 12,500 BCE, to have caused this great upheaval? It is almost impossible to know with any degree of certainty. However, recent discoveries tell us that around this time (the exact date is presently uncertain), a massive meteor struck northwest Greenland, releasing the energy of a seven-hundred-megaton nuclear explosion. This event alone would have caused significant global upheavals but was likely only the catalyst for a whole chain of subsequent and interlinked catastrophic events.

If we imagine that this meteor impact occurred around 17,000 BCE and that it possessed sufficient force to alter the Earth's axial tilt by several degrees, this may have resulted in the North American and European ice sheets being sufficiently shifted into warmer latitudes for them to go into a long, slow meltdown. Eventually, the slowly rising seas brought the Earth's irregular-shaped geoid to a tipping point whereby, circa 10,081 BCE, the planet became unstable and fully tumbled over, Dzhanibekov style, causing the stars and other celestial objects to lose their normal passage across the heavens—perhaps the very event Sūrīd's astronomer-priests had observed. It may be no coincidence that the Giza stellar time line calculations present the midpoint date (perhaps a tipping point) in the Earth's sea-level rise (as noted in fig. 7.20, p. 173).

With this inversion of the planet, it seems that Giza was relocated from around 3° north of the equator to around 30° south (it would be relocated back to the Northern Hemisphere in a subsequent pole shift event some 7,693 years later, circa 2388 BCE). Giza seems also to have been relocated relatively unscathed, perhaps as a result of being in close proximity to one of the pivot points of the inversion. At the same time, the great ice sheets in North America and Europe would have been relocated into even warmer latitudes, thereby causing them to go into further rapid and irreversible meltdown and storing up trouble for the planet in the centuries and millennia to come.

Whatever the exact chain of events and their timings, what the Coptic-Egyptian texts tell us, unequivocally, is that the Egyptian king at that time, Sūrīd, decided he would build great stone pyramids as watertight, impregnable storehouses to try and mitigate the worst effects of the coming deluge. This would have meant storing in each of the pyramids all manner of items: tools, seeds, weapons, papyrus scrolls, pottery, and so on. However, as previously stated, the single most vital aspect of Sūrīd's plan was the placement in the Hall of the Ancestors the mummified bodies of his forefathers, for only they could occasion the revivification of the kingdom.

But if this was the true purpose of these monuments, how did this truth come to be so lost? Why is this picture of our ancient past so blurred and confused? There are a number of factors that contributed to this.

First of all, there were the writings of Herodotus, who tells us that Khufu built the pyramid as his tomb (although Diodorus Siculus tells us that Khufu was not buried there).

Second were the social attitudes and ethnocentric biases of the first Europeans to study these monuments in the early eighteenth and nineteenth centuries, which led them to assume that the smaller, unfinished chamber within the Great Pyramid must have been for Khufu's queen while the larger chamber (with its stone sarcophagus) must have belonged to the king (such notions have since been shown to be utter bunk). In the mindset of the Europeans of this period, "big" = "king" and "small" = "queen." As such, it was likewise assumed by these early pyramid explorers that the small pyramids were for the king's queens, with the giant pyramid being the domain of the king.

In seeing just one sarcophagus in the so-called burial chamber, these early explorers also assumed, not unsurprisingly, that the pyramid was built as the burial place for just one king. These early explorers were unaware that the ancient Egyptians had several different names for large stone boxes because each of them served a different purpose, and they also did not understand that the granite container they believed to be the king's sarcophagus was not, in fact, a sarcophagus for human burial at all but likely served a ritual function related to the revivification, not of the king, but of the Earth. This explains why, in 1818, the Italian pyramid explorer Giovanni Belzoni, upon removing the lid from the granite sarcophagus in the second pyramid at Giza, was disappointed (and not a little puzzled) to discover that it contained nothing more than Egyptian earth and stones. This discovery by Belzoni perhaps explains also why the ancient Egyptians of later dynasties made small, ceremonial replicas of this earth-filled sarcophagus, filling these small stone and wooden boxes also with earth and some grain, then burying them in a small hole in the ground and finally placing a large rock (symbolizing the pyramid) on top.*

---

*See *The Secret Chamber of Osiris: Lost Knowledge of the Sixteen Pyramids*, 205–11.

We can thus begin to see how the idea of the pyramid as the tomb of just one pharaoh became embedded in the mindsets of the early pyramid explorers. These attitudes were compounded by misinterpretation and incomplete readings of the available evidence. However, to be fair to the Egyptologists, their task in making sense of all of this wasn't made any easier when certain unscrupulous individuals manufactured and placed false evidence into the historical puzzle.

In 1837, the British antiquarian and pyramid explorer Colonel Richard William Howard Vyse blasted his way into a series of four hitherto unknown and completely sealed chambers within the Great Pyramid. In these chambers, Vyse claimed to have found Khufu's name (and *only* this king's name) crudely painted onto several wall and roof blocks. Vyse's discovery is held up by Egyptology, even today, as conclusive proof of Khufu's hand in building the Great Pyramid. But more than that, it is seen as proof that the pyramid was built as Khufu's *tomb* and only Khufu's tomb.

From a personal perspective, there is little doubt in this author's mind that most of the painted marks, including all of the royal cartouches, that Vyse claimed to have discovered on the walls of these chambers will, upon any future scientific scrutiny, be found to be fraudulent. A close analysis of Vyse's claims* reveals many serious discrepancies and, as such, places sufficient doubt on his claimed discovery as to render it unreliable and thus inadmissible as evidence. But, to a large extent, the damage has already been done. The corrupting effect of Vyse's alleged discovery helped to solidify the pyramid-as-tomb-of-Khufu narrative in the minds of Egyptologists. This false evidence completely stymied their critical thinking, and they looked no further.

The result of this closed thinking meant that the Coptic-Egyptian texts that speak to us of a completely different narrative for the construction of these monuments were largely ignored and set aside by Egyptology, where they languished in relative obscurity for the better part of two hundred years. This is why it is important to demonstrate,

---

*Many more details regarding this analysis can be found in *The Great Pyramid Hoax* and in the appendices at the end of this book.

with convincing evidence, that Vyse's claimed discovery is entirely bogus for, in removing his false evidence, we may be able to dislodge the tomb-of-Khufu narrative and open our eyes to other possibilities for these monuments; we may then be able to go back to basics and consider more seriously what the Coptic-Egyptian oral tradition tells us about these monuments.

And, as previously mentioned, one of the other important things the Coptic-Egyptian tradition tells us is that the Great Pyramid, Sūrīd's great recovery vault, was built also to secure the mummified bodies of his ancestors. Since not a single one of these ancestor kings and queens has ever been discovered, then it seems self-evident that they must have been placed within a hidden chamber of the pyramid, the Big Void, high up within the monument's superstructure, to ensure the bodies were as high above the coming floodwaters as possible. To protect them from any potential threat, there would be no access passageways—none whatsoever—making it virtually impossible for anyone ever to detect the presence of, let alone gain access to, this chamber. Each deceased king and queen would be placed into the Big Void when its roof was still open during construction, and when the assembly of kings and queens was fully complete, the Hall of the Ancestors would be hermetically sealed as the pyramid was built upward and over it to completion. In this sense, one can regard the chambers within the pyramid that possess passageways and entrances almost as decoy chambers. Who would ever think of looking for a chamber where there was no discernable passageway or hidden entrance?

But the builders still could not be certain that the remains of the mummified ancestor kings and queens could survive the coming upheaval, and so, below this great void chamber, the inaccessible Hall of the Ancestors, they built a second massive chamber that we know today as the Grand Gallery. In accordance with their religious beliefs, into this chamber would be placed a statue bearing the likeness of each ancestor king (and his queen) along the length of and on each of its sides—twenty-seven kings and twenty-seven queens in total. (Some Arabic texts tell us that such statues were indeed found in this chamber when the Great Pyramid was first breached, ca. 820 CE.) The purpose of the statues was a practical one, for should the actual mummified bodies in the great Hall of the Ancestors (above the Grand Gallery) become too decayed, then the stone statue of each king and queen would serve as a surrogate body for his or her soul to take refuge and become an akh. It may be no coincidence, then, that we find the number of kings preceding Khufu, going all the way back to Menes, the first king of the unified kingdom, was twenty-seven in number.

It is also worth noting here that the original burials of some of these ancestor kings (and one queen) were found undisturbed, with the sarcophagi fully sealed and intact. However, upon removing the lid from each of these sarcophagi, no mummy was found inside, even though, in the case of Queen Hetepheres I (Khufu's mother), there is good evidence to indicate that the mummy *did* once occupy the now empty sarcophagus.

Also worth mentioning here is that these sealed and empty sarcophagi all predate the reign of Khufu. Only Khufu's *ancestors* (not any of his successors) have been found to have these peculiar sealed but empty sarcophagi. This phenomenon has puzzled Egyptologists, who find it difficult to rationalize all the circumstances around these peculiar discoveries into a cohesive and sensible picture. However, if we accept the Coptic-Egyptian tradition as to the purpose of the Great Pyramid as offering a sanctuary for these kings and queens against a coming deluge, then these sealed but seemingly abandoned ancestor sarcophagi are precisely what we would expect to find. The bodies of Khufu's ancestors, all twenty-seven kings and queens, were simply removed from their original burial sarcophagi (which were then respectfully and ritually resealed) and relocated to the protection of the great Hall of the Ancestors (the Big Void), high up within the Great Pyramid, from whence, at the appropriate time, they would collectively act, through the agency of the god Osiris, to intercede with the gods and bring about the rebirth of the kingdom. Such was the responsibility and power of these Osirian Kings.

In addition to providing secure storage for seeds and tools and giving sanctuary to the former kings and queens of Egypt, the Coptic-Egyptian legend further informs us that the Giza pyramids (particularly the so-called Queens' Pyramids) appear to have served another, secondary purpose—as a universal stellar timepiece that uses the precessional motion of Orion's Belt to tell us when this great unnatural motion of the stars (the pole shift event) in Egypt actually occurred (ca. 10,081 BCE). Not only this, but this stellar clock also informs us that the *periodicity* of these cataclysmic events is every 7,693 years. With this stellar clock we can then determine when the most recent event occurred (ca. 2388 BCE) and, most important from our own civilization's perspective, when the *next* cataclysm is likely to occur, which, if the interpretation of the Giza stellar time line presented here is correct, won't occur until circa 5305 CE. We can all sleep easily in our beds for a long while yet.

This book began with a "troublesome discovery," the Big Void. To Egyptologists, the presence of another massive chamber within the Great Pyramid makes little sense in terms of their own understanding of these monuments, the pyramid-as-tomb-of-the-king paradigm. And if, as I suspect, the ancestor kings and queens of Khufu are one day discovered within this great Hall of the Ancestors, then Egyptology, as it is presently stands, will crumble. And perhaps deservedly so, for if we take it upon ourselves to cast as mere myth and legend that which the Coptic-Egyptians have to say about their own history and understanding of these monuments, then we arrogantly dismiss these ancient voices at our peril.

Portrait of a Fraud

Analysis of Colonel Vyse's Activities

As stated throughout this book, the discovery of the painted marks presented by Colonel Vyse from the four Vyse Chambers had the effect of Egyptology accepting, uncritically, that Khufu built the Great Pyramid as his eternal tomb despite the fact that early medieval Arabic translations of some Coptic-Egyptian oral traditions (rightly or wrongly) tell us that the pyramids, including the Great Pyramid, were constructed by Sūrīd (Suphis/Khufu) as a great recovery system for the kingdom in anticipation of a civilization-ending deluge.

Notwithstanding the extensive evidence hitherto presented in my previous books and articles that calls into question Vyse's claimed discovery of the painted marks within these four cramped chambers of the Great Pyramid, it seems that the more we analyze the available evidence relating to his discovery, the more errors, anomalies, and inconsistencies we find, all of which adds to the already considerable body of evidence previously uncovered that indicates the strong likelihood of a quite audacious hoax having been perpetrated within the Great Pyramid by Vyse and his closest assistants in the spring of 1837. There are simply too many questions with regard to these painted marks for any objective mind to remotely accept them as being genuine artifacts from the time of Khufu. And Vyse, we should not forget, is a man now known to have perpetrated a major fraud earlier in his life in his bid to become a member of the British Parliament in 1807.* Is he a man who can be taken at his word?

It is unlikely, of course, that we will ever find a signed confession from Vyse or any of his accomplices admitting to this fraud. What we must do instead, therefore, is continue to carefully study what these men left behind, analyzing the inconsistencies, mistakes, and contradictions in the available evidence—the stylistic elements of the marks—this being one of the means by which this hoax can be exposed and this evidence presented by Vyse discredited. Only then, with Vyse's false evidence removed, will we be able to look upon these monuments with fresh eyes and begin to contemplate their true meaning and purpose.

STYLE MATTERS: EXAMINING THE ORIENTATION OF THE MARKS

The painted marks that Vyse presents from the four chambers he discovered entirely distort and muddle the historical picture with respect to the chronology of the pyramid's construction and, by extension, the chronology of the Old Kingdom itself (even in terms of the orthodox chronology). This arises from the paleography of the script used in these marks, which possess a number of stylistic elements that appear to be entirely anachronistic to the period circa 2550 BCE, when the Great Pyramid was supposedly built. A number of these elements find their best stylistic/paleographic matches between the Eighth and Eleventh Dynasties—around six hundred years *after* the conventional date for the pyramid's construction.[†]

A simple comparison of the king's name written in old hieratic script from the Fourth Dynasty period, when the Great Pyramid was supposedly being built, clearly demonstrates some marked differences (fig. A1.1, p. 188). In contemporary papyri from the period, as well as graffiti written elsewhere in Egypt, we find most of the king's cartouches are presented in a vertical fashion (fig. A1.1, *upper*). This

---

*Details about Vyse's quest for Parliament can be found in *The Great Pyramid Hoax,* 32–38.

†See *The Great Pyramid Hoax,* 147–50.

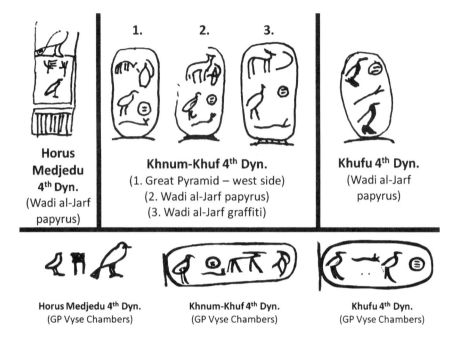

Figure A1.1. A comparison of hieratic text showing how Khufu's name was usually written in hieratic text during the Fourth Dynasty (upper) and the various names of Khufu in hieratic text from the Vyse Chambers (lower). Note also how the Horus name (lower, left) is no longer contained within the rectangular serekh (upper, left), nor does it present the distinctive palace facade motif.

contrasts quite starkly with the various Khufu cartouches supposedly discovered by Vyse within the Great Pyramid, in which the hieratic text, without exception, presents all of the king's various names in horizontal (linear) fashion (fig. A1.1, *lower*). Furthermore, we find that every example of the Horus name of Khufu found within the Vyse Chambers is entirely devoid of the "palace facade" motif (the vertical lines at the bottom of the Horus Medjedu inscription, which symbolize the royal palace and power base of the king) and also the enclosing rectangular frame known as a *serekh,* suggesting it is a much evolved and simplified hieratic version of this particular Horus name (and thus that it comes from a much later period).

Whenever we find contemporary texts of the kings from this period, such as Djedfre's name in both Giza boat pits* or the Khufu, Khnum-Khufu, and Horus names at Wadi al-Jarf (and on some exposed core stones of the Great Pyramid), we find that they are invariably written in a vertical fashion.

It is known, of course, that ancient Egyptian script can be written variously in vertical or horizontal fashion (sometimes even both orientations are used in the same inscription). But the general understanding that Egyptologists have acquired of ancient Egyptian hieratic script is that it was first written in columns and gradually evolved to being written horizontally in rows. In this regard, the ancient Egyptian hieratic expert Hans Goedicke informs us, "The horizontal arrangement evolved slowly . . . the reign of Amenemhet III (1842–1795 B.C.) appears to mark the watershed between vertical and horizontal line arrangement. . . . After the adoption of the horizontal arrangement there were no relapses into the earlier form."[1]

And so, caveats notwithstanding, we see that the general trend in ancient Egyptian hieratic writing was from a vertical to a horizontal form. This evolution in hieratic script appears, unsurprisingly, to have applied also to the quarry gang names.

Applying this general trend to the various names of Khufu (and other associated marks) that were supposedly found by Vyse inside the Great Pyramid, which are written—without exception—in horizontal fashion, suggests that the British pyramid explorer had, bizarrely, found within these chambers painted marks in a style that only arose in a period long after the pyramid was supposedly built, when hieratic script had fully evolved into its horizontal form (fig. A1.2, p. 190).

But how could this be? As a result of his ignorance of the evolution between hieroglyphic and hieratic writing, it is conceivable that Vyse and his accomplices had found authentic but *anachronistic* marks from somewhere else (most likely on the stones in the rubble outside the pyramid, somewhere that they would have been largely protected

---

*The Khufu I boat pit (discovered and excavated in 1954 by Kamal el-Mallakh) was found to contain several vertical Djedfre cartouches but none of Khufu. The Khufu II boat pit, also discovered by el-Mallakh in 1954, was opened and excavated only in 2011 by a Japanese archaeology team from Waseda University. This second boat pit contained just one vertical Djedfre cartouche along with five (vertical and horizontal) Khufu cartouches.

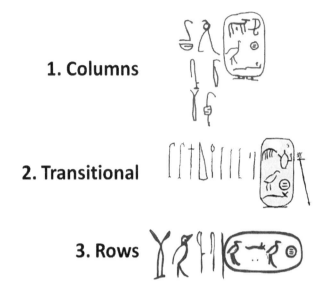

1. Columns

2. Transitional

3. Rows

Figure A1.2. Ancient Egyptian quarry gang names appear to demonstrate the evolution of hieratic script from being written in columns to being written in rows.

and preserved from the elements) and, unwittingly, copied these much younger marks into the four Vyse Chambers.

This hypothesis finds some support from the crudely painted horizontal Khufu cartouches that were found relatively recently in the second boat pit on the south side of the Great Pyramid. Afifi Rohim Ghonim, who was part of the investigating team exploring this boat pit, said of the horizontal Khufu cartouche found therein, "If we make a comparison for this cartouche of Khufu which we discovered on our cover stones [of the second boat pit] with the cartouche found in the five rooms [the cartouche in Campbell's Chamber, one of the four chambers discovered by Vyse], we will find it the same—they used the same techniques, the same colors."[2]

Ghonim essentially tells us that the horizontal Khufu cartouche in the second boat pit is stylistically the same as that within Campbell's

Figure A1.3. The horizontal Khufu cartouche found in the second southern boat pit at Giza.

Chamber, that they have an identical provenance. However, a problem arises when we consider the view of other Egyptologists regarding the Khufu cartouche within the Great Pyramid. On the Ahram Online website, Nevine El-Aref writes, "Ahmed Saeed, professor of ancient Egyptian civilization at Cairo University . . . suggests the [Khufu cartouche in Campbell's Chamber] could have been written during the Middle Kingdom era [ca. 2050–1652 BCE], due to the style of writing used."[3]

Given that Ghonim states that the Khufu cartouche in the second boat pit (see fig. A1.3) is written in the same style as the Khufu cartouche in Campbell's Chamber, then it becomes entirely possible, as Saeed's statement above implies, that the similarly styled horizontal boat-pit cartouche of Khufu might also date to the Middle Kingdom period.

If Saeed is right and the horizontal Khufu cartouches in the second boat pit stylistically belong to the Middle Kingdom period, then this suggests that the second boat pit (at least) had been open and accessible for many hundreds of years after construction, long before perhaps being finally sealed in the Middle Kingdom period. In short, we simply do not know for certain when these boat pits were sealed with their massive fourteen-ton blocking stones, and neither can we be certain if the blocking stones themselves were not repurposed in the Middle Kingdom period (bearing painted cartouches from an earlier period when they were first worked), perhaps taken from some other older construction that may have once existed at Giza (or elsewhere), a practice that was not uncommon in ancient Egypt. And, naturally, when reworking these scavenged stones for the purpose of covering the boat pits, the Middle Kingdom workers would have then painted their own (evolved) gang name marks onto the blocks, thereby giving us the seemingly mixed provenance of cartouches that we observe on these stones today.

It barely needs to be said, but the ramifications of these comments from these two prominent Egyptologists with regard to the provenance of the similarly styled cartouches that Vyse allegedly discovered within the Great Pyramid are huge. How exactly is it possible that cartouches that stylistically belong to the Middle Kingdom period could be found within entirely sealed and inaccessible chambers of a monument dated to the earlier Old Kingdom period?

OFFENDING THE KING

The question arises: If we find these construction crew names painted onto stone blocks within the formerly inaccessible Vyse Chambers, why don't we see any of them painted also on any of the stone surfaces within the accessible passages and chambers of the Great Pyramid? Why are all of these areas completely devoid of such markings? Egyptologists typically answer this by asserting that such marks probably *had* been painted onto the stones in these passages and chambers when the pyramid was still under construction but that these marks would, subsequently, have been scrubbed from the block surfaces so as not to offend the eyes of the funerary procession transporting Khufu's body through these narrow passages to his final resting place in the so-called King's Chamber. They further assert that the crudely painted marks in the sealed Vyse Chambers, however, would never have been seen by the funerary party, so there would have been no need to remove any of these; hence, that's why we find them there today.

It's an explanation of sorts. But it misses a crucial point about the funerary practices and religious beliefs of the ancient Egyptians of this period, who believed that, with a few magic spells, the king's soul could pass through stone. Thus, with such an ability, how, exactly, would these painted marks be shielded from Khufu's soul? In effect, what Egyptology is proposing is that graffiti was removed only from where it might be seen by the eyes of the living (the funerary party) but that is was essentially okay for the king's soul to be exposed to it in the Vyse Chambers.

The Vyse Chambers might not have been within reach of the living, but their inaccessibility, we are told, would have been little problem for Khufu's soul. And given that Khufu's priests would have understood this, then is it not more likely that they would never have permitted even the possibility of such an offense to the king's soul to occur and would have ensured that all marks—even those within the inaccessible Vyse Chambers—would have been scrubbed away? Why risk offending the king and potentially confusing his ka in his afterlife with such profane graffiti? And yet, we are expected to accept that these marks are genuine and that the king's priests would not have objected to their presence on the blocks of the Vyse Chambers as the pyramid was being built.

THE "BROTHER OF SUPHIS" MYSTERY

Such objections notwithstanding, mainstream Egyptology, however, remains steadfast in its opinion that the crudely painted marks presented to the world by the British pyramid explorer are the real deal, genuine artifacts from the time the pyramids were built. Unarguably, the primary reason why the painted marks are considered by Egyptology as being authentic comes from the fact that Vyse's discovery presents something that no one in 1837 could ever have anticipated or, indeed, reasonably explain: there were *two* different king's names (cartouches) found in the chambers (fig. A1.4)!*

Today, Egyptologists insist that these two cartouches belong to the same ancient Egyptian king and that the name Suphis (fig. A1.4, *upper*) is but an abbreviated version of the second cartouche, Sen-Suphis (fig. A1.4, *lower*). However, this was not known in Vyse's time, when it was believed by the leading scholars of the day that these two slightly different cartouches actually belonged to two quite separate kings (two brothers). So why, the critics ask, would Vyse risk drawing scrutiny to his alleged discovery by placing what was believed at the time to be the cartouches of two different kings, two brothers, within these chambers? Why insert two cartouches when placing just one in these chambers would have drawn fewer questions and would have been just as effective in corroborating the writings of Herodotus in attributing the monument to Suphis/Khufu?

Figure A1.4. The two cartouches from within the Vyse Chambers of the Great Pyramid.

---

*The king's Horus name, Medjedu, was also found in these chambers, but this name was not in the distinctive royal cartouche oval and, as such, would not have been recognized by any scholar of the period, let alone Vyse, as being another name for Saophis (Suphis/Khufu).

On the surface, this seems a fairly robust argument against Vyse having perpetrated any fraudulent actions, and for him to have placed two king's names (rather than the safer option of just one) into these chambers would have required some compelling reasons for him to have come to such a bold decision, not to mention the knowledge required to do so. However, when we consider the details of the situation, what we find is that there are, in fact, a number of possible scenarios that could have brought Vyse—contrary to the scholarly view of his time—to the conclusion that both cartouches should be placed within the chambers he had discovered.

Of course, it might reasonably be argued that the very fact that few people would have expected Vyse to have placed both of these cartouches into the chambers when just one of them would have served his needs, may, paradoxically, have been the very reason why he took such a bold action. If the colonel had reasoned that few would believe that he could ever have made such an audacious move, then, it actually becomes the best reason for doing so—a double-down double-bluff that salts the deception with a "whiff of authenticity" on the basis of its sheer audacity.

In short, the conventional view is that the two royal cartouches we find today in these chambers must be authentic because Vyse wouldn't ever have dared doing something so clearly at odds with the prevailing academic knowledge of the day (academia, we may remind ourselves, that was itself still in its infancy in understanding ancient Egyptian writing).

The colonel's actions, of course, would primarily depend on what he was able to learn about these two cartouches and whether any knowledge he was able to obtain was compelling enough to convince him that both cartouches should be placed within the chambers he had discovered. If such information was available at the time that convinced Vyse that there was a good likelihood that these two cartouches actually belonged to one and the same king, then placing both into the chambers would actually have been more of an intuitive and clever decision rather than the complete uneducated gamble it is often portrayed to have been. But was such information available and could Vyse have had access to it at Giza in 1837?

When Vyse embarked on his journey to Egypt in late 1835, the state of knowledge of this ancient country—particularly with regard to the reigns and successions of its many kings and queens—was incredibly vague. This situation is summarized by Vyse himself in his published account from 1840, in which he writes:

> Mr. Wilkinson, the highest authority in these matters, thus expressed himself: "No one is yet sufficiently advanced in the language of antient Egypt to enable him literally to translate an inscription of any length, or moderately complicated, though a general meaning may frequently be obtained." This assertion is unfortunately found to be true, notwithstanding the pretensions set up to the contrary. Nor does it appear that even Mr. Wilkinson has been able to establish any undoubted chronology, or succession of the antient kings, even with the aid of the stone found at Abydos, and of the Greek historians, or to reconcile in any way the differences which exist between the accounts of Manetho, and those of Herodotus.[4]

In Vyse's time, there were a number of conflicting and somewhat contradictory accounts from ancient sources as to the various names and spellings of the builders of the three main Giza pyramids. From these ancient sources, we have the names shown in figure A1.5, (p. 196).

For the purposes of this appendix, I shall mostly refer to these three kings—the Giza pyramid builders—using those names given to us by Eratosthenes, namely, Saophis I, Sen-Saophis, and Moscheres. In his 1828 book *Materia Hieroglyphica,* the British scholar Sir John Gardner Wilkinson had translated the Sen-Saophis of Eratosthenes as meaning the "Brother of Saophis" (Suphis) and had stated that these two brothers were the founders of the two largest pyramids at Giza. Wilkinson, however, was not able to identify which cartouche belonged to Saophis I or Sen-Saophis.*

So we must ask then: If Vyse did perpetrate a fraud within the Great Pyramid, why would he place the cartouches of not one but two different

---

*The accepted view today is that these two cartouches actually belong to the same king (Khnum-Khuf) and that Khufu is simply an abbreviation of the longer name. Our hypothesis, however, must be based only on what Vyse could have understood from the state of scholarly knowledge as it stood in 1837. Later information (information that would come after Vyse had already fraudulently placed the two cartouches into the chambers in 1837 and departed Egypt) could hardly have influenced his thoughts and decisions during his presence at Giza.

	G1 Pyramid	G2 Pyramid	G3 Pyramid
Herodotus (484 BCE):	Cheops	Cephrenes	Mycerinus
Manetho (300 BCE):	Suphis I	Suphis II	Mencheres
Eratosthenes (276 BCE):	Saophis I	Sen-Saophis	Moscheres
Diodorus (90 BCE):	Chembes (or Chemnis)	Kephren	Mycerinus (or Mecherinus)

Figure A1.5. The various historical names given as the builders of the three Giza pyramids.

kings (supposedly two brothers, Saophis I and Sen-Saophis) into the newly discovered chambers? Indeed, the critics argue, for Vyse to have known, in 1837, that these two cartouches were not of brothers at all (as the leading scholars of the time believed) but actually belonged to the same king would have made the British colonel the foremost scholarly authority of his day, exceeding the knowledge of Wilkinson and Ippolito Rosellini.

So how could a complete amateur such as Vyse have confounded the experts of his day and acquired for himself the necessary knowledge to pull off such an audacious, convincing, and lasting fraud?

MARKS ON THE STONES

From his published work, Vyse informs us that he found part of the royal cartouche of Khufu (Saophis I) on a stone among the debris on the north side of the Great Pyramid[5] and that he also found other painted quarry marks on some stones at the south side of the monument.[6] While Vyse presents in his published account only a few of the painted marks that were found on the pyramid's south side, it is entirely likely that many more were found, possibly including the cartouche of Saophis I (and associated marks) and also the king's Horus name (not in a cartouche), which Vyse would not have been able to recognize as a king's name. In the pyramid's north side, the colonel may well have found there, on some stones buried in the great mound of debris, cartouches of Saophis I and Sen-Saophis. Vyse may then have pondered as to why he was finding two different (though similar) royal cartouches on these stones among the debris on the pyramid's north side but only the Saophis I cartouche and other unknown markings among the debris on the pyramid's south side.

Since it was known in Vyse's time that it was Saophis I who built the Great Pyramid, then if the British explorer had been planning to place a fake cartouche within the hidden chambers he had blasted open, he might have wondered if either of the two cartouche types he had (hypothetically) already found among the debris was that of Saophis I, the pyramid builder. And so, before copying any of these marks into the newly discovered chambers, the colonel would first have to be certain that any cartouche he had found was indeed that of Saophis I; he could hardly choose some cartouche at random, copy it into the chambers, and simply hope to pass it off as the cartouche of the pyramid builder. In short, to pull off his hoax, the colonel would have to find some way of checking if either of the cartouches he had (theoretically) found among the pyramid rubble was indeed that of the pyramid builder.

But here's a curious thing: from Vyse's private journal, it is perfectly clear that, during his operations at Giza, he already *knew* which of the hundreds of ancient Egyptian royal cartouches was, in fact, that of Saophis I.* But how and from where could he possibly have obtained such information? There is perhaps a clue to this little mystery in a passage from the *Quarterly Review* periodical, published in the United Kingdom in the spring of 1835, about six months before Vyse departed England for Egypt (fig. A1.6).

The absence of hieroglyphics has usually been adduced as the conclusive proof of the antiquity of the pyramids, showing that they were raised before the use of written characters. Besides the name of Suphis, that of his successor, called Suphis the Second by Manetho, Sensaophis by Eratosthenes (the Cephren of the Greeks), has been copied in the tombs at Geezah. Sensaophis, according to Mr. Wilkinson (Materia Hieroglyphica, part ii. p. 74): and Rosellini, (vol. i. p. 130), means, brother of Suphis. He was the builder of the second pyramid. Mencheres, the name which succeeds in the list of Manetho, is not improbably identified with the third founder of the pyramids, the Mycerinus of Herodotus.

Figure A1.6. Extract from "Egypt and Thebes" in the February and April 1835 edition of the Quarterly Review, *115.*

---

*What did Vyse know and when did he know it? See *The Great Pyramid Hoax*, 173–82.

Had Vyse read this article, then it would have given him a big clue as to where to search for information concerning Saophis I ("Suphis") and possibly learn of the hieroglyphic spelling of his name, that is, his cartouche. In the first instance, he would likely have consulted Wilkinson's *Materia Hieroglyphica,* this book likely being more easily accessible to him. This scholarly tome was published in 1828, some seven years before Vyse embarked on his voyage to Egypt. But, as previously stated, in reading Wilkinson's earlier work, Vyse would have discovered that, while it notes "Suphis" (Saophis I) and "Sensaophis" (Sen-Saophis) as the pyramid builders, it does not actually present their cartouches, the hieroglyphic spelling of these kings' names. With Wilkinson's work being a dead end, Vyse would likely have next obtained a copy of the Rosellini work cited in the *Quarterly Review* article. If Vyse had, indeed, done this, then perusing page 128 of Rosellini's book, *I Monumenti Dell' Egitto E Della Nubia,* he would have read (in Italian), "Among them is a sign that is written in No. 2 on plate I at the end of this volume, which reads Suten Oueb Sciufo, that is to say, the pure King, Priest, or Prophet Sciufo. This name shows a very notable analogy with the Suphis of Manetho, the second king of the IV dynasty (2)."

Even if Vyse could not read Rosellini's Italian text, it would not have been beyond him to have found someone who could have translated the passage for him, such as his Italian colleague at Giza, Giovanni Caviglia (a man who had confided in Vyse of his belief that there were hidden chambers above Davison's Chamber and whom Vyse subsequently sacked and banished from the site). If Vyse then went to Plate 1 at the end of Rosellini's work, he would have found the list of kings' cartouches shown in figure A1.7.

Here we find that Rosellini has identified the hieroglyphic spelling of the Suphis/Khufu and Sen-Saophis cartouches, which would have given Vyse the all-important information he needed to perpetrate a fraud. But what evidence is there that Vyse actually read this *Quarterly Review* article from 1835 and that he had access to Rosellini's 1832 book? While Vyse tells us in his published account that he had with him a book by Wilkinson, he makes no mention of having with him Rosellini's book with its key information. Intriguingly, however, in his private journal entry of October 18, 1836, Vyse writes the following short passage: "Wrote notes from the Quarterly Review abt: Rosellini &

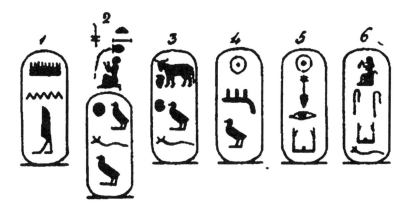

Figure A1.7. Plate 1 in Rosellini's book I Monumenti Dell' Egitto E Della Nubia *(page 130) presents the hieroglyphic spelling of the Suphis/Khufu cartouche* (labelled # 2) *and the Sen-Saophis cartouche* (labelled # 3).

Champollion, our first books, 69 dollars 14.7.6 in half crowns."

The amount Vyse paid for these books by Rosellini and Champollion, 14 pounds, 7 shillings, and 6 pence (paid with 115 half-crown coins), was a substantial investment and would, in today's terms (accounting for inflation), amount to around £1,650 or around $2,000. This was a very serious investment, indeed, and we might legitimately wonder why Vyse considered such a heavy purchase was necessary. We might further wonder here why Vyse writes in the plural, "*our* first books."

A search through the various issues of the *Quarterly Review* from 1835 to Vyse's journal entry of October 1836 reveals only one issue (volume 53, February and April 1835) that gives any mention of the works of Champollion and Rosellini. Thus, given his journal comment of October 1836, it seems that Vyse did, in fact, read this *Quarterly Review* article (fig. A1.6) and that he did go on to purchase Rosellini's book, which would have lead him to find the hieroglyphic spelling of Suphis/Khufu, which, as previously stated, we learn from his private journal, he did, in fact, know during his time at Giza.

And using Rosellini as his reference, the colonel could not have failed to notice that the Italian scholar presented the Saophis I cartouche vertically aligned (fig. A1.7) but that the cartouches he was hypothetically finding painted onto the stones in the debris outside the Great Pyramid were oriented horizontally (because they were likely from a much later period). Vyse would have been entirely unaware of the anachronistic style of these genuine builders' marks he theoretically had found, and he would have blithely copied them from the stones outside the pyramid into the newly discovered inner chambers, ensuring also to replicate any pattern of distribution these painted marks may have presented (more on this shortly).

With further consideration of Rosellini's work, Vyse may have noticed that the Italian scholar had also identified the other cartouche that the colonel had hypothetically found among the debris at the base of the pyramid's north front and that the learned Italian had accepted Wilkinson's interpretation of this second cartouche as meaning the "Brother of Saophis." Further analysis of the works of Rosellini and Wilkinson may also have brought Vyse to a series of logical deductions that would, inexorably, lead him to the realization that these two cartouches he had theoretically found in the debris around the pyramid could not, in fact, be the names of brothers at all, but that they both actually belonged to the same king. As such, this would then have compelled the colonel to place not one but *both* of the royal cartouches he had found into the Vyse Chambers of the Great Pyramid, albeit for an erroneous reason.

To be clear—the question here is not so much that the early academics such as Wilkinson and Rosellini believed that Sen-Saophis was to be understood as meaning the "Brother of Suphis" and that this brother built the second pyramid, but is rather more about how these scholars could possibly have come to such a translation in the first place when it surely should have occurred to them that the translation of Sen-Saophis as meaning "Brother of Suphis" is:

1. Such a nonsensical name for any ancient Egyptian parent to name their son, and,
2. The name Saophis I and the "Saophis" part of Sen-Saophis logically cannot both be translated into the hieroglyphics for the two Greek names of these kings, Cheops and Cephrenes. This is to say that the Greek name Cheops and the Greek name Cephrenes, being significantly different, cannot both translate back to the name Saophis (or its hieroglyphic spelling) and that these scholars should have realized this simple logic. That they didn't is baffling.

ONE AND THE SAME

A study of the painted marks within the Vyse Chambers reveals that Wellington's Chamber and Lady Arbuthnot's Chamber bear only the Sen-Saophis cartouche while the topmost, Campbell's Chamber, presents only the Saophis I cartouche. (Nelson's Chamber has no obvious cartouches.) We will now consider a number of hypothetical scenarios that may help explain why Vyse might have felt compelled to place both of these royal cartouches into these chambers.

First of all, one of the interesting things the ancient historians tell us of Saophis I and Sen-Saophis is the great length of time that they each reigned. Herodotus gives us reigns of fifty and fifty-six years, respectively, whereas Manetho gives reigns of sixty-three and sixty-six years, respectively. Such lengthy reigns have led a number of later commentators to take the view that these two kings must have reigned together in a co-regency. Vyse may also have seen from the works of Wilkinson and Rosellini that Saophis I and Sen-Saophis were believed to have been brothers. Were Vyse, in 1837, to have considered this information, then it becomes conceivable that he may also have come to the view that these two brothers were likely to have been co-regents. This thought may well have been reinforced if he was actually finding the cartouches of these two kings among the debris on the outside of the pyramid, and, given this, it would not have been unreasonable to him that these two cartouches should then also be found within the pyramid.

Second, in Vyse's time it was believed (via the historian and bishop Eusebius, citing Manetho) that it was actually Suphis II (also named the Sen-Saophis of Eratosthenes) who built the Great Pyramid. And so, if Vyse had come upon and accepted this remark given by Eusebius, then this would easily explain his placement of the Sen-Saophis cartouche within the lower chambers. However, in the fourth and final chamber opened by Vyse we find only the Saophis I (Khufu) cartouche. What this may indicate is a late change of mind by Vyse (perhaps he later came to believe that the structure had been built by Saophis I), and so he placed only this cartouche within the final chamber. However, he could hardly now remove the Sen-Saophis cartouches he had previously placed in the chambers below as these had already been independently witnessed on the walls there by others, with copies of them having already been sent to the British Museum in London. Admittedly, this possibility is much less likely to have influenced Vyse's decision because, Eusebius aside, the prevailing view in Vyse's time was that Saophis I had built the Great Pyramid.

A third possibility and more likely scenario arises from a study of the cartouches and texts in the academic books that would have been available to Vyse in 1837. One of the first questions that almost certainly would have crossed Vyse's mind with regard to the cartouche of Sen-Saophis presented in these early Egyptology books (some of which we now know he actually purchased) would have been why the name within this royal cartouche was being interpreted by scholars as "Brother of Saophis." In this regard, Rosellini writes, "Sensciufo (Chephren) autore della seconda piramide. . . . In questo Scencsciufo poi ritroviamo evidentemente il nome del successore di Suphis, che sebenne nei cataloghi di Manetone si chiami semplicementi Suphis II e pero con piu precisione chiamato nella lista di Erastothenes Sensuphis o Sensaophis. E Sensaophis significa (come l'avverti giustamente il dotto Wilkinson) fratello di Saophis."[7]

Translation: "Sensciufo (Chephren) author of the second pyramid. . . . In this Scencsciufo then we clearly find the name of the successor of Suphis, which in Manetho's list is called Suphis II but more precisely named in the list of Eratosthenes as Sensuphis or Sensaophis. And Sensaophis means (as the learned Wilkinson rightly stated) 'brother of Saophis.'"

Here was a royal cartouche of an ancient Egyptian king that Wilkinson and Rosellini wrongly believed was to be read as "Brother of Saophis." Had Vyse read this passage, he could reasonably have pondered why on Earth two ancient Egyptian royal parents would have named one of their sons the Brother of Saophis (a.k.a. the brother of another of their sons, or brother of the king). *What kind of a name is that?* Vyse might well have pondered. As a king's royal name (within a cartouche) it makes zero sense. Indeed, upon taking the throne, why would this king, Sen-Saophis, still wish to be known as the Brother of Saophis? Surely, this brother of Saophis, this new king would have desired his very own king's name upon ascending the throne. Was "Brother of Saophis" really the actual royal name of the builder of the second Giza pyramid?

In pursuance of this particular train of thought and the obvious absurdity of such a king's name, Vyse could then have considered the names that Herodotus gave as the builders of these monuments, namely:

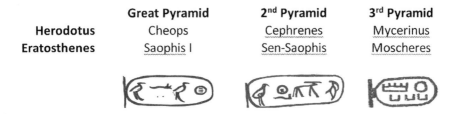

	Great Pyramid	2nd Pyramid	3rd Pyramid
Herodotus	Cheops	Cephrenes	Mycerinus
Eratosthenes	Saophis I	Sen-Saophis	Moscheres

Figure A1.8. The names of the kings who built the pyramids, as given by Herodotus and Eratosthenes, along with their hieroglyphic equivalents.

Cheops, Cephrenes, and Mycerinus. Compare these Greek names with the counterpart names given by Eratosthenes, shown in figure A1.8.

In consideration of the various kings' names given by Herodotus and Eratosthenes, Vyse might logically have concluded that the first three signs in the Sen-Saophis cartouche (fig. A1.9, *dashed box*) represented the name Saophis (because these signs were the same as those in the Saophis I cartouche). The remaining two signs of the Sen-Saophis cartouche (fig. A1.9, *solid box*) the colonel probably deduced, erroneously, to be the word *brother*.

Pursuing this line of thought further, Vyse might then have wondered, if the Cheops of Herodotus = the Saophis I of Eratosthenes (fig. A1.8), why then should the Saophis element of the Sen-Saophis of Eratosthenes = the Cephrenes of Herodotus, a completely different name? In short, Vyse may have wondered how it was possible that the name Saophis could translate into Cheops and also translate into Cephrenes (fig. A1.9).

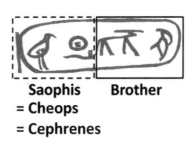

Saophis   Brother
= Cheops
= Cephrenes

Figure A1.9. Based on the contemporary understanding of his time, Vyse may have believed that the first three signs in the Sen-Saophis cartouche represented the name Saophis (dashed box) and that the last two signs (solid box) represented the word brother.

	Great Pyramid	2nd Pyramid	3rd Pyramid
Herodotus	Cheops	Cephrenes	Mycerinus
Eratosthenes	Saophis I	~~Sen-Saophis~~	Moscheres

Figure A1.10. The Sen-Saophis cartouche logically cannot belong to Cephrenes since (Sen-)Saophis = Cheops, thereby implying that the name Cephrenes must consist of different hieroglyphics and a different cartouche. In removing its association with Cephrenes, the Sen-Saophis cartouche then becomes disconnected from the second pyramid and it thus effectively becomes homeless.

Vyse would likely have concluded, rightly, that this simply wasn't possible and must, therefore, be wrong. Thus, by simple deduction, the colonel could reasonably have concluded that if the Saophis part of the Sen-Saophis cartouche must also = Cheops, then this cartouche simply cannot belong to Cephrenes, who must, therefore, have a different (as yet unidentified) cartouche. And since Herodotus tells us it was Cephrenes who built the second Giza pyramid, then, by logical deduction, the Sen-Saophis cartouche cannot belong to the builder of the second pyramid, and it effectively becomes homeless; this cartouche must, logically, mean something else and belong to someone else (fig. A1.10).

And so, if Vyse had deduced that the Sen-Saophis cartouche logically could not belong to the Cephrenes of Herodotus, whom the academics in Vyse's time believed to be the builder of the second pyramid, then the colonel's next thought, naturally, would be to wonder precisely who this king Sen-Saophis actually was, where exactly this king fitted into the list of ancient Egyptian kings, and why he was (hypothetically) finding this king's name painted onto stones among the debris at the pyramid's north side.

VYSE'S KING'S GAMBIT

Well, first of all, there's a very obvious clue to answering this question that Vyse could not have failed to notice—quite simply, both cartouches present the name Saophis. Might they not be connected with each other in some other way? The answer to this particular question may have presented itself to Vyse from information that had long been publically available, even before he had ever embarked on his journey to Egypt in late 1835. With further consideration of Wilkinson's *Materia Hieroglyphica,* we find that the British scholar informs us of some intriguing aspects of the royal cartouche, or "oval."

1. That the phonetic names are always contained in the oval . . . which I shall distinguish by the word "nomen."
2. That the other oval, or prenomen, always contains a title, derived from the name of one, or more deities, which serves to point out more particularly the king, to whom both the ovals belong. . . .
4. That these prenomens, or titles being sometimes mentioned together with the nomens, have led to that disagreement, which exists amongst ancient scholars, in the names of the kings; they have confounded the prenomens with the nomens, or mistaken the one for the other . . . for it does appear in a few instances that Manetho has introduced both the nomen and the prenomen.[8]

Thus, through a series of simple deductions from the available knowledge—such as it was in 1837—it was perfectly feasible that the British explorer could have erroneously concluded that the two slightly different cartouches of Saophis I and Sen-Saophis were not, in fact, two different kings or two brothers at all, but that they could actually represent the nomen and prenomen cartouches of just *one* king.* This idea could have been reinforced in Vyse's mind with this comment from Wilkinson:

5. The prenomens were often varied, by the addition of other titles, but not by any omission of the original characters; thus, in many of the prenomens, we find more hieroglyphics than usual, and yet, the original title is still traceable.[9]

---

*Later studies of the Sen-Saophis name by the Prussian Egyptologist Karl Lepsius concluded that the "Brother" aspect had actually come about as the result of a scribal error in the king list of Eratosthenes. The finding of Lepsius was published in 1839 and, as such, could in no way have influenced Vyse's thinking and decisions in 1837.

This is to say that the name in the shorter cartouche of Saophis I can still be perceived in the longer prenomen cartouche of Sen-Saophis, as presented in figure A1.4 (p. 193). And so, once more, upon reading the above passage from Wilkinson and then perhaps by a study of the cartouches presented by Rossellini, it is quite conceivable that Vyse could have erroneously concluded that these two slightly different cartouches he had hypothetically found on the stones outside the Great Pyramid were but the nomen and prenomen of the same king. Consequently, he could have decided that both cartouches should be copied into the newly discovered chambers that he had blasted his way into.*

Vyse may, of course, have regarded the decision to place both of these cartouches into the chambers as something of a gambit, but if he had followed the information that was easily available in the academic texts of his time (and which we know he did have with him), then it would have been an educated gambit based on logical deductions that would have led him, inexorably, to the conclusion of "two cartouches, one king."

HOW COULD THIS HAVE HAPPENED?

As outlined earlier, these speculative painted blocks would have been recovered from the debris mounds on the north and south sides of the pyramid and, in analyzing them, Vyse would likely have observed their pertinent features and may have noted that:

- The painted marks were found only on limestone blocks, not on granite blocks.
- The painted inscriptions were confined to single blocks.
- Blocks recovered from the debris to the north and south of the pyramid bore the cartouche of Saophis/Khufu.
- The cartouche of Sensaophis/Khnum-Khuf was present only on blocks recovered from the pyramid's north side.
- The king's Horus name (Medjedu) was present only on blocks recovered from the pyramid's south side.

---

*Commenting on these marks in Vyse's book, the Egyptologist Samuel Birch of the British Museum came to this same, erroneous conclusion as it was not known in Vyse's time that this practice only began with the pharaoh Neferirkara Kakai in the later Fifth Dynasty.

With the other groups of marks (which he almost certainly could not read) being found alongside or close to the one cartouche that Vyse *could* recognize outside the pyramid, the colonel would ensure that all of these other marks were copied into the various chambers he had blasted open, being careful to ensure that any distribution pattern of the marks he might have observed on the stones recovered from the debris outside the pyramid was replicated within the chambers. This would mean, for example, confining the marks of the king's Horus name to the south wall (and the southern end of the west wall), the Sensaophis/Khnum-Khuf cartouche to the north wall (and the northern end of the west wall), and the Saophis/Khufu cartouche to both the north and south sides of Campbell's Chamber (an observation that might actually have been a replication mistake by his hired fraudsters). Vyse would further ensure that the painted marks were copied onto limestone blocks only and that the text was constrained to single blocks.

However, in Lady Arbuthnot's Chamber we observe that the distribution of these quarry gang names is not entirely consistent, whereby one partial name, White Crown of Khnum-Khuf (Sensaophis), has been painted onto the south wall of the chamber, whereas all others of this type have been painted onto the chamber's north wall (as well as the northern portions of the east and west walls). In short, the distribution of the gang names (with their associated king's names), while generally conforming to a pattern, presents some distribution anomalies. And it is the anomalies that are interesting, for they may be indicative of Vyse's assistants erring slightly in emulating the distribution pattern that had theoretically been observed on the limestone blocks among the debris outside the pyramid's north and south sides.

And, of course, after Vyse had studied and retrieved the inscriptions from the various blocks, having fulfilled their use, the blocks would likely have been broken up and discarded. (This action would ensure that the marks found on them could never be compared with the marks copied into the Vyse Chambers, thereby potentially exposing the colonel's fraudulent activities.)

And so, what the critics believed would have been an impossible task for Vyse could, in actual fact, have been achieved by him relatively easily with a simple reference to the available texts of his day, mainly the published works of Wilkinson and Rossellini, and thereafter by following a series of simple, logical deductions from those texts. Finding authentic painted marks on stones in the debris outside the pyramid, he could simply have followed any distribution pattern of the marks observed there and replicated them within the pyramid chambers. Job done.

I do not insist, however, that this is exactly what happened. It's hypothetical. All that is sought here is to demonstrate various scenarios whereby Vyse *could* have obtained the necessary knowledge needed to execute a convincing and lasting hoax.

And the rest, as they say, is history.

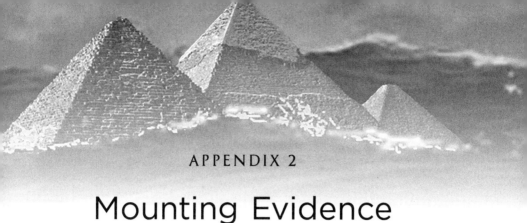

Mounting Evidence

New Confirmation of Vyse's Deceit

The evidence presented in my previous book, *The Great Pyramid Hoax,* concerned itself primarily with the painted quarry marks from the lowest of the Vyse Chambers, Wellington's Chamber, and the uppermost, Campbell's Chamber. We will now consider a whole raft of new evidence that has only recently come to light from the other two Vyse Chambers (Nelson's and Lady Arbuthnot's) and that further indicates a hoax having been perpetrated within the Vyse Chambers of the Great Pyramid in 1837.

NELSON'S CHAMBER

Over the years, as I wrestled with the cryptic handwriting in Vyse's private journal (sometimes for days and weeks on end), slowly but ever so surely the fog clouding his nearly impenetrable script gradually receded, revealing ever more insights from his journal that had been overlooked for almost two hundred years.

On April 25, 1837, Nelson's Chamber became the second of the small chambers or apartments that Vyse blasted his way into, and in his published account of that day, he describes what he found when he first entered the chamber.

Notice in the description from figure A2.1, of the day Vyse opened and first entered this chamber, that he states, "Several quarry marks were inscribed in red upon the blocks, particularly on the western side."

April 25th.

Reis, 9.   Men, 111.   Children, 134.

Great Pyramid.—Excavation in southern front.

—————   Excavation in northern front.

—————   Wellington's Chamber.

—————   Northern Air-channel.

Third Pyramid.—Interior.

Fourth Pyramid.—Interior.

Harvest having commenced, very few able-bodied men came, and the works at Campbell's Tomb, the Queen's, and Belzoni's Chambers, were necessarily discontinued. In the course of the day the chamber, subsequently called Nelson's, was discovered. It was entirely empty, had no regular entrance, and was floored with the reverse of the granite blocks of Wellington's Chamber, which it much resembled, as it had these dimensions, thirty-eight feet nine inches, by sixteen feet eight inches. The ceiling was of polished granite, and resembled those in the other chambers ; but the northern and southern sides of the room were not entirely of that material. Several quarry-marks were inscribed in red upon the blocks, particularly on the western side. This apartment was evidently intended for the same purpose as those below it, viz. to carry off the weight of the building from the King's Chamber.

Figure A2.1. Extract from Vyse's published account of April 25, 1837, the day Vyse first opened and entered what would come to be called Nelson's Chamber. Vyse, Operations Carried On at the Pyramids, *vol. I, 234–35.*

Prior to the discovery of the painted marks in Nelson's Chamber, only one other example of similar painted marks had apparently been made within the Great Pyramid (in Wellington's Chamber). As such, the discovery of additional inscriptions in Nelson's Chamber would naturally have been regarded as a highly important discovery in its own right, and, as we might expect, Vyse would have wasted little time in writing of this important discovery in his daily journal, as we observe in his published account in figure A2.1.

However, as I have come to expect with Vyse's writings, things are never so straightforward or quite what they at first seem to be. When we now consider Vyse's private diary account of the very same day—April 25, 1837—we find a quite different account with some glaring and highly significant omissions to the events of this day.

25th Sent off the people, breakfast, went to the temple, blew up
stones north front of pyramid, Mr Perring came, rest, was sent for by
Mr Raven, full width into hole called Nelson's Chamber, apparently like
Wellington's, floored with the reverse of the blocks [that] are below;
&c &c, paid off the people, dinner, & bed. *

As we can see in in Vyse's private journal—where he gives us his unedited, uncensored, private thoughts of that day's main events—there is no mention whatsoever of a discovery of any quarry marks in Nelson's Chamber, as claimed in his published account of this day. And let us be clear here—had painted quarry marks actually been present on the west wall of this chamber when Vyse first entered it, we can be absolutely certain that the colonel would not have been remiss or shy in making note of such an important discovery in his private notes of that day; this would not have been an event that could easily have slipped his mind. That Vyse, in his private account, makes no mention on April 25 of such an important discovery (contrary to his published account) strongly suggests that there were, in fact, no marks present in the chamber at that time for him to comment on in his private notes, hence the complete silence here.

Given that it is simply inconceivable that Vyse could have failed, in his private journal, to have made mention of such an important discovery, we must ask the obvious questions: Why does Vyse present two quite different accounts of this particular day, and further, what is the true version of the events? What truly happened on this day in 1837, and is there anything that might help us get nearer to the truth?

Alas, Vyse's published account of the following day, April 26, barely makes matters any clearer (fig. A2.2, p. 212).

What is curious about Vyse's comments in his published account here is that he actually goes out of his way to say "hopes of an important discovery were not yet given up," thus implying that, at this date, no important discovery had actually yet been made in Nelson's Chamber (and presumably Wellington's below it). This remark also implies that

---

*All transcribed entries and illustrations are from Vyse's private journal, the Centre for Buckinghamshire Studies Archive Center, London, reference number D121/2/35. Transcribed by the author. Words in square brackets are either uncertain or unknown.

April 26th.

Reis, 9.   Men, 71.   Children, 72.

Great Pyramid.—Excavation in northern front.

———   Excavation in southern front.

———   Nelson's Chamber.

———   Northern Air-channel.

Third Pyramid.—Interior.

Fourth Pyramid.—Interior.

All hopes of an important discovery were not yet given up, and the best quarrymen were employed to get above the roof of Nelson's Chamber. I was sorry to have so few men, but the excuse, viz. the harvest, would not allow of a complaint. I sent an account of our discoveries to Mr. Hamilton.

Figure A2.2. Extract from Vyse's published account of
April 26, 1837. Vyse, Operations Carried On at the Pyramids,
vol. I, 235.

Vyse did not consider the discovery of these chambers, of themselves, to be of any great significance (presumably because they contained no sarcophagus or treasure).

The quarry marks supposedly discovered in this chamber on April 25 (according to Vyse's published account) were only the second example of ancient Egyptian script ever found in any pyramid in Vyse's time. Such a discovery in Nelson's Chamber would have been an important discovery, and Vyse most assuredly would have understood that to be the case from the very moment he first set eyes on those inscriptions (had they truly been there). And we can be absolutely certain that Vyse *would* have understood the import of these painted inscriptions because, some weeks later, on May 9, he writes in his published account:

Notwithstanding that the characters in these chambers were surveyed by Mr. Perring upon a reduced scale, I considered that facsimiles in their original size would be desirable, as they were of great importance from their situation, and probably the most antient inscriptions in existence. I requested therefore Mr. Hill to copy them. His drawings were compared with the originals by Sir Robert Arbuthnot, Mr. Brettel (a civil engineer), Mr. Raven, and myself, and are deposited in the British Museum.[1]

As we can see, the painted characters/inscriptions in these chambers were, in Vyse's stated view, "of great importance," and so much so, in fact, that he had two separate copies of them made (one set by Mr. Perring to be used in Vyse's future book and another by Mr. Hill for the British Museum). Later still, on May 19, the colonel even arranged for a group of independent witnesses to attest to the accuracy of Hill's drawings of the inscriptions he had made from the chambers opened by Vyse up to that point.

Thus, with his casual remark on April 26, 1837, about still hoping to make an important discovery, and given his clearly expressed views on the importance of these quarry marks, it seems that the contradictory nature of these two comments appears to have Vyse inadvertently tripping himself up. The logical implication of his comment of April 26, after having just opened Nelson's Chamber and still hoping to make an important discovery, is that, by simple deduction, the discovery of the important quarry marks in Nelson's Chamber could not actually have occurred by this time, as Vyse claimed in his published account, a claim that is evidently contradicted by his private account.

By claiming in his published account of a discovery of the quarry marks when he first entered Nelson's Chamber on April 25, Vyse is merely backfilling his story. These quarry marks fill the entire length (sixteen feet and eight inches) of the chamber's west wall and so would be virtually impossible to miss, especially so given that Vyse had apparently discovered quarry marks in the chamber below and, in anticipation of finding similar marks in Nelson's Chamber, would naturally have checked the walls here extra carefully. It would thus have looked entirely suspicious of him to claim in his published account that he only found this wall full of quarry marks after three days, thus his backfill comment on April 25 in his published account. But the complete silence of such an important discovery in his private account exposes the truth of the situation: there were no quarry marks in this chamber on this first day.

Consulting Vyse's private account of April 26, matters remain just as curious.

26th Sent off the people, breakfast, rest, assisted surveying the great with Mr Perring & Mr Mash; &c, read, wrote to Mr Hamilton; [enclosed for] Col. Campbell, rest, read, Paid off the people, rest &c dinner, &c bed. Ibrahim came back from Cairo.

Again, contrary to his published account, how is it possible that after two days there is not a single mention being made of the quarry marks from Nelson's Chamber in Vyse's private account? Did no one spot these quarry marks on the west wall of this chamber in these two days and mention them to Vyse (assuming here—contrary to his published claim—that Vyse hadn't actually noticed them in the chamber himself on the twenty-fifth)? There's simply nothing in the private account in these first two days relating to the discovery of quarry marks in this chamber, which is surely highly peculiar. It is not until April 27, 1837—the third day after their supposed discovery—that we first read of the quarry marks from this chamber in Vyse's private account and when we next hear of them in Vyse's published account.

As we can see in the published account (fig. A2.3), Vyse tells us that the "quarry-marks in Nelson's Chamber were copied." He does not say who copied the marks, but we know that they probably were not copied by Hill because Vyse only instructs Hill to make copies of the chamber quarry marks on May 9, some two weeks or so later. However, from his private journal of this day, we find that Vyse himself had made a copy of some of the marks in Nelson's Chamber, which we shall consider shortly.

First of all, however, it may help us here to actually familiarize ourselves with the quarry marks that were supposedly found in Nelson's Chamber; see Perring's survey drawing of them in figure A2.4.

The first thing we notice here is that these marks have been painted upside down onto two large wall blocks at the western end of Nelson's Chamber (note the two upside-down birds, fig. A2.4, stone #1). The inscriptions on the two stones are believed to represent the names of two quarry gangs: "Pure ones of the Horus Medjedu" (stone #1) and "The Gang, the White Crown of Khnum-Khuf is Powerful" (stone #2). What is believed to be the cartouche of Khnum-Khuf (left side of stone #2) is mostly obliterated. The mark on the extreme right of stone #2 may be an ouroboros (a snake eating its own tail) and is probably not related to the (partial) gang name inscription on this block. (Note: the vertical line to the left of the ouroboros sign is actually a painted red line on the block and does not demarcate a third block).

April 27th.

Reis, 9.   Men, 50.   Children, 52.

The same works were repeated.

The quarry-marks in Nelson's Chamber were copied.
Several Arab Sheiks called. Every evening just before
sunset there were strong gusts of wind, chiefly from the
north and north-west.

*Figure A2.3. Extract from Vyse's published account,
April 27, 1837. Vyse,* Operations Carried On at the Pyramids,
vol. I, 235–36.

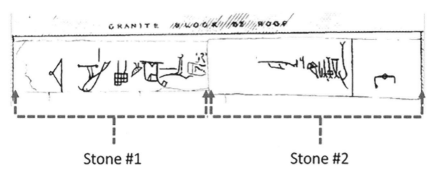

Stone #1   Stone #2

*Figure A2.4. The quarry marks on the two limestone
wall blocks of the west end of Nelson's Chamber.
Vyse,* Operations Carried On at the Pyramids, *vol. I, 285.
(Drawing by Scott Creighton,
based on original by John Shae Perring)*

If we now consider the events of this day, April 27, as described by
Vyse in his private account, matters are not quite as straightforward as
he describes them in his published version, and this raises a number of
questions.

*27th Sent off the people (very few came owing to the harvest). Col:
Campbell's Tomb. & the Queen's Chamber, & also Belzoni's Chamber
not been worked owing to the want of men for 2 days: Mr [?]
worked within [at] night in Nelson's Chamber; Operations today, 1st
Pyramid south, and northern sections, air supply, Nelson's Chamber,
3rd Pyramid 4th Pyramid and surveying. Breakfast, [???, ??] & [got*

lost]: went into Nelson's Chamber, Mr Hill came, [ran pretests] of
[letters] &c, [?] the Sheikh was inside [& drew] figures,

on the western side of calcerous stones as [?]
[Selin] paid the people off, dinner & bed.

As we can see from the private account of this day, Vyse seems to have had someone working in Nelson's Chamber overnight. He does not explain why this person was there or what they were doing. The name of this individual in his private journal is unclear (looks like "Mr. James") and is quite unlike any of the other regular names the colonel writes in his journal. Who was this individual, and what was he doing in Nelson's Chamber overnight? The next curious aspect of the private account here is where Vyse writes "the Sheikh was inside, [& drew] figures, [sketch of hieroglyphic signs] on the western side of calcerous stones as [?]"

If this reading is correct, a sheikh drawing hieroglyphic figures onto the west wall of Nelson's Chamber is quite an astonishing statement by Vyse in his private journal. Admittedly, the words "& drew" are uncertain here (as indicated by their placement within the brackets), and it should be said, there is another (though more vague) possible reading of them that shall be considered later. There is, however, some evidence to suggest that this particular reading, "[& drew] figures," may very well be the correct reading.

Who was this sheikh, and why was he in Nelson's Chamber at that time? In his published account, Vyse mentions only that several Arab sheikhs came by that day but makes no mention of any of them actually being inside Nelson's Chamber. Was this sheikh perhaps employed in placing these figures onto the wall of this chamber by the colonel? If so, is there any evidence that might point to such an arrangement?

From his published account, we know that Vyse had a high regard for the knowledge of some of the local Egyptians and that he took copies of the marks he allegedly discovered in these chambers to them. He wrote:

The Shereef had got Major Felix's book on hieroglyphics, talked much about the Pyramids, and said that he had himself entered the great one. I offered to shew him Mr. Perring's drawings, and the few things of interest that had been found at Gizeh, and he appointed three o'clock for that purpose. . . . I returned at three o'clock with the drawings, &c. The Shereef was more intelligent than any Arab I had ever met with. . . . I gave the Shereef a copy of the cartouche of Suphis, and of some of the hieroglyphics found in the chambers of the Great Pyramid.[2]

But what actual evidence is there that might show that an Arab sheik was responsible for painting these marks onto the west wall of Nelson's Chamber, as Vyse's comment above—assuming a correct reading—suggests?

Comparing Vyse's journal sketch of the painted marks from this wall with Perring's drawing of the same marks (fig. A2.4), we find, somewhat bizarrely, that the colonel copied only the marks on the right side of the west wall (only those marks painted onto stone #2 in fig. A2.4). Why would Vyse have neglected to also copy the marks on the left side of the wall (the marks on stone #1)? But the more pertinent point here is that, as a Westerner, the most natural approach for the British explorer in copying the painted hieroglyphics from this wall would surely have been to commence copying them from left to right. So, once again, why does Vyse copy only the marks on the right side of this wall?

This anomaly is further emphasized if we then consider the five facsimile drawings made by Hill of the very same marks from this wall of Nelson's Chamber, where we find that he has numbered each of his drawings in such a way as to indicate to us how he had gone about copying the marks on this wall. His drawing numbering clearly indicates that he commenced his drawing of the painted marks on this wall from left to right, as we might expect a Westerner to do (fig. A2.5, p. 218).

Indeed, an examination of Hill's drawings from the walls of the other Vyse Chambers shows that he consistently began his copying work from the left side of each wall. Thus, if Hill commenced all of *his* drawings from left to right, why does Vyse draw only half of the marks on this wall of Nelson's Chamber, why only from the second stone on

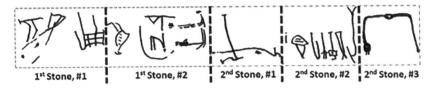

| 1st Stone, #1 | 1st Stone, #2 | 2nd Stone, #1 | 2nd Stone, #2 | 2nd Stone, #3 |

Figure A2.5. Impression of Hill's five facsimile drawings of the quarry marks on the two wall blocks of the west end of Nelson's Chamber. Note that the numbering sequence indicates Hill made his drawings from left to right. (Drawing by Scott Creighton, based on originals by J. R. Hill)

the right side of the chamber wall, and why from right to left when a Westerner would naturally and instinctively have commenced copying them from left to right?

And finally, in Vyse's sketch of the marks from Nelson's Chamber, we find that he places a rather curious sign between the left and right parts of his sketch, as indicated by the arrow in figure A2.6.

This peculiar mark is not replicated by Hill or Perring in their drawings of these particular marks. We observe it only here in Vyse's journal sketch, and it makes little sense. Why place something in this journal sketch that, according to the drawings of Hill and Perring, isn't actually present on this wall block?

Upon closer analysis of this peculiar mark, I realized that I had actually seen it many times before throughout Vyse's private journal, for it appears, in fact, to be Vyse's "&" sign (though slightly incomplete on the left side). Now, it may seem a trivial point, but we have to ask: Why would Vyse have felt the need to insert this "&" sign into his journal sketch, thus effectively segmenting his sketch into two parts—a left and a right section—almost as though his own drawing here had initially been presented as two parts that were put together as one inscription? Why not simply copy the marks from the wall block into his journal as they supposedly appeared on the wall? Why the embellishment with this "&" symbol?

Is there any scenario that can explain all of these contradictions, inconsistencies, and anomalies?

Perhaps.

If we presume that Vyse found no quarry marks at all in this cham-

Figure A2.6. Impression of Vyse's sketch of the quarry marks on the second wall block (right side) of the west end of Nelson's Chamber. Note the anomalous sign indicated by the arrow. (Drawing by Scott Creighton, based on original by Vyse in his private journal, April 27, 1837.)

ber when he first entered it (as his private journal indicates), then it seems that by the third day, April 27, he had acquired some quarry marks from a source (as yet unknown)* and that these were then replicated throughout the various chambers. Vyse may have copied these source marks (gang names) from stones found among the debris outside the pyramid onto a series of small "copy cards," being careful to ensure that any longer inscriptions copied over two or more cards were carefully referenced to ensure the correct reading order was maintained. In particular, the marks we observe on the right side of the west wall in Nelson's Chamber (stone #2) may have been a long inscription on a single stone somewhere outside the pyramid, but they were copied by Vyse onto *two* small copy cards (fig. A2.7, p. 220).

Taking our hypothetical scenario further, Vyse may then have decided, in keeping with any distribution pattern he may have observed, to have these marks copied onto the northern and southern ends of the chamber's west wall because this was of limestone construction, whereas the north and south walls were both of granite construction. In preparation for the copy job, he may have employed someone overnight to clean or otherwise prepare the west limestone wall to receive the painted marks from his series of copy cards. This preparation may have been carried out by the unknown person Vyse had working through the night of April 26–27.

---

*Vyse's published account, as we learned previously, makes it clear that he found painted marks on stones in the debris on the north and the south fronts of the Great Pyramid.

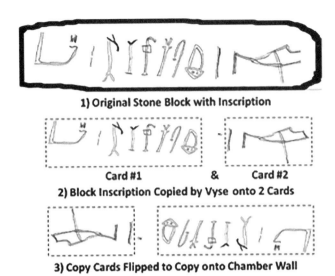

1) Original Stone Block with Inscription

Card #1   &   Card #2
2) Block Inscription Copied by Vyse onto 2 Cards

3) Copy Cards Flipped to Copy onto Chamber Wall

Figure A2.7. Postulated copy sequence of the quarry marks from an original stone block (perhaps found on stones among the debris outside the pyramid), theoretically copied onto two copy cards and finally onto the chamber wall. (Drawing by Scott Creighton)

For reasons of plausible deniability, it would have been natural that Vyse would want to keep some distance between himself and the actual paint job, so he employed a local Egyptian sheikh to undertake the actual copying and gave him his copy cards, instructing the sheikh to paint the marks onto the two wall blocks upside down in order to give the impression that the marks had been painted onto the blocks while they were at the quarry, thereby giving them the appearance of authenticity. The sheikh began his task and—being Egyptian—he naturally commenced the copy job from the *right side* of the chamber's west wall (at Hill's stone #2). (As we shall see later, there is additional evidence within these chambers that may further indicate that a local Egyptian had been used to help copy the marks into these chambers.) A short time later, Vyse visited to check the sheikh's progress and found that the right side of the west wall, where the sheikh began his copying task, was now replete with upside-down painted markings that Vyse then copied into his journal, and he departed, leaving the sheikh to finish the left side of the wall (Hill's stone #1).

This then may explain why Vyse copied only some of the text from this wall into his private journal and only that text from the right side of the wall, whereas, assuming the marks were genuinely present, we might reasonably have expected him to have copied everything and that he would have commenced his copying from the wall's left side, just as Hill had done. And if Vyse did have inscriptions copied from stones from somewhere outside the pyramid onto two or more copy cards, then this might also explain why he placed this "&" symbol between the left and right aspects of his sketch; he is inadvertently indicating with this symbol that his original source for his journal sketch was too long to copy onto just one copy card and that it had to be copied onto two copy cards—a left "&" right card—hence the placement of the "&" symbol in the middle of Vyse's journal sketch of these particular marks.

It is impossible, of course, to prove that the scenario outlined above presents the true version of events in this chamber at that time. What *can* be said, however, is that the scenario presented here makes much better sense of the available evidence while also explaining the anomalies and contradictions that we find exist between Vyse's private and published accounts of the events at Giza between April 25 and 27, 1837.

LADY ARBUTHNOT'S CHAMBER

Lady Arbuthnot's Chamber was the third of the four chambers that Vyse blasted his way into with his gunpowder archaeology. It was named after Lady Anne Arbuthnot, wife of Sir Robert Keith Arbuthnot, a Scottish civil servant who worked with the Bombay Civil Service.

A consideration of Vyse's remarks in his published account of the opening of the four Vyse Chambers and the discovery therein of the painted quarry marks throws up a rather curious situation with regard to Lady Arbuthnot's Chamber. In the published account, Vyse writes:

March 30th
    The hole into Wellington's Chamber being practicable, I examined it with Mr. Hill. . . . Mr. Perring and Mr. Mash having arrived, we went in the evening into Wellington's Chamber, and took various admeasurements, and in doing so we found the quarry marks.[3]

Comment: There are only a handful of quarry marks in Wellington's Chamber, and they were reportedly discovered (upon a second visit to take measurements) on the same day the chamber was opened.

> April 25th
> In the course of the day the chamber, subsequently called Nelson's, was discovered. . . . Several quarry marks were inscribed in red upon the blocks, particularly on the western side.[4]

Comment: The quarry marks in Nelson's Chamber were reportedly found on the same day the chamber was opened (according to the published account, that is).

> May 6th
> The chamber above Nelson's (afterwards called Lady Arbuthnot's) was opened, and in the course of the afternoon I entered it with Mr. Raven. . . . [three days later on May 9] Lady Arbuthnot's Chamber was minutely examined, and found to contain a great many quarry-marks.[5]

Comment: No quarry marks were reportedly found on May 6 but only upon a second visit three days after the chamber had been opened.

> May 27th
> The chamber over Lady Arbuthnot's (subsequently called Campbell's) was opened and minutely examined. . . . There were many quarry marks similar to those in the other chambers.[6]

Comment: The quarry marks were reportedly found on the day the chamber was opened.

As can be seen from the above excerpts, Vyse's published work shows us that, with the single exception of Lady Arbuthnot's Chamber, the discovery of quarry marks was reported upon the very day each of the Vyse Chambers was opened. Given the fact that Lady Arbuthnot's has more of these painted marks on its walls than all of the other chambers combined (fig. A2.8), why then, we have to ask, did it take the colonel four days to report the discovery of a single one of them

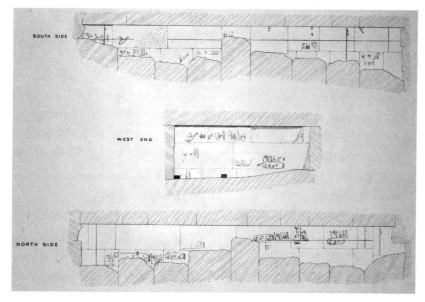

*Figure A2.8. The quarry marks on the three walls of
Lady Arbuthnot's Chamber. These include four full and
four partial cartouches of the pharaoh Khnum-Khuf and many
other hieratic signs. (Original drawing by John Shae Perring)*

and then only after having conducted a second, minute examination
of the chamber?

As was shown previously, we learn from his private account that Vyse
backfilled the date of his "discovery" of the quarry marks in Nelson's
Chamber in his published account by two days to coincide with that chamber's opening. If he could be so brazen as to alter this detail for Nelson's
Chamber, then why didn't he do likewise in his published account for the
discovery of the quarry marks in Lady Arbuthnot's Chamber? Conflating
the date the chamber was opened with the discovery date of the quarry
marks would surely have been as easy to do with Lady Arbuthnot's
Chamber as it was to do with Nelson's Chamber, so what, if anything,
might have prevented him from doing so with Lady Arbuthnot's?

As we now consider Vyse's public and private journal accounts of
the events surrounding the opening of Lady Arbuthnot's Chamber and
the obvious delay in the reporting of the painted quarry marks therein,
we may come to a rather surprising conclusion.

Analysis of Published vs. Private Accounts

Lady Arbuthnot's Chamber was opened on May 6, 1837, and the moment of entry into the chamber is described in Vyse's official account thus:

> May 6th
>
> The chamber above Nelson's (afterwards called Lady Arbuthnot's) was opened, and in the course of the afternoon I entered it with Mr. Raven. We found this apartment of the same description, and nearly of the same dimensions as the others below it, being thirty-seven feet four inches by sixteen feet four inches. Like the rest it was quite empty, and built in the same manner, but with less care, and with a greater proportion of calcareous stone on the north and south sides. The excavation was continued, in order to get above it. In the evening I returned to Cairo with Mr. Perring and Mr. Mash.[7]

Notice in the above passage from Vyse's published account of this day, May 6, the complete absence of any mention of painted quarry marks having been discovered on the walls of this chamber. And we can be absolutely certain that this wasn't a mere oversight in Vyse's recollection of the events of that day (as if it were even possible to so quickly forget a discovery of such importance), because three days later, he writes the following in his published account:

> May 9th
>
> Lady Arbuthnot's Chamber was minutely examined, and found to contain a great many quarry-marks.[8]

With this entry, Vyse effectively confirms that the painted quarry marks on the walls of Lady Arbuthnot's Chamber were first "discovered" three days later, on May 9, after a second, minute examination of the chamber had taken place and that he hadn't simply overlooked making mention of their presence in his published journal entry of May 6. In short, the quarry marks in this chamber had, it seems, gone entirely unnoticed by Vyse and Raven during the initial visit to this chamber and apparently required this second visit three days later, on May 9, to discover them.

The first person to read Vyse's published account and make mention of this inordinate delay in the reporting of quarry marks in Lady

Arbuthnot's Chamber was the international bestselling author and historian Zecharia Sitchin. In his book *The Stairway to Heaven,* Sitchin writes, "On May 7, the way was blasted through into one more chamber above Nelson's, which Vyse temporarily named after Lady Arbuthnot. The journal makes no mention of any quarry marks, although they were later on found there in profusion."[9]

This breaching of Lady Arbuthnot's Chamber actually occurred on May 6 and not May 7, as Sitchin states. More importantly, in this short passage, Sitchin is drawing our attention to the delayed discovery of the quarry marks, seemingly implying that since there is no mention of the quarry marks in Vyse's initial published entry of May 6, the colonel had not yet had time to place any fraudulent marks into this chamber. Although Sitchin might have chosen to pursue this question further, he did not provide more detailed evidence for his allegation.

There is a bigger, more obvious, and pertinent question here that needs to be properly addressed and plausibly answered by those who insist that the quarry marks Vyse claimed to have found in these chambers are genuine ancient artifacts. To understand this question, let us assume here that the painted marks in Lady Arbuthnot's Chamber are indeed genuine and that they *were* present on the chamber walls prior to Vyse blasting his way in on May 6, 1837. As mentioned above, this chamber presents (by some considerable margin) the largest amount of painted quarry marks of any of the four Vyse Chambers. Indeed, as previously noted, there are possibly more painted quarry marks in Lady Arbuthnot's Chamber than all of the other chambers combined. Most of the painted marks here are large (each between twelve and eighteen inches tall, the cartouches between twenty-four and thirty-six inches wide). They are also bold, run the full length of three walls, and yet, astonishingly, neither Vyse nor Raven seem to have observed a single one of these red ochre marks (around 120 of them), including four fully formed and four partial royal cartouches, during their initial inspection on May 6, the day this chamber was breached. Did these two men fail completely to notice any of the painted marks at this time thus explaining the absence of a report of their discovery on this date?*

---

*Photographic images of the painted marks from Lady Arbuthnot's Chamber are extremely rare, but of those that have surfaced from this chamber (in books or from TV documentaries), many of the painted marks are very clear and seem no less observable than the

If that is the explanation, then just how feasible is it that both Vyse *and* Raven could have entirely missed seeing any of the large, bold quarry marks that we observe today on its walls? In Vyse's published account, we learn that during the initial inspection on May 6, 1837, he and Raven were able to observe a number of features of Lady Arbuthnot's Chamber.

1. It was empty. (There was no secret Khufu burial.)
2. It was constructed with less care than the chambers below.
3. It had more limestone wall blocks on its north and south sides than the other chambers below.
4. Its dimensions were similar to the other chambers below.
5. There was another chamber above. (To determine this, Vyse would have to have spent some time inside the chamber looking for a gap between the ceiling blocks to slip a long reed through. If the reed went all the way through, then he could be sure there was another chamber above.)

And yet, despite all the observations made in this chamber on May 6, both men seemingly managed to overlook around 120 painted quarry marks on the chamber walls, including a total of eight royal cartouches, the most cartouches in any of these chambers and certainly the most obvious royal cartouches found up to that point. What we have to keep in mind here is that by this time in his operations at Giza, Vyse had already breached two similar chambers below (Wellington's and Nelson's) and had allegedly discovered painted quarry marks on the walls of those chambers, reporting each "discovery" (in his published account) immediately afterward. Given this, it is surely not unreasonable to suggest that these two pyramid explorers would have been fully anticipating a similar discovery on the walls of this third chamber and, as such, would have been actively scrutinizing the walls there for further quarry marks in the hope of finding another royal cartouche (the one previously found in

---

(*cont. from p. 225*) painted marks from the other chambers. And, of course, the marks in this chamber were certainly visible and clear enough for Perring and Hill (and later, the Egyptologist Alan Rowe) to observe and make copies of them, so this fact alone begs the question as to how Vyse and Raven could both have missed them entirely on their first visit.

Wellington's was fairly sketchy) and thereby giving Vyse the important discovery he had hoped for. But from Vyse's official account, both men apparently saw nothing; not a single mark was reportedly found during their first inspection. How could that possibly be?

It has been suggested that perhaps the lighting the men used was too poor. However, this is simply not a credible explanation because the two explorers would have used similar lighting (candles or oil lamp) when inspecting the chambers below and were seemingly able to find the much smaller number of quarry marks in those chambers on the very first day of exploration (according to Vyse's published account). Furthermore, the two men were quite able to take measurements of Lady Arbuthnot's Chamber, which would have required them to be able to read their measuring rods and note down the results, so if they could have read the measuring rods (with their much smaller markings), why couldn't they have seen any of the much larger painted markings on the chamber walls during this measuring activity? Indeed, in his discovery of the painted marks in Wellington's Chamber, Vyse tells us in his published account:

> March 30th
> Mr. Perring and Mr. Mash having arrived, we went in the evening into Wellington's Chamber, and took various admeasurements, and in doing so we found the quarry marks.[10]

They found the painted quarry marks (just a handful) in Wellington's Chamber during the course of measuring that chamber, the very same activity they were doing in Lady Arbuthnot's Chamber. So, again, how is it possible that Vyse and Raven could both have missed over a hundred large painted marks on the walls of Lady Arbuthnot's Chamber when he and his men had been carrying out a near identical task of measuring the chambers like those below and, as stated, when they would surely now have been fully anticipating such marks being present on the walls?

Some have suggested that the chamber was filled with dust (from blasting), which perhaps covered the walls, making it difficult to see any of the painted marks (and thus difficult to breathe also). But the wall surfaces of this chamber would have been little different from the chambers below after blasting, and, as already noted, given the previous discoveries, even if the walls of Lady Arbuthnot's Chamber had some-how been coated with a layer of dust, the two men would surely have been actively clearing it away, trying to see if there were any quarry marks underneath. And in any case, from what Vyse tells us, we can immediately discard this notion because, in his later published writings concerning Campbell's Chamber (the final chamber, immediately above Lady Arbuthnot's), the colonel writes:

> May 27th
>
> When we first entered this chamber, the floor was covered with the same deposit of dust which we had observed in the apartments below it, and, in addition, the calcareous stones were covered with an exudation, which had the appearance of white feathers, and resembled that afterwards found in the Third Pyramid. There were many quarry marks similar to those in the other chambers.[11]

According to Vyse, this white feathery exudation was not covered with black floor dust and neither the wall exudation nor the floor dust prevented him from observing the quarry marks in this chamber on the very day it was opened. Furthermore, Vyse specifically tells us where else this wall exudation had occurred: "in the Third Pyramid." He makes no mention of such detritus on any of the walls in any of the other Vyse Chambers below. On this basis, we have to discount dust or other detritus, though it may have been present, as a possible barrier to Vyse and Raven from observing the quarry marks on the wall blocks of Lady Arbuthnot's Chamber.

One other possible reason suggested for the apparent oversight of both Vyse and Raven is that the men were in a hurry, so much so that they missed all the quarry marks on the walls. Again, this is a barely credible explanation. With only three feet between floor and roof, the two men would have spent all of their time in this chamber on their hands and knees, crawling through it to measure its dimensions, and, as such, they could hardly have been going so fast that the walls would have been a blur to them. In addition, we know that upon finding this chamber empty, Vyse immediately ordered that his men begin excavating above it, which implies he knew at that point that there was another chamber above Lady Arbuthnot's. He could only have come to know this by being inside the chamber and pushing a long reed through a gap into the chamber above, a process that, again, would have taken time (along with measuring the chamber), which also supports the view that the air could hardly have been choked with dust; the men were able to properly breathe during these time-consuming activities.

Others have suggested that Vyse simply wasn't interested in the quarry marks or their importance, hence, why he neglected to make any mention of them in his private journal after the initial chamber inspection with Raven.

Once more, this suggestion simply does not stand up to scrutiny. On the very day that Lady Arbuthnot's Chamber was breached, Vyse had been at the temple of the pyramid of Khafre, copying hieroglyphic signs from the temple blocks there precisely *because* he understood their importance. Indeed, throughout his entire published work, Vyse presents numerous examples of hieroglyphic signs he had observed and copied from the walls of various temples and tombs and, indeed, from some stones among the rubble on the north and south sides of the Great Pyramid itself. With regard to the quarry marks in general, Vyse later writes in his published account:

May 9th
Lady Arbuthnot's Chamber was minutely examined, and found to contain a great many quarry-marks. Notwithstanding that the characters in these chambers were surveyed by Mr. Perring upon a reduced scale, I considered that facsimiles in their original size would be desirable, as they were of great importance from their situation, and probably the most antient inscriptions in existence. I requested therefore Mr. Hill to copy them.[12]

From this statement, it is self-evident that Vyse understood the importance of the painted quarry marks he had allegedly found in these chambers. And with specific regard to the royal cartouches of the king, Vyse well understood their paramount significance, for in his published account (some three days before he first entered Lady Arbuthnot's Chamber on May 6) he writes:

May 3rd
I examined the rocky ground to the westward of the Great Pyramid, and the tombs and buildings to the north of the Second.

Foundations might everywhere be traced under the sands; and shafts lined with unburnt bricks, amongst which probably a cartouche might be found, which would determine the date of the constructions. . . . Much information might possibly be obtained from the cartouches on the bricks in the various ruins in Egypt.[13]

Thus, from his published writings, it is clear to see that the colonel well understood the importance of the quarry marks being discovered within these chambers in general and the critical importance of finding a royal cartouche among them that could potentially impart useful information that might help date the pyramids. All of which comes back to the same obvious question, Why would it have required a minute examination to finally find and report so many large, boldly painted signs in Lady Arbuthnot's Chamber, especially given that their presence would almost certainly have been fully anticipated by Vyse even before this chamber was blasted open?

All things being equal—and Vyse offers nothing in his published or private accounts to suggest otherwise—these painted quarry marks should easily have been observed by these two men during their initial inspection of this chamber on May 6 and this important discovery reported by Vyse on that date. For Vyse to imply that both he and Raven completely overlooked all of these painted marks during their initial inspection of Lady Arbuthnot's Chamber and that they were found only after a second, minute examination three days later simply makes no sense and surely stretches credibility to breaking point.

Frankly, that Vyse could even consider that any rational person could ever consider such an account plausible (let alone probable) is insulting to the intelligence of all objective people. Only those lacking in critical thinking and analytical skills could possibly conceive of Vyse's account of May 6 as being even remotely plausible, let alone credible. In all probability, however, Vyse was likely aware that this aspect of his account was less than convincing, but as we shall shortly see, it seems that events somewhat conspired against him, which meant, ultimately, that there was precious little he could do about this incredibly weak aspect of what, in effect, amounts to a cover story, a very weak cover story at that. All he could hope for was that this glaring anomaly in his published work would go unnoticed, hoping perhaps that his fudging of the events over these five days would be enough to gloss over this gaping chasm in his official account of the events at Giza in early May 1837.

But when something lacks credibility, when it so blatantly assaults and insults our logic and common sense, it is often a sure sign that there's something deeper going on that is, as yet, unseen or undetected, and this situation, as presented in Vyse's published account, sorely smacks of an attempted cover-up of something, a massaging of the actual events in order to hide a deeper, more sinister truth.

But what?

In order to answer this question, we must now focus our attention on Vyse's *private* account of these few days of his explorations at Giza, beginning with the pivotal day, May 6, 1837.

> *S. 6*
> *. . . Mr Raven returned from the Great Pyramid, and was pleased we were ready for a look into the room above Nelson's, we then paid the people off &c, Mr Raven, Mr Perring, Mr Mash, & myself came to Cairo, I took a bath & dined with Mr Brettel, & robed Armenian Effendi who had been educated in England, & who spoke good English.*

And that is it. In this original version of the events of this day, there is no mention of Vyse or Raven actually entering Lady Arbuthnot's Chamber at all, only that they "were ready for a look into" the chamber, which, of course, indicates that the chamber had indeed been opened on May 6. But there is no mention in the private journal at all of Vyse or anyone else actually being inside the chamber, nothing of this chamber's poorer workmanship, or any details of the measuring of the chamber that Vyse tells us in his published account took place on this first day. That said, it may well be that Vyse and Raven did enter the chamber on this first day, but of what occurred once inside, the private journal falls completely silent.

If we consider that Vyse had not, in fact, entered the chamber on this day with Raven, then that may well go some way to explaining why his published account (and also his private account) fails to mention the discovery of any quarry marks on this day. However, if that were the case, then why mention *anything* about this chamber at all on this day in his official account if he had not actually entered the chamber? Why fabricate an account of a visit if such a visit had never actually taken place? Why not simply stick to the truth of what actually happened at Giza on this day in 1837?

Continuing with the scenario that Vyse had not entered the chamber on May 6 and that he was perhaps merely backfilling the events of later dates to this day for his published account, then why not backfill the discovery of the painted quarry marks also to that first day? After all, we observe that Vyse did precisely that for the alleged discovery of the quarry marks in Nelson's Chamber, where it is clear from the private account that the quarry marks in Nelson's are first mentioned on the third day after that chamber had been opened, and yet, in the published version, Vyse backfills the account and tells us he discovered the quarry marks in Nelson's Chamber on the very day he first entered it. So, again, why not simply do the same with Lady Arbuthnot's Chamber? Why backfill *some* of the story (wall blocks, poorer workmanship, chamber measuring, and so on) but leave out the most important discovery of all—the quarry marks? It makes little sense.

It rather seems that, in all probability, Vyse and Raven most likely did enter Lady Arbuthnot's Chamber shortly after it had been breached on May 6, 1837, and carried out the tasks therein as described in the later published work, though not mentioned in the private account. As we see from comments elsewhere in his book, Vyse would undoubtedly have desired to have been the first to enter each of the newly breached chambers, to have been the one to make the discovery of all discoveries—Khufu's true sepulchral chamber, a truly important discovery that would have immortalized Vyse's name in the annals of world history. Given this, then Vyse most certainly would not have wanted such a potentially historic discovery to be claimed by anyone but himself and, as such, would have gotten himself into each compartment the moment it had been breached to establish if it was indeed Khufu's true burial chamber (with all its attendant treasure). Primacy of discovery was as relevant and important in 1837 as it is today.

From Vyse's private and published accounts, we know that he went to Cairo on the evening of May 6 and returned to Giza two days later, in the afternoon of May 8. From these accounts, there is no mention of Vyse entering Lady Arbuthnot's Chamber upon his return to Giza on May 8, and we further learn from his private account that he did not visit the newly opened chamber on May 9, either.

T. 9
. . . Mr Raven, and Mr Hill have gone into Lady Arbuthnot's Chamber,
I should have done the same, but I am unwell, and I know that I must
go tomorrow. *

W. 10
. . . Sent off the people (100 men came) had [?], wrote to Mr Brettel;
(hot weather) Sir Robt. & Lady Arbuthnot went to the pyramid;

Although Vyse states in his private account of May 9 that he "must go [to Lady Arbuthnot's Chamber] tomorrow" (presumably as host to the visit to the pyramid by the Arbuthnots), it seems his esteemed guests visited the monument on May 10 without Vyse being present, he having remained behind, possibly still unwell.

And so, between the dates of May 7 and 10, we can be virtually certain that Vyse made no visit to Lady Arbuthnot's Chamber. During this period, we also know for certain that Raven and Hill *did* go into this chamber (Hill a couple of times) and possibly also Perring, the Arbuthnots, and "Mr. Fitzgerald" (Lady Arbuthnot's brother). In other words, had Vyse not inspected the chamber on May 6, when it was first blasted open, then he would have been leaving any potentially massive discovery for a number of others to make.

In summary then, if Vyse wanted to lay claim to what would surely have been the discovery of all time—Khufu's true burial—then the date of May 6, when the chamber was first opened, was his best and seemingly only opportunity to have done so. And given that Vyse would have known that he would be detained in Cairo for at least a couple of nights, then it stands to reason that he simply must have entered Lady Arbuthnot's Chamber on May 6, and that is, of course, what he tells us happened in his published account (and implied in his private account).

---

*There is no mention here in Vyse's private account (or, indeed, in his published account) of this chamber being breached on this date (May 9), only that Raven and Hill (in the private account) had "gone into" the chamber (thereby supporting the statements elsewhere from Vyse and Perring that the chamber had already been opened before this date). Note also here that the chamber has now been named Lady Arbuthnot's Chamber. The chamber's name seems to have been agreed to on the previous day, May 8, when Vyse had talks with Sir Robert Keith Arbuthnot.

All of which brings us full circle. Accepting Vyse's published account that he and Raven *did* enter and explore Lady Arbuthnot's Chamber on May 6, why then did Vyse fail to make any mention on this date of the numerous quarry marks we see today on the walls of this chamber when it would surely have been virtually impossible for two explorers to have missed them? And even if Vyse did find these marks some days later (as his published account tells us), why not simply backfill the published narrative to say that he *had* found the marks upon the first inspection (as he has evidently done with Nelson's Chamber)?

As we know, the painted marks in this chamber are numerous, bold, and large (each approximately twelve to eighteen inches tall). Would it really have required a further minute examination of this chamber by potentially three men in order to discover such marks? One man methodically working his way around the chamber, inspecting the walls and making copies of what was found, would surely have sufficed for this purpose. And that is exactly what Vyse tasked Hill with—to copy each of the quarry marks on a one-to-one scale from all the chambers. In this regard then, Raven's presence in the chamber along with Hill on May 9 seems somewhat superfluous, as would Vyse's presence have been (had he not taken ill).

Unless, of course, we consider the elephant-in-the-room scenario—that no marks were discovered at all during the initial inspection on May 6 because no quarry marks were actually present on any of the chamber walls when the chamber was first opened, and that is the real reason for the complete silence on this matter in Vyse's private and published accounts of this day. In this scenario, it becomes perfectly understandable that it would require a second visit of two or three men to prepare and paint so many markings onto the chamber walls, especially if time was of the essence—which it would have been given that the Arbuthnots were planning to visit the Great Pyramid and possibly Lady Arbuthnot's Chamber the following day. Thus, when the colonel writes in his private journal of Raven and Hill going into Lady Arbuthnot's Chamber (which, remember, he also wanted to do but was unwell), it perhaps wasn't to minutely examine the chamber walls for the quarry marks that Vyse and Raven had bizarrely managed to overlook the first time around, but rather to check on and assist Vyse's Egyptian worker (who had probably been tasked with this job prior to Vyse departing for Cairo) prepare and paint fraudulent marks onto the chamber walls before the arrival of the Arbuthnots. And this visit of the Arbuthnots to the Great Pyramid (they arrived at Vyse's encampment on the evening of May 9, 1837) was to be pivotal to Vyse's machinations, machinations that would shortly backfire on him in quite dramatic fashion.

A Practice to Deceive

From both of Vyse's accounts (private and published), it is plainly clear that Lady Arbuthnot's Chamber had been breached on May 6 (fig. A2.9). However, the chamber's dedication inscription to Lady Arbuthnot, which was painted onto the chamber wall by Hill, contradicts this May 6 date and actually gives the chamber's opening date as having occurred three days later, on May 9 (fig. A2.10, p. 236).

To be clear, this date of May 9 does not reflect the date when Hill actually painted the inscription itself, but, just like the dedication inscriptions in the other chambers, it states the chamber's *opening date*. We can be certain of this since it was confirmed by Hill in no less than six of his facsimile sheets from this chamber, in which he writes on each sheet, "opened on the 9th of May 1837." Furthermore, these facsimile sheets were duly signed by a number of witnesses, including Sir Robert Arbuthnot, Raven, Hill, Brettel, and even Vyse himself, all testifying to this May 9 opening date. Here then we have a glaring contradiction as

INSCRIPTIONS.

Great Pyramid.

Basement stones	-	Excavated 1837.
North-eastern excavation		—
North-western excavation		—
Northern air-channel	-	Opened May 22d, 1837.
Southern air-channel	-	— May 29th, 1837.
Wellington's chamber	-	Wellington's chamber, March 30, 1837.
Nelson's chamber	-	Nelson's chamber, April 25, 1837.
Lady Arbuthnot's chamber		Lady Arbuthnot's chamber, May 6, 1837.
Col. Campbell's chamber		{ Col. Campbell's chamber, May 27, 1837; { H. Raven and Hill.

Figure A2.9. In the "Inscriptions" entry for the Great Pyramid in Vyse's published account, he misreports the date given within the inscription in Lady Arbuthnot's Chamber as May 6, 1837.

Figure A2.10. The dedication inscription in Lady Arbuthnot's Chamber. The actual date in the chamber is given as May 9, 1837, contradicting Vyse's private and published accounts. (Photo courtesy of Patrick Chapuis)

to when this chamber was actually opened: both of Vyse's journals tell us May 6 (as does Perring's account), but Hill has written May 9 on the chamber wall and also on no less than six of his verified facsimile drawings. Something is clearly afoot here.

So what's going on? It is evident that Vyse saw Hill's date of May 9 on the chamber wall during the attestation of the chamber marks that took place on May 19, so why does the colonel contradict this date by stating in his later published account that the dedication inscription reads "Lady Arbuthnot's chamber, May 6, 1837," when evidently it does not say this? Why did Vyse, upon seeing this contradiction painted onto the chamber wall and Hill's facsimile sheets, not instruct Hill to correct this date? Indeed, why should such a glaring contradiction even exist at all between these various documented sources? Why did Perring (in 1839) and Vyse (in 1840) claim an opening date of May 6 while the chamber's dedication inscription and Hill's facsimile drawings state May 9 as the opening date? Why such a blatant contradiction?

What we may actually be observing here is but yet another calculated attempt by Vyse to manipulate events at Giza, just as he had previously conflated and fudged the dates of Nelson's Chamber. In this instance, however, Vyse was not (at least initially) attempting to backfill the events to the earlier date of May 6 as being when the chamber was actually opened but, rather, was attempting to shift the opening date of the chamber (and the claimed discovery of the painted marks therein) *forward* in time by three days to May 9, and for a very specific reason.

The colonel, naturally, would have wanted it to be known that the discovery of the painted marks in this chamber occurred on the very same day the chamber was opened because, during any initial exploration, he would have realized that such an obvious oversight by two men would surely have raised some eyebrows and probably some awkward questions. As such, the three-day time lag between the chamber's actual opening and the discovery of the painted marks needed to be compressed (read: vanish), and Vyse's solution was to shift the date of the chamber's actual opening, moving it a few days forward in order to give himself time to have the quarry marks painted into the chamber by his Egyptian worker (with Raven and Hill likely complicit in this nefarious activity). And, naturally, as part of his plan, Vyse would have instructed Hill to place the dedication inscription with the date of May 9, 1837, on the chamber wall to show to the world that *this* was the date the chamber was opened (as opposed to the true date of May 6) and that this May 9 date was also the date that a "great many quarry-marks" therein were also discovered. Awkward time gap gone.

To be absolutely clear here, the wording of the dedication inscription placed in Lady Arbuthnot's Chamber would have been wholly the responsibility of Vyse—not Hill. This chamber was Vyse's discovery. The naming of each chamber was entirely his prerogative. And the text of the dedication inscription would also have been his prerogative. It is simply inconceivable that the colonel would have delegated the wording of the chamber's dedication inscription to Hill. Vyse would have totally called the shots on this, deciding exactly what text, including the date, was to be placed on the chamber wall.

Consider then that Vyse's published account tells us (without any indication whatsoever that he had actually altered this date) this chamber was opened on May 6, 1837. There is no question or ambiguity about this: this chamber *was* opened on May 6. And yet Vyse, for some reason, instructed Hill to change this date to May 9, 1837, in the chamber's dedication inscription. This, right here, is a complete fabrication, an outright lie. This, right here, is clear proof of Vyse knowingly and surreptitiously misreporting actual facts. This, right here, is clear evidence of an attempt to conceal his botched deception. There is simply no getting around this. Vyse instructed Hill to paint a false opening date onto the wall of Lady Arbuthnot's Chamber (see fig. A2.10), a false date that can be observed in this chamber to this very day.

Critics will undoubtedly respond to this by suggesting that Hill somehow got muddled and painted the wrong date onto the chamber wall. While that remains a possibility, it is highly unlikely for a number of reasons.

1. This was an important piece of text that Hill was placing on this wall—the chamber's dedication inscription! Is it realistic to believe that Hill could get something so important so wrong?

2. If Hill had made a simple mistake by painting a "9" instead of a "6," then it would have been easy enough to correct, but it wasn't corrected and Hill's "error" remains on the chamber wall to this day. Furthermore, if Hill had been using stencils for his inscriptions (not unlikely), then the very fact that a "9," when inverted, can become a "6" would have made it all the more likely that he would have been extra careful with this particular number, ensuring that he had it the correct and desired way up before painting the number.

3. Is it really likely that Hill and Vyse somehow managed between them to come up with the wrong chamber opening date when that event had occurred only a few days earlier? The date this inscription was actually painted onto this wall by Hill also happened to be May 9. As such, in painting the opening date (that day's date) onto the wall, Hill would surely have known that this chamber had not been opened that *same day,* but rather three days earlier (when he would have been in Cairo at the time), and yet, for some unfathomable reason, he ignored that glaring chronological disparity and continued to paint "May 9th" onto the wall rather than the earlier true opening date of May 6.

4. Hill specifically wrote May 9 as the chamber opening date on six of his facsimile sheets (the accuracy of which was attested to by Vyse and other witnesses).

5. Hill, whom Vyse describes as "a very intelligent person," appears throughout Vyse's operations at Giza to have been a thoroughly

dependable man, having made no mistakes of any kind with the dedication inscriptions in any of the other chambers.

On the balance of probability then, it does seem that Hill painted onto the wall the dedication inscription he would have been instructed to paint. There was no mistake, and he painted the inscription exactly as it would have been given to him. And so, May 9, 1837, was to be the date that Vyse planned to tell the world that Lady Arbuthnot's Chamber was first opened and when the painted quarry marks were found on its walls. Thus, in this planned scenario, there is no problematic time lag that needed explaining between the date the chamber was opened and the date the quarry marks therein were discovered. In this scenario, there would have been no mention whatsoever in the colonel's future published account of the actual truth (i.e., that the chamber had, in fact, been opened three days earlier on May 6 and that no quarry marks had been found in the chamber on that date). It was not intended that any of this be known, and, had everything gone to plan, the true opening date of this chamber, May 6, would have been entirely expunged from Vyse's official account.

And so, everything was in place, and the colonel's plan was nicely coming together. The chamber was now ready for the visit of Sir Robert and Lady Arbuthnot the following day, and, naturally, with the chamber being named in honor of Lady Arbuthnot, it would have been quite likely that these esteemed guests of Vyse would have desired to see inside this chamber. The perfect witnesses.

But the best-laid schemes o' mice an' men, often go awry. Vyse's carefully crafted deception was about to unravel and the truth of his mendacity exposed in quite spectacular fashion.

The Wheels Loosen

Intriguingly, Vyse's fraudulent activity at Giza was apparently witnessed by one of Vyse's workers, a man named Humphries Brewer.* Brewer wrote letters back to his family in England about his travels through Egypt and the Holy Land and, it seems, about his time working with Vyse at Giza. Brewer eventually emigrated to the United

---

*For more on Brewer, see *The Great Pyramid Hoax,* 69–90.

States, and the letters he had written to his parents were apparently passed down the family line (presumably after the death of Brewer's parents). While researching his family history with his mother and some elderly aunts in 1954, Walter Allen of Pittsburgh, Pennsylvania (Brewer's great-grandson), came to learn of his great grandfather's time with Vyse at Giza and recorded the details of the family discussion in his ham radio logbook at the time. In these notes, Allen recounts the following story of his great grandfather's time with Vyse at Giza: "He joined a Col. Visse exploring Gizeh pyramids. Rechecked dimensions 2 pyramids. Had dispute with Raven and Hill about painted marks in pyramid. Faint marks were repainted, some were new. Did not find Tomb . . . had words with a Mr. Hill and Visse when he left."

The statement in the short passage seems clear enough. Allen's great grandfather, Humphries Brewer, worked for Vyse at Giza and, at some point, seems to have had a dispute with Raven and Hill, Vyse's two closest assistants. About what? This seems equally clear—about painted marks in the pyramid. Some of these painted marks, we are told, were repainted while others were new. This statement from Allen's notes is about as clear an inference of fraudulent activity occurring at Giza as one could hope to obtain short of it being explicitly and unequivocally attested by Vyse himself. Soon after this incident, it seems that Brewer was dismissed by Vyse (and presumably permanently banned from the site), whereupon he continued on his travels to the Holy Land, but not before having some choice words with Vyse and Hill prior to his departure.

Even though Allen's logbook page bears elements that would have been very difficult for a hoaxer to have known (thus imbuing the account's authenticity with a high degree of confidence), typically, crtics of the account point out that there is no mention in any of Vyse's published volumes of Brewer ever having been in the colonel's employ, implying that he had never actually worked with Vyse at Giza at all and thus could never have witnessed any fraudulent activity there. Without Brewer's original letters to corroborate his great-grandson's later logbook account, the critics insist that this evidence from Allen is, at best, hearsay and, at worst, itself fraudulent. In their view, with no corroboration of the story, Allen's account becomes inadmissible to the debate.

But, of course, Brewer's original letters (which appear to have been lost sometime after 1954) are not the only place we should be looking for corroborating evidence of Allen's story. If such an incident really had occurred at Giza in 1837, then it is highly unlikely indeed that Vyse would have made any mention of it in his published work, for to have done so, if he could not disprove the allegation, would have fatally undermined his word on the authenticity of the Khufu cartouches he claimed to have discovered within the Great Pyramid, something the colonel would, naturally, have wished to avoid. However, while Vyse, understandably, may have entirely expunged such an unpleasant event and the antagonists involved in it from his published volumes, he may not have been so concerned in doing so with his private account, an account that was, after all, for his eyes only. So is there anything in Vyse's private notes that might lend support to Allen's logbook account?

Vyse's private field notes (his daily diary of events at Giza) consist of around six hundred foolscap pages covering the period from December 1835 to August 1837. The pages most likely to mention the Humphries Brewer incident would, logically, be found in the period when the colonel was blasting open the four Vyse Chambers, from March 30, 1837, to May 27, 1837—a period of around eight weeks. However, given that Lady Arbuthnot's Chamber contains more quarry marks than all of the other chambers combined, it is reasonable to further suppose that if any fraudulent activity had been occurring in the Great Pyramid during this eight-week period, then it is more likely to have been witnessed shortly after the opening of this particular chamber (between the dates of May 6 to May 10, 1837). The logic here is simple: more forged chamber marks require more preparation time, need more paint, more chamber visits, and generally more journeying back and forth to this chamber by the forgers—all of which add up to an increased probability of any fraudulent activity being spotted and witnessed by a third party between those particular dates. After checking Vyse's private notes, we find that these five days amounted to just three foolscap pages—a considerably less arduous task to check, especially given the very difficult nature of the colonel's handwriting.

So what, if anything, is present within these three pages of Vyse's private notes between these specific dates of May 6 to May 10, 1837, that might point to fraudulent activity within Lady Arbuthnot's Chamber? Is there any corroborating evidence in Vyse's private account from these critical days at Giza—these three pages—that might lend support to Allen's story about his great-grandfather calling foul on forgery within the Great Pyramid and being subsequently dismissed by Vyse?

Quite remarkably, it would appear that such an account is indeed present in Vyse's private journal during this very time frame. However, as is typical when transcribing the colonel's incredibly difficult handwriting, it comes with something of an unexpected twist to the account relayed to us by Allen.

Witness M: The Truth Erupts

On May 9, after the arrival of the Arbuthnots to Vyse's encampment, Hill is sent with an inkpad up to Lady Arbuthnot's chamber, presumably to paint the chamber's dedication inscription onto the chamber wall (and probably also to make facsimile copies of the fake inscriptions that had been placed there earlier).

> *T. 9*
> *. . . Sir Robert & Lady Arbuthnot, & Mr Fitzgerald arrive, &c talked, dined, &c Mr Hill went up to copy the inscription[s] in Lady Arbuthnot's Chamber &c; had inkpad in the sack, Mr Hill [returned from] the pyramid, the [name] is very curious, I now recollect that Prince Muskau [Pückler] said that we should find an inscription in our apartment.*

Upon his return from this task in Lady Arbuthnot's Chamber it seems that Hill then told Vyse that someone (the name used here in the private journal is unclear) was "very curious." What was this individual curious about? Alas, Vyse doesn't say. However, the colonel's very next thought, his very next sentence, may be instructive in this regard when he writes, "I now recollect that Prince Muskau [Pückler?]* said that we should find an inscription in our apartment."

Linking Vyse's thought stream here, it seems then that someone

---

*It appears in his private journal that Vyse has transposed the forename and surname of this prince. The name in his private journal was likely intended to have been Prince Hermann von Pückler-Muskau, whom Vyse mentions (with the correct name) a number of times in his published account. More on this prince later.

was "curious" (suspicious?) about "inscriptions" in one of the chambers*
(presumably Lady Arbuthnot's) and seems to have relayed his concerns
to Hill who subsequently relayed them to Vyse. That was the end of
Vyse's private journal entry of that day, May 9, 1837. It was the calm
before the storm for this, it seems, wasn't the end of the matter for this
curious individual. The very next day his name appears again, exploding onto the pages of the colonel's private journal and, almost certainly,
this person laid waste Vyse's carefully planned deception. On this day,
May 10, the colonel writes:

> W. 10
> . . . breakfast, I sat out here, Sir Robert & Lady Arbuthnot sat in
> [their] tent, Mr Perring, & Mr Mash came; rest, [name] quarreled with
> Mr Raven, I discharged [name], &c, paying him by a receipt received
> & bills for him to sign, walk with Sir Robert & Lady Arbuthnot, &c,
> dinner, &c bed.

Here then we have someone in Vyse's employment, an individual
who was seemingly "very curious" about the painted inscriptions within
the Great Pyramid, who subsequently had a quarrel with Raven, and
who, as a result of this dispute, was instantly dismissed by Vyse. Do
these events sound at all familiar?

While Vyse does not elaborate on the specifics of this incident in
his private journal (and nothing at all of them appears in his published
account), it cannot be denied that, in these brief passages from his private field notes of May 9 and 10, 1837, the events the colonel writes of
bear clear similarities with the key elements in Allen's account of his
great-grandfather, Humphries Brewer, having had a dispute with Raven
and Hill about some painted marks in the Great Pyramid and then
being dismissed from the site by Vyse. Thus, what we might in fact have
with these private journal entries is actual independent corroboration of
the Allen story from the very pen of Vyse himself.

Except, however, for one very considerable fly in the ointment. This
indecipherable "name" (this witness) who quarreled with Raven and

---

*Vyse sometime would refer to these small chambers he was blasting his way into as
"apartments."

who was subsequently dismissed appears three times in Vyse's private notes during these two critical days. This indecipherable name is about six to eight letters in length, begins with a capital letter *M,* and appears to end with the letters *ing* or *iq.* Clearly then, this name categorically *cannot* be Humphries or Brewer. (For the sake of simplicity and clarity, this unknown individual will henceforth be referred to as Witness M.)

And so, if this incident Vyse writes of in his private account was indeed the very same incident recalled in Allen's account from 1954, then we seem to have a contradiction as to who this witness to Vyse's fraud actually was. Allen cites his great-grandfather, Humphries Brewer, as the witness, but Vyse's private account seems to indicate someone else, a person whose name begins with *M* and appears to end with *ing* or perhaps *iq.* And yet, this contradiction aside, the fact remains that the key elements of this incident in both accounts are strikingly similar.

If Witness M was the true witness to fraudulent activity at Giza (rather than Brewer), what are we to make of this? Where does Brewer fit into the picture, if at all? Did Allen simply invent this story of his great-grandfather witnessing fraud at Giza, as some have suggested? If that were the case, however, then it has to be considered a quite astonishing insight by Allen that in 1954, almost 120 years after these events took place, he was able to recount with good accuracy some pertinent details involving Vyse and his team at Giza in early May 1837. This is to say that if Allen's great-grandfather had not been present at Giza at all during this time, how then could Allen have possibly known these details since Vyse never published any of them in his official account?

There are, however, a couple of possible explanations that might help us reconcile the apparent contradiction between the accounts of Vyse and Allen. A close analysis of the indecipherable name in Vyse's private journal informs us that there is no salutation such as "Mr.," "Sheikh," "Sir," "Captain," and so on, preceding it. This suggests the word is possibly a forename that is being used or even a nickname that is perhaps associated in some way with Brewer's actual name, his occupation, his status, or perhaps even an attribute of Brewer himself, such as his personal character or physical appearance, a nickname that Vyse might have used for Brewer that began with a capital *M* and ended with *ing* or *iq.* This idea of a nickname is given more weight when we observe that the first appearance of this name on May 9 is preceded with the word *The* (i.e., The M***ing). We know that Brewer was a young man, being only twenty years of age in 1837. If he was also of short stature, Vyse could have referred to Brewer as "The Manling" or simply "Manling"—a young or short man. This, of course, is but speculation, and we will never know the truth of this with any degree of certainty until such time as this indecipherable name can be definitively transcribed from Vyse's private journal.

Another—and it has to be said—more likely possibility is simply that this unknown "name" (our Witness M) was not Humphries Brewer at all but was actually someone else altogether whose name began with *M* and ended with *ing* or possibly *iq*.* However, it may also be that when the quarrel with Witness M and Raven erupted, Brewer was standing nearby and witnessed the dispute take place (as undoubtedly some others would also have done, including Sir Robert and Lady Arbuthnot, who Vyse tells us were in their tent in his encampment at the time). As such, Allen's great-grandfather may not have been the primary witness to the forgery per se, but in this scenario he *could* have been a primary witness to the *accusation* of forgery, hearing it firsthand as Witness M hurled it at Raven (and possibly also Hill and perhaps even Vyse himself) during the dispute. Brewer may also have been looking on as Vyse intervened and had Witness M instantly dismissed from his service as a result of the seriousness of the accusations being made. All of which Brewer could have faithfully reported in his letters to his family back in England. Indeed, it may even be that Brewer was so appalled by what he had witnessed on this day that he himself (assuming here that he was not Witness M) decided to express some choice words of his own with Vyse and Hill about their actions, words that perhaps prompted his own early departure from the colonel's employment, along with a permanent ban from the site and a guaranteed exclusion from Vyse's published works to boot.†

But, of course, with family histories—especially when most of the written record is lost and the story is passed down only via oral means—

---

*This indecipherable name could also be of Arabic origin, such as Mussadiq (one who verifies another) or Mushiq (friend).

†There are a few examples elsewhere in Vyse's private account that may be the name Brewer.

events can become muddled, characters can become conflated or transposed, and before we know it, we find that it is Brewer himself who has become the main protagonist of the story, the one who witnessed the forgery firsthand, who then argued with Raven (and perhaps Hill), and who was subsequently dismissed by Vyse. Such are the perils of the oral transmission of family histories.

A Second Witness: The Prussian Prince

If we now consider more fully Vyse's private journal entry of May 9, 1837, concerning Prince Pückler-Muskau, matters become even more damning for the colonel.

Apparently, Vyse had held a discussion some time previously at Giza with Prince Hermann von Pückler-Muskau (fig. A2.11), a Prussian traveler and adventurer, in which the prince had said to Vyse that the British pyramid explorer would find an inscription in an "apartment." (As previously stated, the word *apartment* is sometimes used by Vyse in his writings to describe these newly discovered chambers.)

This is a very peculiar statement by the Prussian prince. How exactly could Pückler-Muskau have correctly predicted that Vyse would find an "inscription" in an "apartment"? Even more peculiar here is that, according to Vyse's official account, Pückler-Muskau arrived at the colonel's encampment at Giza on February 22, 1837, but was refused permission by Vyse to camp there, being directed instead to a large mastaba tomb in the plain that was often used by travel-

Figure A2.11. Prince Hermann von Pückler-Muskau.

ers. The Prussian prince's stay at Giza was brief, and he departed for Upper Egypt just three days later. What this means, of course, is that any discussion between Vyse and this prince about inscriptions being found within a pyramid's "apartment" would have taken place over a month before Vyse had even breached any of the hidden chambers. How could this Prussian prince have known this in advance of Vyse entering any of the chambers? Was the Prussian prince privy to some secret, wider conspiracy to have inscriptions placed within the Great Pyramid?

Pückler-Muskau was certainly a man known to have circulated in the highest echelons of Egyptian society at the time and, perhaps significantly, is known to have met Vyse's former disgruntled business partner, Giovanni Caviglia, during his stay in Cairo. We can only imagine what conversation Caviglia might have had with Pückler-Muskau regarding Vyse, who had only recently banished Caviglia from Giza. Was it during this meeting with Caviglia in February 1837 that the prince learned that Vyse was planning to find an inscription in the chamber he was attempting, at that time, to blast his way into? Or had the prince perhaps heard of a Vyse plan from among the people with whom he had encamped during his brief stay at Giza? With this peculiar comment in Vyse's private account, it seems quite possible that Pückler-Muskau was perhaps hinting to Vyse that he knew what the colonel was up to, that he knew Vyse was planning to make an "important discovery" in these sealed chambers by placing fraudulent inscriptions therein after gaining access to them.

After concluding his adventures through North Africa, this Prussian prince published his own travelogue of his extensive travels in 1845 in two volumes, titled *Egypt under Mehemet Ali*. In the first of these volumes he writes the following:

> For, after all, these rude beginnings of art, without sculpture, and without hieroglyphic writings, were nothing more than tumuli of stone, though, at the time of Herodotus, they were again surrounded with the ornaments of art, (which had improved in the meantime) with temples, sphinxes, colossi, courts, and avenues, all of which had hieroglyphics, while the primeval monuments were left with religious awe in their original simplicity.[14]

Pückler-Muskau repeated the above passage (with a slightly different translation) in a separate publication in 1847.

> For after all we cannot give any other name than tumuli of stone to these rough beginnings of art, without any sculpture or hieroglyphics, although in the time of Herodotus, they were again surrounded by the ornaments of an advanced art, with temples, sphinxes, colosses, court yards, and splendid avenues, all of which were ornamented with hieroglyphics, whilst the old monuments were left with a holy veneration in their primitive simplicity.[15]

What these passages clearly show is that the Prussian prince believed that although later Egyptian monuments had been decorated with hieroglyphics, the ancient monuments (by which he means the Giza pyramids) were devoid of all such hieroglyphic inscriptions and that they had always existed in this "primitive simplicity." That is what he appears to have believed during his time in Egypt visiting these monuments. Why then, weeks before Vyse had blasted open the first of the sealed chambers, Wellington's Chamber, would Pückler-Muskau predict that the colonel would find an inscription inside it? Why, if the prince believed these monuments, from the time of their construction, were intended to have been devoid of all hieroglyphic inscriptions and built with "primitive simplicity" (without any hieroglyphics), would he then assert that Vyse would go on to find an inscription in Wellington's Chamber? Why does he further write:

> I have confidence in the gallant and worthy Colonel Howard Vyse, and that by his perseverance and acuteness, he, sooner than any others, will at length make important discoveries.[16]

Here we observe that Pückler-Muskau believed that Vyse was more likely to make important discoveries than any of his peers in Egypt at the time. But why should the Prussian have held such a view? Is it, perhaps, because he had suspicions that Vyse was planning to place painted hieroglyphics into these chambers and that what is being expressed in this passage is not so much a compliment of the British colonel's determination but rather a veiled indictment of his fraudulent aspirations? If that were the case, then what evidence is there directly from Pückler-Muskau himself that actually shows that he did indeed suspect Vyse of fraudulent practices? In his 1847 publication, Pückler-Muskau writes the following truly astonishing passage:

> The hieroglyphics which Major Wyse* pretends to have just discovered in the great pyramid are not cut in the stone, but merely drawn on the wall, and perhaps recently too, with a finger, dipped in colour.[17]

Thus, from the explosive remarks in his published works, it is quite evident that Pückler-Muskau appears to be questioning the provenance of the painted marks Vyse claimed to have discovered and thus their authenticity, stating that Vyse was merely *pretending* to have discovered them and that the marks were "merely drawn on the wall [ergo, in situ], and perhaps recently too." It seems that, for whatever reason, Pückler-Muskau was deeply skeptical and somewhat suspicious of Vyse's activities at Giza. And, significantly, the prince was certainly not afraid to go public with his suspicions by putting them into print, which suggests he had, if called upon, the ability to produce the evidence to back up his very public accusation of fraud against Vyse. It may also be signficant that Vyse did not ever refute or challenge Pückler-Muskau's clear accusation against him.

The Lost Symbol

Let us now turn our attention to some of the actual quarry marks that Vyse claimed to have found in Lady Arbuthnot's Chamber after the minute examination on the second visit. While a number of anomalies of the painted marks in this chamber were identified and presented in my previous book, *The Great Pyramid Hoax,* additional anomalies have since come to light from this chamber that, upon detailed scrutiny, we find are also strongly suggestive of fraudulent activity having occurred in this chamber in 1837.

---

*Pückler-Muskau's original text had been written in German, and in this English translation, he keeps the German spelling of Vyse (Wyse). In 1846, Vyse was promoted to the rank of major-general, which Pückler-Muskau refers to simply as "major."

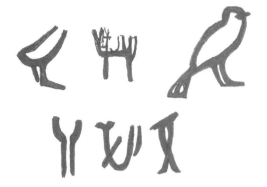

Figure A2.12. Impression of the marks copied by Perring from Lady Arbuthnot's Chamber. Note that one sign (lower row, far right) is the only sign in this inscription that is upside down.

In the course of his survey of Lady Arbuthnot's Chamber, Perring made a drawing of marks from a block on the eastern side of the south wall of this chamber (fig. A2.12).

These painted marks (known as old hieretic or linear hieroglyphic, that is, painted rather than chiseled hieroglyphic signs) present something of a curious anomaly. All the hieratic signs on the two rows of the inscription on this particular wall block are upright with the exception of one: the very last sign on the second row is, bizarrely, upside down. This is a fairly common sign used for this type of inscription to represent the names of construction gangs, in this case, the Pure Ones of the Horus Medjedu. The upside-down sign is transliterated as *apr,* which means "gang" or "team." We see it used many times in these Vyse Chambers as part of other gang names.

Aside from the mixed orientation of signs that we find on this block, which itself is a rare occurrence for such inscriptions, the anomaly here arises because the gang sign on this block is not actually needed for this particular piece of text. This gang sign is entirely superfluous to this piece of text since another—more crudely drawn—version of this sign is already presented (upright) as the first character of the second row of the inscription (fig. A2.13). This gang sign is never used twice in the same piece of text and never with two different orientations like we see in Perring's drawing of the marks presented on this block.

In response to this observation, critics have suggested that the ancient Egyptian scribe placing this inscription onto the block (presumably at the quarry or mason's yard) possibly began by first painting the upside-down gang sign in its proper upright manner but for some rea-

Figure A2.13. The gang sign in the dashed box (on the left) *is an upright and more crudely drawn version of the upside-down gang sign in the dashed box* (on the right).

son changed his mind, stopped, had the block rotated 180°, and began again, completing the full inscription as observed in Perring's drawing of it. This suggestion makes little sense, however, since it would mean the scribe would have started this inscription by painting the very *last* word in this piece of text (the gang sign) onto the block *first* (before rotating the block 180° to begin again). It would be unlikely in the extreme for an ancient Egyptian scribe to begin a piece of text by painting the final word in the sentence onto the block first; it's simply not how writing is done. As such, the presence of this gang sign, in this context, is entirely baffling and without parallel; there's just no logical way to explain its presence on this stone block in terms of conventional ancient Egyptian scribal writing because, as stated, with such an ensemble of signs, the gang sign would always be written last and never first.

But what is even *more* peculiar about this block inscription on the south wall of this chamber is Hill's one-to-one facsimile drawing of it (fig. A2.14, p. 252).

The anomalous upside-down gang sign is *gone!* Vanished! Disappeared!

A close analysis shows that there are a number of minor differences between the drawings of Perring and Hill of the signs on this particular wall block, but as we can see, the most striking and significant difference between the two is that the bizarre upside-down gang sign that we clearly observe in Perring's drawing (A2.12) is entirely missing from Hill's! It simply no longer exists.

And we can be absolutely certain that this gang sign is no longer present on the chamber wall because as we know, on May 19, 1837, Vyse

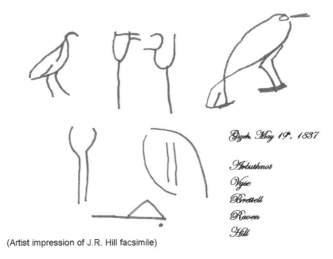

(Artist impression of J.R. Hill facsimile)

Figure A2.14. Impression of Hill's facsimile copy of the marks from the same block as Perring's drawing (see fig. A2.12). Note the five witness names signed on the drawing (lower right).

Figure A2.15. This upside-down gang sign is entirely missing from Hill's facsimile drawing.

arranged for a number of witnesses, including Sir Robert Arbuthnot, to attest to the accuracy of Hill's facsimile drawings against the actual marks in the various Vyse Chambers (with the exception of Campbell's Chamber, which had not yet been opened). Notably, Perring—a man whom Vyse had commissioned to make a plan survey copy of all the painted marks in these chambers and who would have known them fairly well—was not among the five witnesses to verify the accuracy of Hill's drawings. The absence of the upside-down gang sign is confirmed also by the Egyptologist Alan Rowe, who copied this group of marks in the 1920s (fig. A2.16).

What we also observe in Hill's and Rowe's drawings of the signs from this block is the inordinate amount of empty white space on the right side of the bottom row of the inscription in figure A2.16, almost as though a sign *had* once existed in this position, thereby causing the

Figure A2.16. This block inscription by the Egyptologist Alan Rowe also shows that the upside-down gang sign is no longer present on the block. (Note: Rowe did not make exact copies of the painted wall marks and would often fill in missing elements to complete what he believed a particular sign was meant to be.)

other two signs we observe on this row to be shifted leftward. Had this inscription been painted upright onto the stone at the quarry, then the ancient Egyptian scribe, writing right to left, would likely have placed the first sign of the second row directly under the first character of the first row, thereby placing this white space on the left of the bottom row and not, as we observe, on the right (fig. A2.17).

So here we have a situation in which Perring copies what is a well-documented hieratic sign, but one that, being superfluous to this inscription, is highly peculiar in this particular ensemble of marks and clearly out of place among the other upright signs on this block. But by the time Hill comes to copy the same group of marks, the anomalous symbol has vanished—*gone!*

Figure A2.17. Impression of how this two-line inscription would likely have been painted onto the stone by an ancient Egyptian scribe. Note how when writing right to left, the white space ends up on the left (at the end of the inscription) and not the right side of the second row.

What on earth happened to it? More pertinently, what are the chances that the most anomalous hieratic sign presented from these chambers—a superfluous sign—just also happens to be the only sign to have mysteriously vanished from the chambers? How can the sudden disappearance of this sign be reasonably explained? Before we consider a possible answer to this, it is worth examining some of the explanations critics have made for the complete absence of this sign from the drawings of Hill and Rowe.

Poor Lighting

First of all, it is suggested that the lighting conditions (most likely from candles or oil lamps) might have resulted in Perring copying a sign that wasn't actually on the block, a sign that didn't actually exist (i.e., it is contended that Perring wholly *imagined* something that simply wasn't there). This scenario is highly improbable, for if this were true, then we would likely find a number of other such striking anomalies between the work of Perring and Hill, and we just don't. Yes, there are minor variances between the two men's work in the way certain signs have been drawn (which is to be expected), but for Perring to have imagined entirely the presence of a bona-fide ancient Egyptian hieratic gang sign is on a different level of improbability altogether. Furthermore, Perring would have spent a fair bit of time observing and copying the marks from this wall block; this would not have been a fleeting glimpse that he would have had of these particular marks. It is one thing to perhaps miss some small detail that does exist in a particular inscription but an altogether different matter for someone to somehow observe and copy an entire sign that simply doesn't exist on the stone and for that imagined sign to then actually have meaning, to be a common, recognizable hieratic symbol as opposed to a series of random brush strokes made in the dim light that would more likely have created a meaningless blob of paint. And, as outlined above, the white space being on the right side of the second row (as opposed to the more natural left side) is indicative of something having once been present in this position on the wall block that was removed, thereby creating the inordinate amount of white space on the right-hand side of this row of the inscription.

Lithographer Mistake

Secondly, critics point out that in Perring's publication we have only a lithographer's copy of Perring's original drawings. It is thereby inferred that somewhere along the line, a mistake was made during the production of the lithographic plates from which the subsequent impression prints were made for Perring's published account (and presumably Vyse's also).

But once again this particular possibility simply does not stand up to basic scrutiny. As stated, these lithographic plates would have been created using Perring's original artwork. It is the lithographer's job to ensure an accurate lithograph is made from the original artwork. These lithographs (usually made of stone, hence "litho") were not easy to make and would likely have had the lithographer spending many hours carefully studying the original artwork before etching a reverse image of the artwork onto the stone (in order to make a positive print). Is it reasonable to suggest that, given the considerable skill, time, and effort involved, the lithographer could have made such a basic mistake, that the lithographer had somehow imagined (for a lengthy period of time) a symbol that simply wasn't present in Perring's original artwork and then to etch a reverse image of it? Seriously?

Over and above this possibility, standard publishing practice would have ensured that proof copies were made from the lithographic negative and that the proofs, importantly, would have needed to be approved by Perring before final publication. It is simply inconceivable that a proof check would not have taken place for a drawing of such considerable importance. As such, we must accept that the lithographer would have made a true and accurate copy of Perring's original artwork and that Perring himself would have approved the lithographer's proof copy for publication. In fact, Perring's signature actually appears on the plates of these drawings in his publication of them in 1839, a year before Vyse published them in his own book.

It is also worth pointing out in this regard that a separate, slightly different version of this inscription (including the upside-down gang sign) appears in Vyse's *Operations Carried On at the Pyramids of Gizeh in 1837,* from 1840 (fig. A2.18, p. 256, *left*). A comparison of this inscription with the one from Perring's *The Pyramids of Gizeh,* from

Figure A2.18. Two separate lithographic prints were made of the upside-down gang sign (indicated by arrows): left, *from Vyse's* Operations Carried On at the Pyramids of Gizeh *(1840), and* right, *from Perring's* The Pyramids of Gizeh *(1839).*

1839 (fig. A2.18, *right*), shows some minor differences in the rendering of the drawings, thereby indicating the use of two separate lithographs.

If we are to imagine that two different lithographic plates were produced using just one original source—Perring's drawing—then just how likely is it that the lithographer(s), working for hours on each of the two different lithographic plates, somehow imagined the upside-down gang sign on two occasions in Perring's drawing? This is surely highly unlikely indeed, and, as such, on the balance of probability, we must conclude that Perring *did* make at least one actual drawing (possibly even two—one copy for Vyse's use and another for Perring's own book) in which this upside-down gang sign *was* present in his original artwork. This was *not* a mistake by the lithographers: they would have copied and produced exactly what they saw in Perring's original source drawing(s).

And so, if this cannot have been a mistake by the lithographers and we accept that Perring made a true and accurate copy of the signs he observed on that wall block in Lady Arbuthnot's Chamber (possibly two copies), then the subsequent and mysterious disappearance of this bizarrely placed, upside-down hieratic gang sign (its disappearance being verified by no less than five people in 1837 and subsequently also by Alan Rowe in 1924) must surely set alarm bells ringing. There is surely something very seriously amiss here.

An Arabic Hand

But if these marks *were* faked by Vyse's assistants (on the colonel's instruction), how did such a glaring mistake come to be made in the first place and how did the upside-down gang sign come to be present in Perring's drawing and then become absent from Hill's (and Alan Rowe's)?

There is another possible explanation.

Virtually all of the painted marks in the Vyse Chambers are presented either upside down or sideways on the wall blocks. Indeed, this inscription is the only one in all the Vyse Chambers that is presented on the stone in an upright manner. Of course, statistically speaking, we would surely expect to observe some inscriptions on these wall blocks presented in an upright manner. Indeed, were we to have found no inscriptions presented in the upright manner, then this would surely have been considered an anomaly. Perhaps what we are witnessing with this upright inscription is just such a statistical realization having dawned on the forger of these wall marks: he needed to present at least one inscription in the upright manner.

If we were to imagine that Vyse employed a local Egyptian to copy this particular inscription onto this wall block (as evidence in Nelson's Chamber analyzed earlier in this book also suggests) and that this Egyptian began copying the inscription onto the wall using an upside-down master source, then, being Arabic and writing from right to left (and top to bottom), the first sign he naturally would have copied onto the wall block would have been the upside-down gang sign (fig. A2.19, p. 258).

However, it seems that after painting the first sign onto the wall—the upside-down gang sign—the forger changed his mind (perhaps realizing the statistical issue mentioned above), rotated his master source 180°, and began again, now copying all of the signs upright onto the wall block (fig. A2.20), resulting in the sign for "gang" being presented twice on the second row of the inscription and oriented in two different directions. The Arabic forger would, of course, have been fully aware of his upside-down "false start" sign and would have likely planned that this now superfluous and erroneous sign would be removed from the wall block some time later (perhaps with a chisel or sandpaper), thereby resulting in the inordinate amount of white space to the right of the inscription.

Alas, however, before the forger got around to removing the

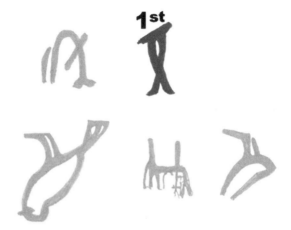

*Figure A2.19. Proposed master source inscription (upside down).
Were this inscription copied with this orientation onto a wall
by an Egyptian employee of Vyse, then, being Arabic and writing
from right to left and top to bottom, the first sign he would have
copied onto the wall block would have been the upside-down
gang sign (top right).*

superfluous and erroneous gang sign, unbeknownst to him, Perring, as part of his ongoing survey of the chamber marks, entered Lady Arbuthnot's Chamber and made his own copy of this group of signs, including the duplicate upside-down gang sign that had not yet been removed. The forger would likely have arrived a short time after Perring to remove the "false start" sign, perhaps unaware that Perring had already copied all the signs from this wall block. It may also be that the forger *did* know that Perring had copied the duplicate gang sign but was reluctant to say anything to him about it lest the fraudulent activity he was engaged in be revealed to Perring.*

---

*This may explain why Perring was not present at the attestation of Hill's facsimile copies of the quarry marks on May 19. It was perhaps feared that Perring might have brought along his own drawings of these painted marks to compare with Hill's and that he would undoubtedly have spotted the sign now missing from the chamber wall and would perhaps have begun asking awkward questions in the presence of Sir Robert Arbuthnot, who, speculatively, may have previously seen Vyse being subjected to some very awkward questions about the marks in this chamber from Witness M on May 10, 1837.

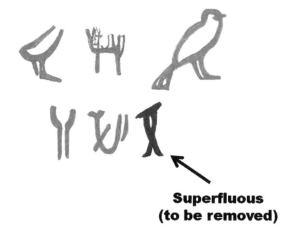

**Superfluous
(to be removed)**

*Figure A2.20. Having copied the initial sign onto the
wall block upside down, the forger seems to have changed his
mind, rotated his master source 180°, and began again, copying all
the now upright signs onto the block, resolving to have his
"false start," the initial upside-down sign,
removed from the block at a later time.*

With the duplicate gang sign now removed, Hill then entered the chamber shortly afterward and made his own facsimile copy of the block inscription, now minus the superfluous upside-down gang sign (see fig. A2.14, p. 252) and, in so doing, created the contradiction that we observe today between his copy of these marks and that of Perring.

If this hypothesis is correct, then what we have here is further evidence of a local Egyptian Arabic writer having been employed by Vyse to copy marks onto the walls of both Nelson's and Lady Arbuthnot's Chambers. But more than that, the evidence of this particular inscription strongly suggests that this Egyptian used a master source (a guide or template) from which to copy these inscriptions onto the various wall blocks in these chambers. A master source initially being held upside down (to create the illusion of authenticity) explains why the gang sign (see fig. A2.20, *bottom right*) is transposed to the top-right position (see fig. A2.19) and, as such, would be copied first by an Arabic hand when, in natural hieratic writing convention, it should have been written last.

An ancient Egyptian scribe would have had little need for any master source; he would simply have painted the upright inscription straight onto the block from memory and without any false starts.

To reiterate, the only feasible way that this gang sign would appear twice on this block with two different orientations, at the bottom left and bottom right of this inscription (as presented in Perring's drawing, see fig. A2.12, p. 250), is to propose that two separate attempts were made at painting this particular group of signs onto the wall block from a master source that was initially oriented upside down and subsequently rotated to be upright. Had this inscription been created by an ancient Egyptian scribe, it is unlikely that we would have ever seen two gang signs with two different orientations present on the block. Being at the quarry and having full access to the stone, it would have been easy enough for such an ancient scribe to simply use and incorporate any upside-down gang sign (if such had been placed onto the block) into the intended inscription by painting the remaining signs with the appropriate orientation above and to the right of the already existing gang sign. By using an existing gang sign in the intended inscription, there is no need to draw a second gang sign on the stone or, indeed, to remove any erroneous signs from it. In short, it is highly unlikely that such a situation of two gang signs with two different orientations being present in one inscription (as we observe in Perring's drawing) could have arisen in an ancient Egyptian quarry.

What this evidence seems to demonstrate is a deliberate act of copying an upside-down sign onto this block of stone. Given that there is no plausible reason whatsoever for an ancient Egyptian scribe to paint signs in this manner onto any block, then we must conclude that this was the action of a modern forger making two separate attempts at copying this inscription from a master source onto the chamber wall. And with the change of mind in the orientation of the inscription, it then became necessary to later remove the initial upside-down gang sign, the false start, and that is precisely what we observe in Hill's and Rowe's drawings of this inscription. The forger of this inscription clearly knew which sign was a duplicate, and that is why that particular sign was subsequently removed from the chamber wall. In short, what we are witnessing here is clear evidence of blatant fraud—pure and simple.

A Reconstruction

And so, using information from Vyse's private journal along with that in his published account, it now becomes possible to reconstruct a tentative, hypothetical sequence of the full events at Giza during the period of May 6 to May 10, 1837.

MAY 6

- Vyse opens his third chamber (yet to be named) and, along with Raven, enters and explores it but finds nothing—no secret burial of Khufu, no treasure, and not a single quarry mark (because there are no quarry marks present on any wall block at this time).
- Before leaving for Cairo, Vyse gives one of his Egyptian workers a set of quarry marks from his secret cache, instructing him to paint the marks, large and bold, onto some wall blocks in Lady Arbuthnot's Chamber.
- Shortly after Vyse and his assistants had departed for Cairo, Witness M enters the newly opened chamber, perhaps to store his tools for the night. He has a look around and, just like Vyse and Raven earlier, he finds nothing.

MAY 7

- In Cairo, Vyse calls on Colonel Patrick Campbell and is introduced to Sir Robert and Lady Arbuthnot, both of whom express great interest in Vyse's explorations at the pyramids. Vyse tells them of his discoveries thus far but says nothing of having already entered the new chamber, perhaps telling them that he expects to breach it soon. (He needs time to have his Egyptian worker paint the fake marks into the chamber and to have his work checked).

MAY 8

- In Lady Arbuthnot's Chamber Vyse's Egyptian worker, as instructed, begins painting fake marks onto a number of wall blocks using Vyse's secret cache as his guide. On one of the blocks he begins painting a group of signs upside-down. Having painted the first sign, he changes his mind and rotates his master guide 180° and begins painting the same signs upright, resolving to come back the following day to remove his initial upside-down sign from the block.

- Vyse calls again on Sir Robert and Lady Arbuthnot as he has had an idea, and they talk. The colonel invites the Arbuthnots to visit the Great Pyramid on May 10 to be among the first visitors into the new chamber, which he tells them is certain to have been opened by then. (It's already open.) He asks Sir Robert if he would act as a witness to the discovery of the quarry marks in the chambers thus far opened and perhaps other marks in the new chamber if any are discovered when the chamber is finally breached, and in return for this service, he offers to name the new chamber after Sir Robert. Sir Robert is flattered by Vyse's generous offer but agrees to the colonel's request only on the condition that the new chamber be named in his wife's honor, a condition that Vyse gladly accepts. The colonel now has a reputable and distinguished witness ready to testify to the authenticity of his discoveries.

- Vyse and his assistants return to Giza from Cairo late that afternoon.

MAY 9

- Early in the day, Raven and Hill enter Lady Arbuthnot's Chamber to check upon the progress of Vyse's Egyptian worker. (Vyse should have gone with them too, but he was unwell.) The Egyptian is nowhere to be seen but his handiwork is now plainly evident on the chamber walls. The two men inspect his work and decide that some of the fake marks needed repainting to make them bolder and clearer and so they set about this task, perhaps adding some fake marks of their own.

- Later, (with the "inspection" of Lady Arbuthnot's Chamber now complete), Vyse then instructs Mr. Perring to begin a survey of all the quarry marks in the Great Pyramid, beginning with Lady Arbuthnot's Chamber.

- Some hours later, after Perring had completed his survey of the quarry marks in Lady Arbuthnot's Chamber, Vyse's Egyptian worker returns to the empty chamber and chisels away the erroneous upside-down sign from the wall block, unaware that it had already been copied by Perring earlier that day.

- The Arbuthnots arrive at Vyse's encampment. Vyse tells them that their timing is excellent as the new chamber had just been opened and that a great many quarry marks had been discovered on its walls, which he would like them to witness.

- After dinner that evening, the Arbuthnots agree to the wording of the dedication inscription, and Vyse sends Hill to the Great Pyramid to paint the inscription onto a chamber wall in order that his guests might witness it during their visit the following day, making sure that the dedication text bears that day's date (May 9) as the chamber's opening date. He also asks Hill to bring back facsimile copies (in the original size) of some of the chamber inscriptions discovered earlier that day so that the Arbuthnots might witness them on the very day of their "discovery."

- Meanwhile Witness M comes again to deposit his tools in Lady Arbuthnot's Chamber after the day's work. He is utterly shocked to see that three walls of the chamber are now resplendent with a profusion of fraudulently painted hieroglyphic marks. As he is about to leave, Hill arrives to paint the dedication inscription (and make his facsimile copies). Witness M tells Hill that he suspects the painted hieroglyphic marks on the chamber walls are fraudulent as he had not noticed them before, and perhaps further states that he suspects Raven of perpetrating the fraud as, earlier that day, he saw Raven exiting the pyramid, carrying a bucket of red ochre paint and some brushes. Hill is taken aback and answers that he knows nothing of this. Witness M further tells Hill that, back in February, Prince Pückler-Muskau had confided in him that he suspected Vyse was planning to place fraudulent marks within the chambers. Again, Hill refuses to engage in the discussion, perhaps suggesting that Witness M take his concerns directly to the colonel.

- Upon returning from the pyramid, Hill gives Vyse his facsimile copies of the painted marks (now minus the superfluous upside-down sign that Perring had managed to copy before Vyse's Egyptian worker had it removed.) He also relays the suspicions of Witness M to Vyse, to which the colonel euphemistically writes in his private journal that Witness M "is very curious." Curious about what? The colonel doesn't say, but his very next thought is to recollect a conversation from February of that year in which Pückler-Muskau—even before any chamber had been opened—said that Vyse would find an inscription in an apartment. Vyse is perhaps wondering here just how much the Prussian prince knew of his plans and whether he was the source of Witness M's "curiosity" (seemingly of the quarry marks in Lady Arbuthnot's Chamber). However, the die was cast. The quarry marks and dedication inscription had already been painted onto the chamber walls and the Arbuthnots invited to visit the pyramid the following day. There was no going back for Vyse now, even if he had wanted to.

MAY 10

- Sir Robert and Lady Arbuthnot go to the Great Pyramid while Vyse remains behind. They return some time later and go to their tent to escape the hot weather.
- Having mulled things over through the night and seeing no action from Vyse, Witness M decides to take matters into his own hands. Later that afternoon, in Vyse's encampment, he seeks out and challenges Raven directly, accusing him (and possibly also Hill) of painting fake marks onto the walls of Lady Arbuthnot's Chamber. An almighty quarrel erupts between Raven and Witness M. Raven claims he was merely painting over faint marks that were already present on the stones, simply to make them clearer. But this is countered by Witness M who insists that there were no signs present on any chamber wall days earlier and that these marks were new. The argument rages on in full earshot of Vyse, the Arbuthnots, and probably also a certain Humphries Brewer. Witness M further insists to the assembled onlookers that the chamber had been opened and inspected by Vyse and Raven on May 6, three days previously, that no quarry marks had been reported to have been found by either of them during their initial inspection, and that Vyse had used the intervening days to have Raven (and perhaps Hill) place fraudulent marks into the chamber, then had Hill paint a false opening date of May 9 onto the chamber wall so that there would be no time lag between the chamber being opened and the painted marks supposedly being

discovered. Witness M demands of Raven to admit that this is the truth. Raven, seeing that the Arbuthnots were looking on at the spectacle from their nearby tent, waiting for him to respond, can only look to Vyse for guidance.

- Vyse, horrified by what Witness M had revealed to his distinguished guests, the Arbuthnots, intervenes and instantly dismisses the man from his service, charging him with scurrilous and outrageous accusations and of behavior thoroughly unbecoming of a gentleman.
- A short time later, the colonel, realizing the Arbuthnots had been witnesses to the allegations made by Witness M, invites them both for a walk, possibly to smooth things over and explain to them the "truth" of the situation with the newly opened chamber. But it would seem that the strength of Witness M's allegation was too overwhelming for Vyse to dismiss outright the man's claim that the chamber had actually been opened and explored days earlier, on May 6. He explains away this discrepancy perhaps by telling the Arbuthnots that the chamber had only been partially opened and was not easily accessible on May 6. He insists that the chamber was only fully accessible on May 9 and that this is why he had Hill paint the later date onto the chamber wall. A barely credible fudge. He explains further that because he was needed in Cairo on the evening of May 6, he and Raven were able only to make a short inspection of the chamber and that there was no time to inspect the chamber walls more thoroughly at that time for any painted markings. He adds, however, that the chamber walls were minutely examined on May 9 by Raven and Hill, and upon the second inspection, a great many quarry marks were then found. The Arbuthnots smile politely at Vyse's explanation and thank him again for naming the chamber in Lady Arbuthnot's honor.
- Humphries Brewer, a witness to the altercation and the accusations of fraud being made by Witness M against Raven (and possibly also Hill), would report the incident to his family back in England, telling them what he had witnessed that fateful day, writing ". . . had dispute with Raven and Hill . . . faint marks were repainted, some were new."

MAY 19

- Sir Robert Arbuthnot, in attendance with some other witnesses, testifies to the accuracy of the facsimile drawings of the chamber marks made by Hill. He notices that in Lady Arbuthnot's Chamber, the dedication inscription still reads "May 9th, 1837," as does the date on all of Hill's various drawings from this chamber. He quietly suggests to Vyse that the true opening date of the chamber (May 6, 1837) be recorded in the colonel's future publication. Vyse nods in subdued acquiescence to this. Sir Robert then adds his signature to Hill's drawings.

Such *might* have been the scene at Giza during those five highly charged days in May 1837. With this altercation exploding in Vyse's face, and most likely in full public view of Sir Robert and Lady Arbuthnot who were in their nearby tent, then whatever was said in the heated exchange between Witness M and Raven seems to have made it impossible for Vyse to later claim (in his published account) that Lady Arbuthnot's Chamber was first opened and entered on May 9, and neither was it now possible for him to claim (as he had likely planned) that the painted quarry marks had been discovered on the same day the chamber was first opened (now May 6). And neither could he now backfill his May 6 published entry to say that the quarry marks had been discovered on this earlier date (as he had done with Nelson's Chamber). It was too late as he had likely already declared to the Arbuthnots (and others) that the quarry marks in this chamber had been discovered on May 9 after a second inspection and, as such, would have been deeply suspicious to also retract and alter this.

Were Vyse to have continued fully with his plan in his official account, claiming that the chamber had been opened on May 9 and the quarry marks discovered also on this day, then the Arbuthnots, upon reading such an account and then recalling the dispute of May 10 between Witness M and Raven, and Vyse's subsequent walk with them, would surely have known the claim to be false and quite possibly could have called Vyse out on it. Vyse simply could not take such a risk and, it seems, was forced by circumstances beyond his control (whatever was revealed during the quarrel between Witness M and Raven) to curtail his plan and revert in his published account to the true opening date of the chamber—May 6, 1837.

Having been forced by unforeseen events to abort the May 9 opening date, and unable to retract the "discovery" date of the chamber's quarry marks from this day, the marks were then left high and dry with a highly peculiar and unrealistic time lag of three days before their discovery. To explain away this peculiarity, Vyse concocts what can only be described as a barely credible cover story: that this chamber (unlike the others) somehow required a second minute examination on May 9 before any of its numerous, large painted hieroglyphic marks could be found; marks whose presence, by this time, would have been entirely anticipated by Vyse and Raven in this near identical chamber, and thus should have been no more difficult to discover during the first inspection than those found in the chambers below.

Had the quarrel with Witness M and Raven never occurred, then the true opening date of the chamber on May 6 would likely have never been revealed to the Arbuthnots (and other possible witnesses) and in that scenario, Vyse's published volume would almost certainly have declared to the world that the opening of this chamber and the discovery of the painted marks therein had occurred on the very same day, May 9, 1837. The key events of May 6 would have been airbrushed out; we were simply never meant to know the true opening date of this chamber.

Complicating matters further for Vyse was the publication of Perring's account in 1839, a year before Vyse published. Here Perring states that Lady Arbuthnot's Chamber was opened on May 6. Consequently, Vyse was likely forced to revert to this true date, and also to misreport the chamber inscription date as May 6 to ensure there was no contradiction in his book, lest he face some awkward questions. In short, a cover up.

The dedication inscription that we observe today on the south wall of Lady Arbuthnot's Chamber bearing the date of May 9 speaks against the truth of the events at Giza in May 1837 and stands in silent testimony to the planned deception of Vyse, which, as a result of unforeseen events, was partially aborted by him. The legacy of this botched deception is there to see also in the facsimile sheets from this chamber drawn by Hill. Unsurprisingly, the colonel makes no mention of nor attempts to explain anywhere in his published account the contradictory May 9 date Hill had painted into Lady Arbuthnot's Chamber and onto his six facsimile sheets, which Vyse witnessed and signed. This glaring contradiction is completely and—one has to suspect—conveniently ignored by him. As well it might, for to have presented the chamber's contradictory May 9 opening date in his published account would have required Vyse to offer a full and cogent explanation for its occurrence, a situation that appears to have proved just too awkward and difficult a task for the colonel to even attempt. A case of "least said, soonest mended," in the hope that no one would ever notice his false reporting of the evidence and join up the dots.

What may also be significant and somewhat revealing in all of this is the fact that in Vyse's published account we learn that, for various reasons, he discharged a total of four men from his service throughout the course of his operations at Giza, all of which he recounts and clearly documents. However, this fifth incident of a worker being discharged on May 10 that we read of in the colonel's private account has, somewhat curiously, been entirely expunged from his official narrative. There is not a single word spoken of this particular incident in any of Vyse's three published volumes, and we are surely entitled to ponder why he would opt not to publicly document any of the circumstances around the dismissal of Witness M. Was this incident of May 10, 1837, so bad, so highly controversial, so personally detrimental, incriminating, and damaging to Vyse's reputation and work that he felt compelled to exclude it entirely from his published version of events at Giza?

Crew Cuts

In her book *Egyptian Phyles in the Old Kingdom,* the Egyptologist Ann Macy Roth presents a hypothesis that describes the organization of labor during the time the Great Pyramid was being built (and beyond). Roth proposes that these phyles (part-time groups of workers in the service of the king and/or other senior officials) were subdivided into smaller crews, gangs, and divisions to effect the task of constructing various ancient monuments. Each of these work gangs would have its own unique name, and often one of the king's various names would form a part of the gang's own name, such as, for example, the Friends of Khufu gang or the Drunkards of Menkaure gang.

From Roth's study, it seems that the names painted onto the quarried and dressed stones we observe in some of these ancient monuments were those of the gangs whose responsibility it was to actually maneuver and set into its final position each stone within a particular construction, be it a mastaba, temple, palace, pyramid, or whatever. So while these marks, it seems, were painted onto the finished blocks at the quarry, these inscriptions were not the gang names of the quarry laborers or masons working there, but rather appear to have served as a sort of "delivery address" for the installation gangs at the actual construction site. Roth explains:

> The geological layering in these blocks shows that they were frequently placed together in the temple wall just as they had been in the earth. In some cases one can see a vein of softer rock running the length of a wall. These core blocks were generally laid in segments, having previously been fitted together, probably at the quarry. The simplest procedure would have been to fit together a row of blocks that had been quarried from the same area. At this point, each of the series of fitted blocks would have been marked with the hieroglyph of the division that was responsible for placing the block correctly in the temple.[18]

As implied in Roth's statement, it would make sense that a mason's yard would be close to each of the various quarries (of which there were several along the length of the Nile), ready to receive each roughly hewn stone from the quarry laborers, whereupon a team of stonemasons would then set about sizing and shaping the stone to a regular block of a required size—each stone made to measure and to fit within the overall dimensions of a particular structure, such as a chamber wall.

Having the stones cut and shaped at or close to the quarry would, naturally, be much more efficient in terms of the transportation of any given block, a sizable number of which would have to travel many miles down the Nile, across the desert, and then up the steep pyramid slope itself. It makes no sense to haul large, uncut, and unfinished blocks any considerable distance, when hauling a smaller, finished stone would be easier and waste fewer resources. Thus, we can be fairly certain that only dressed blocks (stones cut to a required size and shape), having been appropriately "addressed" with the relevant installation gang's name painted onto the block, would have been sent up to the working level of the pyramid and, after installation, smoothed and polished as necessary.

It makes sense, of course, to address each stone only after the masons had completed their cutting and shaping work and the block was ready to be dispatched. Prematurely painting the addressee's name onto unfinished blocks makes little sense since, as the stone is still being worked, any painted marks made on the stone at this early stage could become scuffed and worn, parts of the addressee's gang name could end up having to be cut off to bring the stone to a particular length or height, or the team waiting to receive the stones could have been moved to another part of the construction site or even rotated out of service by the time the block was ready for dispatch. In such cases, the stone might still be going to the same physical location but the addressee's name would now need to be changed to reflect the name of the new gang now working at the intended destination. So, as previously stated, best then that addressing the stone with painted marks was done only after the stone was finished and ready for dispatch. Perhaps the addressee's name would even need to be checked at this stage to ensure the intended installation gang was still present at the delivery location.

Upon a stone's arriving at its intended location in the pyramid, it is reasonable to expect that some level of refinement might have been required for a particular block, but this would likely, by this time, have been only very minor adjustments. Having already (one must presume) been correctly measured, shaped, sized, and checked at the quarry before being dispatched, then, all things being equal, there should have been little need, at this stage, for any major reworking of the stones during their final installation at the pyramid.

In the mortuary temple of Menkaure at Giza, which Roth describes at length in her book, we find around thirteen examples of the gang name the Drunkards of Menkaure and two of the Friends of Menkaure—a total of fifteen gang inscriptions. Each of these gang names was carefully copied from the temple blocks by Alan Rowe when he was exploring the temple with George Reisner in the 1930s. Rowe's drawings of these gang names (figs. A2.21a and A2.21b), while not always showing the actual orientation of a particular group of signs, nevertheless are careful to show where lines have been slightly scuffed (which he completes with a dotted line) or where signs have been entirely worn away (which he indicates with the lighter shading.

What is immediately noticeable about the fifteen gang name sketches made by Rowe from the blocks in this temple is that not a

Figure A2.21a. The gang name Drunkards of Menkaure.

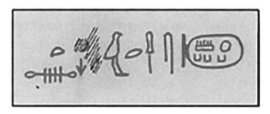

Figure A2.21b. The gang name Friends of Menkaure.

single one of them is presented with any loss of the gang name due to cutting or trimming of the particular block, either vertically or horizontally, suggesting that these painted delivery addresses of the installation gangs had been, as Roth proposes, painted onto the blocks only after the block was finished by the stonemasons at the quarry and was ready to be dispatched to the installation crews at the temple.

It seems that, upon arriving at Menkaure's temple installation site, there was little need for further cutting of the wall blocks, as evidenced by the completeness of the painted gang inscriptions and as we might expect to find. As such then, theoretically at least, we should expect to find a similar completeness with regard to the painted gang names in the Vyse Chambers of the Great Pyramid. However, a cursory examination of the painted gang names on the blocks in these chambers, from drawings of the marks made by Perring,* presents us with a quite different and somewhat perplexing picture.

Roth explains that a line of blocks, such as those forming a course

---

*The reader should be mindful that the drawings of the wall markings in these chambers made by Perring and Hill (and later by Rowe) are but impressions of the actual wall markings as observed by these men; they are not photographs nor, indeed, of photographic quality. It is assumed here, however, that the key features in their drawings are sufficiently detailed and accurate enough for the purposes of this particular inquiry.

layer of a wall, would likely have been placed together in segments at the quarry. For the purposes of checking the bedding layers and the overall height of a particular wall, this would have been a necessary, practical, and commonsense approach. And given the different bedding layers in the walls of Lady Arbutnot's Chamber, it would likely have required that the different courses were actually laid one atop the other or perhaps simply laid tight against each other on their sides at the quarry in order to check that the wall was of the required, preordered height and was consistent in this height along its full length. Having made these checks, and with everything in order, the wall blocks would then be individually addressed and duly dispatched to the installers up at the pyramid, ready to be set in place without too much fuss. At least, in theory.

On the north wall of Lady Arbuthnot's Chamber, we find a total of seven examples of the gang that called itself the Powerful White Crown of Khnum-Khufu. Two examples of this gang name appear on the chamber wall blocks sideways, while the remaining five examples appear on the blocks upside down. Of the seven blocks on which these gang names appear, we find that five of them, somewhat bizarrely, appear to have been significantly reworked upon arriving at their final destination at the pyramid, suggesting that the stonemasons down at the quarry, for some unfathomable reason, made a complete mess of measuring, shaping, and cutting the various blocks—stonemasons who, we must assume by this time, had considerable experience in cutting the blocks for the three similarly sized chambers below Lady Arbuthnot's.

On two of the five reworked blocks (and on two different course layers), we find clear evidence of parts of painted gang names having been truncated horizontally along the top of the block (figs. A2.22a and A2.22b), suggesting that a sizeable chunk at the top of these blocks was removed post-dressing (upon their arrival at the pyramid for installation).

On the three remaining reworked blocks, it seems that the gang name has been truncated slightly on the left side of the block, suggesting these blocks were shortened vertically with a cut down their left side, seemingly at some point after arriving at the pyramid for installation.

That we apparently have so many gang names cut off on the wall blocks in this chamber when, at least in theory, we shouldn't be finding any makes little sense and, given the observations from Menkaure's

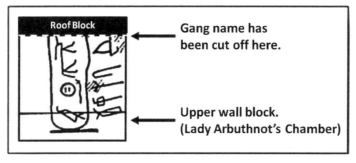

Figure A2.22a. The top part of this gang name on an upper-layer wall block in Lady Arbuthnot's Chamber has been cut off in order to properly fit the block into the chamber wall.

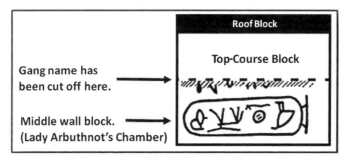

Figure A2.22b. The top part of this gang name on a middle-layer wall block in Lady Arbuthnot's Chamber has been cut off in order to properly fit the block into the chamber wall.

mortuary temple, appears to run entirely contrary to what we might have expected to find. In short, what we have here is yet another anomaly. And when we consider this anomaly in a bit more depth, we find it becomes even more peculiar than at first glance.

If we first consider the upper masonry (fig. A2.23, next page, *blocks a* and *b*), we notice that block *b*, placed to the immediate upper right of block *a*, sits on a slightly higher bedding layer. In order to fit block *b* (with the cut crew name) into the wall with the required height, it appears that block *a* required a small L-shaped notch to be cut from its top-right corner to make a level bedding layer for block *b*. It stands to reason that in cutting this notch to create a level bedding layer for the upper blocks, the stonemasons doing this would have known at this time:

**Cartouche cut off indicating the top of the block was
cut again after the gang name was painted onto the block.**

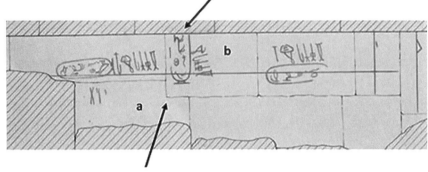

**L-shaped notch cut in lower block to
prepare bedding layer of upper block.**

*Figure A2.23. Particular wall blocks of Lady Arbuthnot's Chamber
where an L-shaped notch has been cut.*

1. The distance (height) from this bedding level to the underside of the chamber ceiling.
2. The height of block *b* (at that time and presumably before the top was trimmed off).

Given that the builders would have known these variables, then surely, simply cutting a slightly deeper bedding layer (which had to be cut anyway) in the lower layer of blocks would have entirely eliminated the need to also slice a chunk off the top of the upper blocks (fig. A2.24). By not cutting the slightly deeper bedding layer in the lower blocks, the builders effectively gave themselves double the work. And that makes no sense whatsoever.

But when we now consider the middle row of blocks in this chamber wall, things become even more peculiar, whereby we find another stone where an entire row of signs forming part of the gang name has been sliced away (fig. A2.25, *block 1*), suggesting that the top part of this stone was also cut away after the stone had been finished and dispatched from the quarry (upon arriving at the pyramid for installation).

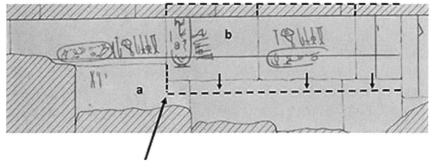

Had a deeper L-shaped notch been cut in the lower block (a) (creating a deeper bedding layer) this would have eliminated the need for the upper blocks to be cut again.

Figure A2.24. By failing to cut a deeper bedding layer in the lower blocks, the builders gave themselves double the work.

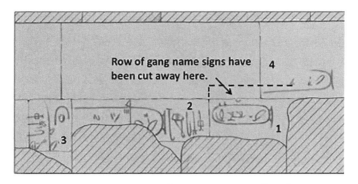

Figure A2.25. An entire row of gang name signs has been cut away from the top of block 1.

This suggests that the height of block 1 (and presumably all of the blocks in this bedding layer) had to be trimmed down by a substantial amount, probably somewhere between six to twelve inches, or possibly more, in order to lower the upper layer of blocks and bring the wall height down to the desired level. Except, however, this error then becomes compounded by the fact that the top row of blocks *also* appears to have required a reduction in height, which raises the very obvious question, Why cut the blocks in both rows? If it was found that this preassembled wall, upon reassembly at the pyramid, needed to be lowered in height by a certain amount, then why give yourself double the work by reducing the height of two rows of wall blocks (presumably by similar smaller amounts) when reducing the height of just one row (by the required total amount) would have achieved the same end result?

A similar situation also arises with the painted marks on blocks 2, 3, and 4, all of which appear to have been slightly truncated on their left side, perhaps indicating that the length of these preassembled wall blocks had to be shortened after having arrived at the pyramid for reassembly. Once again, however, it makes little sense to shorten the length of two separate blocks sitting on the same course level by smaller amounts when shortening just one of them by the required larger amount would have achieved the same result for half the effort.

All of which raises the obvious questions: How is it possible that the stonemasons at the quarry who originally measured and cut the blocks to make up this chamber wall appear to have gotten it so terribly wrong, both in terms of height and length? Are we to believe that they were so utterly incompetent in measuring and cutting these wall blocks to assemble a wall of a required dimension that many of the blocks had to be reworked upon arriving for installation at the pyramid? And to compound matters, when the blocks finally reached the pyramid and it was noticed that the wall was too high and too wide, why did the stonemasons there cut *two* courses of blocks by smaller amounts instead of the more efficient single, larger cut to the relevant blocks? It is seemingly incompetence laid upon incompetence by skilled workers who had, as stated earlier, already successfully completed three chambers of similar dimensions, so we have to assume that they knew what they were doing and that they had, by this time, developed the best and most efficient means of achieving their objective.

Now, there may very well be some set of circumstances that can somehow bring all of the above anomalous observations into a perfectly rational explanation, such as, for example, the repurposing of blocks from some other construction that had previously been abandoned but that still bore the names of the gang that had originally been designated to set those blocks in place. Perhaps this other theorized construction required larger wall blocks, and, once they were abandoned, these larger blocks were simply scavenged and cut down to the required size in the mason's yard at the quarry to suit the smaller dimensions of the new wall in Lady Arbuthnot's Chamber, thereby perhaps explaining the truncated nature of the gang names we see today in Perring's and Rowe's drawings of the painted block marks in this chamber.

While this explanation remains possible, it has to be said that there are many questions and complications in this scenario that render it unlikely, not least of which is the presence of the many other and more difficult to explain anomalies that we find associated with these very same painted marks in this chamber and in the other Vyse Chambers. Given all of this, then the more likely explanation here is that what we may actually be witnessing is nothing more than the further handiwork of a small group of determined and devious fraudsters. If a fraudster wanted to give the impression that the painted markings on these wall blocks were truly ancient, then what better way to achieve this than by painting the gang names onto the blocks in the truncated manner that we observe them? This gives the impression that the gang name must have been cut off when the block was *first cut* at the quarry, ergo giving the illusion that the painted marks are contemporary with the original block cut and thus that the marks themselves must be genuine artifacts from the time of the pyramid's construction. It is an ingenious illusion, for sure, but all things considered, almost certainly not something the builders would ever likely have done.

CAMPBELL'S CHAMBER'S ODD NUMBERS

As explained in chapter 5, early hieratic letters and numerals essentially consisted of cursively painted equivalents of the sculpted hieroglyphic signs, and, as such, their early orthography was not so far removed from their counterpart sculpted signs, although, as the millennia passed, the two forms would diverge greatly from each other. One of the key differences between the early hieratic script and its sculpted hieroglyphic equivalent is that hieratic script (like that allegedly discovered in the Vyse Chambers) would always be written and read only from right to left—never from left to right. On the other hand, monumental sculpted hieroglyphics could be written and read from left or right, and the flow of the reading for a particular line of hieroglyphic text would usually be indicated by the direction in which some animal or person in the script was facing. Both forms would also be read from top to bottom.

In 1837, hieratic script was barely understood and most certainly would not have been known to Vyse, let alone understood by him. Vyse, as we see from his published works, regarded the script in these chambers merely as painted hieroglyphics (by the quarry gangs) rather than painted hieratic marks. This is to say that Vyse would wrongly have believed these hieratic marks were but painted hieroglyphics and, as such, could be written and read from *either* direction—a lack of knowledge that was to bring Vyse into making a grave error in forging some hieratic number signs onto the roof blocks in Campbell's Chamber.

To anyone viewing these painted numbers they will immediately observe that they are upside down. The conventional explanation for this apparent haphazard arrangement of these signs (and the signs throughout these small chambers) is that the marks would have been painted onto each block upright at the quarry and that the builders of these chambers, upon receiving the pre-shaped blocks, would have rotated the blocks to find the most efficient means of placing each within the chamber, a notion that runs contrary to Roth's theory that the walls would have been preassembled at the quarry and the gang's name painted onto each block at that time. Given also the particular shape of these roof blocks in Campbell's chamber, there is actually only *one* way that they could have been installed. It is further worth noting here that were all of these blocks in all the Vyse Chambers oriented with their writing the right way up, we would find that all the text from all these chambers has been written onto each block in a right-to-left manner, as was customary with hieratic script. In this regard, Hans Goedicke writes, "The individual signs, when determinable face right. This direction becomes universal for all practical purposes; there is one hieratic inscription dating to the sixth dynasty which is written facing left."[19]

In hieratic script, a vertical stroke | symbolizes the value 1 while a ∩ sign symbolizes the value 10, thus | | ∩ = 12 and | | | ∩ ∩ = 23. In

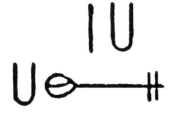

Figure A2.26. Hieratic number sign for the number 21 painted onto the roof blocks of Campbell's Chamber showing the actual upside-down orientations (Image based on original by Alan Rowe, 1931)

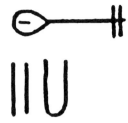

Figure A2.27. Hieratic number sign for the number 12 painted onto the roof blocks of Campbell's Chamber. (Image based on original by Alan Rowe, 1931)

hieratic numbers the units with the highest numerical value are always placed to the right of the units with lower values (the highest values are always placed farthest right and read first). And this is where we see Vyse made a grave mistake, for if we rotate the painted hieratic numbers in these chambers so that they become upright, what we then find is that the lower unit value (|) has been incorrectly placed to the *right* of the higher ∩ value, which has been incorrectly placed to the left (fig. A2.28), meaning that the lower value will be read first, and that is simply wrong in hieratic script.

Critics of the fraud theory have proposed that these back-to-front numbers were actually intended to be read sideways, from top to bottom (fig. A2.29). In this top-down reading of the sideways-rotated number sign, then the higher unit value (the ∩) is now placed above the lower unit values and thus read first.

However, there are considerable problems with this proposal. When we consider all of the other signs painted onto the blocks within the various

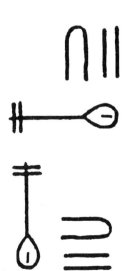

Figure A2.28. Rotating the numbers upright shows that this number on the roof block of Campbell's Chamber has been incorrectly written with the higher value placed to the left instead of to the right. (Image based on original by Alan Rowe, 1931)

Figure A2.29. It has been proposed that the hieratic signs can be rotated sideways in order to fix the anomalous order in which the sign is read when upright. (Image based on original by Alan Rowe, 1931)

Vyse Chambers and how they would have originally been painted upright onto the blocks when at the quarry, we find that every line of text has been written linearly, right to left and *not* top to bottom. This proposal asks us to accept that the quarry scribes were writing their signs, without exception, onto the blocks in these chambers horizontally, but for these particular number signs, for some inexplicable reason, they decided to change to writing their signs onto the blocks vertically. This seems highly unlikely.

This observation aside, it is known that the ancient Egyptians did actually write hieratic numbers sideways in the manner shown in figure A2.29, but this, however, was only ever done when writing calendar days of the month. In his book *Numerical Notation: A Comparative History,* Stephen Chrisomalis writes, "When used to express days of the month, hieratic numerals, like hieroglyphic numerals, were often rotated ninety degrees counterclockwise to reflect their function. Given the nature of the Egyptian calendar, these forms exist only for numerals less than 30."[20]

However, when expressing calendar days, these number signs are *always* accompanied by the solar disc sign to signify the function of the number signs (i.e., that they reflect the ordinal days of the month rather than a cardinal number; fig. A2.30).

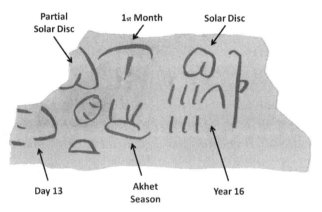

Translation from right to left:
"Year [of the] 16th occasion, 1st month [of the] Akhet Season, day 13."

Figure A2.30. Hieratic script showing the year 16 (with solar disc) and the first month (with upright numerals and solar disc) but with only the numerals for the day of the month (day 13) rotated 90° (sideways). (Image based on original drawing by Karl Lepsius; lithographer: Maximilian Weidenbach from Siliotti, Guide to the Pyramids of Egypt, *50.)*

We find this convention also used in the papyri cache recently discovered at Wadi al-Jarf (fig. A2.31) and at Abusir (fig. A2.32).

This convention of placing calendar day numbers on their side is confirmed by the Egyptian language expert Sir Alan Gardiner, who writes, "In hieratic the tens and units, when referring to the days of the month, are invariably laid on their side."[21]

Gardiner's comment is consistent with the old hieratic paleographic record. As stated above, to represent the days of the month, the ancient Egyptians used the unit and ten number signs turned on their sides. However, on no occasion in the old hieratic paleographic record do we

(Day 24)   (Day 23)   (Day 22)

Figure A2.31. Author's impression from the Wadi al-Jarf papyri with hieratic script showing (from right) *calendar days 22–24, each day with a solar disc above the number value; the signs are rotated 90° (sideways).*

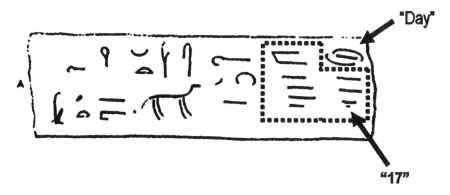

Figure A2.32. Date signs in the pyramid of Neferirkare at Abusir. The sideways calendrical date signs (dotted area) *are accompanied with the hieratic solar disc sign for a calendar "day"* (top right). Vyse, *Operations Carried On at the Pyramids, vol. III, 20. Note: a clearer rendering of these date signs can be viewed in Dobrev et al.,* Old Hieratic Palaeography I, *sign NE08 on page 31 and 68.*

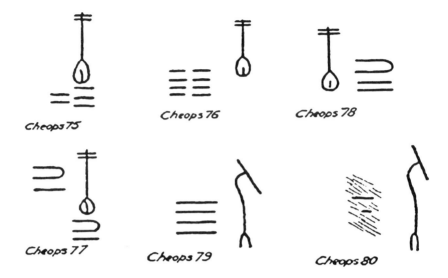

Figure A2.33. Hieratic numbers painted onto the roof blocks of Campbell's Chamber. None of these number inscriptions show any evidence of the solar disc sign being present to indicate that the numbers were to be read sideways, as dates. (Image based on original drawings by Alan Rowe, 1931)

find the ∩ sign, when used as a cardinal number, i.e., *without* the solar disc, turned on its side.

Given the complete absence of the solar disc sign from all of the number signs in Campbell's Chamber, it is therefore highly unlikely that these number signs represent calendar days. As such, these signs should *not* be read sideways (from the top down) but upright from right to left. And since ancient Egyptian scribes were unlikely to write the hieratic cardinal number ∩ upright with the lower unit values placed on the right, then the number signs in Campbell's Chamber are clearly anomalous.

What we are therefore likely witnessing here is the work of someone who did not understand that ancient Egyptian hieratic script, unlike hieroglyphics, can only be read and written from right to left. That genuine hieratic numbers were simply flipped (as opposed to rotated 180°) and painted onto these blocks to make them look as though the signs were painted onto the blocks at the quarry is one simple way of explaining this anomaly (fig. A2.34).

1. Vyse finds genuine hieratic numbers somewhere outside the pyramid.

2. Vyse 'flips' hieratic number signs onto roof blocks (to make it appear as though painted at the quarries).

3. Vyse fails to understand that, as hieratic text, it can only be read from right to left and thus cannot now create a valid number when read upright.

Figure A2.34. A possible explanation for the anomalous numbers in Campbell's Chamber.

A second possibility is that Vyse found a means to teach himself how to write simple ancient Egyptian numbers. In his quest for information about ancient Egypt (see chapter 5), the colonel may have inadvertently stumbled across scholarly material that would have shown him how to do this. Such a book could have been Wilkinson's *Materia Hieroglyphica* (1828), in which, as early as page three, Wilkinson presents the numbers 48 and 20 written in ancient Egyptian hieroglyphic form (fig. A2.35).

Being a hieroglyphic inscription, the text on this page of Wilkinson's book has been written left to right (as opposed to right to left in hieratic script). As a result of this, the ∩ (10) value is presented before the | (1) value. Had Vyse read this hieroglyphic inscription on this page, then he could very easily have worked out how to write ancient Egyptian hieroglyphic numbers such as ∩ | | (12) or ∩∩ | (21), and so on. However,

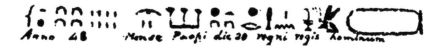

Figure A2.35. Page three of Wilkinson's Materia Hieroglyphica *presents the numbers 48 and 20 written in Egyptian hieroglyphic form.*

what he would also have mistakenly understood from this inscription in Wilkinson's book is that the hieratic ∩ (10) should be placed to the *left* of the | (1) sign. At this early stage in the understanding of ancient Egyptian writing, Vyse simply would not have been aware of the difference in the reading and writing order between hieroglyphic and hieratic inscriptions. And so, if he had used Wilkinson's example hieroglyphic inscription as a teaching aid, it is easy to see how he could have formed the Egyptian ∩ | | (12) and simply rotated this number 180° to wrongly give | | ∪ and had this painted onto the roof blocks of Campbell's Chamber, along with the other numbers on other blocks. A simple mistake being made through a complete lack of knowledge of hieratic script and of the grammatical rules that we understand today between hieroglyphic and hieratic text—this just wasn't known in Vyse's time.

THE SOURCE DRAFTS

One of the main issues critics of the hoax hypothesis often cite is the absence of the original source marks that Vyse is hypothesized to have used as his template to copy into the chambers he blasted open within the Great Pyramid. Unless the original source text can be found, the critics assert, there is simply no case to answer. It is a ploy that has become the standard means of critics to dismiss the hoax hypothesis in its entirety.

But it's a patently ridiculous argument. Imagine, for example, we were to find someone lying in the street with gunshot wounds, surrounded by empty shell casings, with gunshot residue on his clothes and with eyewitnesses to the shooting. Can we seriously argue that no shooting ever took place simply because the gunman ran off with the primary evidence—the gun? Isn't there sufficient circumstantial evidence left behind at the crime scene for us to reasonably conclude that a crime had indeed occurred? Do we really need to find the primary piece of evidence—the gun—in order to prove a shooting had occurred?

The fact of the matter is that even in the absence of the primary evidence—Vyse's source material—there exists a substantial body of circumstantial evidence that is highly indicative of a fraud having been perpetrated by Vyse and his closest assistants within the Great Pyramid in 1837. But even in the absence of the source material (Vyse's secret cache), we can be reasonably certain that the original source material appears to have been obtained locally because none of the painted inscriptions on these stone blocks had ever been published in any book at that time; they were just too obscure in nature.

Furthermore, as noted previously, finding out where Vyse actually obtained his draft material from will itself determine the likelihood or otherwise of any such source material having survived and being found. As stated in appendix 1, most likely Vyse would have had all such source material broken up and discarded. We know, for example, that Vyse found particular groups of painted marks on stones among the rubbish on the north and south sides of the Great Pyramid, as well as a small stone partially inscribed with the cartouche of Khufu on the pyramid's north side. Had any of these stones presented Vyse with the painted quarry marks we find today in the Vyse Chambers, then it would have been easy enough for Vyse to have had those stones broken up and discarded elsewhere or simply to have had the painted markings on the stones removed, thereby obliterating any trace of the source. Indeed, the colonel may well have resorted to even more drastic measures, as we read in his private journal entry of April 24, where he writes:

M. 24
. . . *blew up stones north front of pyramid* . . .

This blowing up of stones with gunpowder outside the pyramid may well have been for an entirely innocent reason—or it may have been to break up incriminating evidence in order that it might be more easily removed and dispensed with. The truth of Vyse's source is perhaps hinted at when we consider this curious passage from May 18, 1837, in Vyse's published book:

Dr. Walne applied, through Mr. Perring, for copies of the characters found in the Great Pyramid, in order to send them to M. Rosellini. I requested Mr. Perring to express my regret that I could not accede to his request, and received from that gentleman a satisfactory and obliging answer.[22]

Dr. Alfred Septimus Walne is a curious character who apparently departed for Egypt in 1836—about a year after Colonel Vyse first arrived. Although Walne was originally a practicing medical doctor (Vyse's private journal tells of him receiving from Walne some boxes of collyrium, a medicated eyewash, for the colonel's workers), he was appointed as the British vice consul at Cairo in June 1837 and full consul four years later on August 16, 1841, in which capacity he was largely responsible for encouraging Abbas Pasha, the *wāli* (ruler) of Egypt, to construct the railway line between Alexandria and Cairo and then on to Suez.[23]

Walne was clearly a fairly senior figure in British political circles of this period, with important connections that went far and wide. So why then did Vyse refuse Walne copies of the quarry marks from the Great Pyramid?

Alas, Vyse does not write of his reason for this refusal, but primacy of publication may have been one motivation to decline Walne's request, perhaps fearing that Walne's friend, Ippolito Rosellini, would publish the discovery of the quarry marks before Vyse had done so himself. This possible motive seems unlikely, however, because Vyse could simply have secured an assurance from Walne and Rosellini that the Italian would not publish anything regarding the marks until after Vyse had done so. This would not have been an unreasonable request and a condition that Rosellini likely would have acceded to.

It is puzzling also because we know that Vyse had no qualms in giving copies of the quarry marks, along with the cartouches, to others, including the shereef of Mecca and Samuel Birch of the British Museum, who eventually went on to comment on the marks in Vyse's published account. Thus his reluctance to extend this courtesy to the British vice consul in Egypt seems even more curious.

Furthermore, on May 19, 1837 (the day after refusing Walne's request), Vyse had assembled a group of five witnesses, which included himself, Sir Robert Arbuthnot, Brettel, Raven, and Hill, to testify to the discovery and accuracy of the various quarry marks present on the walls of the various chambers that had been opened up to that point. This attestation from these witnesses would have made it very difficult indeed for anyone, including Rosellini, to even attempt to usurp and claim Vyse's discovery.

So if not primacy of publication, what other motivation might Vyse have had in refusing Walne's request for a copy of the quarry marks? Interestingly, during his time in Egypt, which lasted until his resignation in 1861, we learn that Walne had interests that went beyond his official capacity as vice consul for the British government. Here, for example, we read in *The Literary Gazette* from December 1836: "Egyptian Society—The *Augsburg Gazette* states, that a scientific society under this name has been formed at Cairo, by a British physician, Mr Alfred Walne, long resident in Egypt, and *a zealous student of hieroglyphic and Coptic literature.* The Society has hired a house for the reception of travellers, and are collecting a library of books likely to be useful to such as explore the Egyptian provinces in Africa and Asia. One Turk has subscribed, but the members are chiefly English, with some French and German"[24] (emphasis added).

And in the periodical *Voyages and Travels,* J. L. Stephens writes: "The author is personally acquainted with many of the members [of the Egyptian Society], particularly with Mr Walne, Hon. Sec. who, besides being a gentleman of high literary and professional attainments, has devoted much attention, and with great success, to the study of hieroglyphics and Egyptian antiquities."[25]

Is it mere coincidence that the *Augsburg Gazette* article was published just two months after Vyse had procured his books by Champollion and Rosellini (at considerable cost), which he did with some other unidentified persons? From this article, we learn that Walne was something of a "zealous student of hieroglyphic and Coptic literature" and that, as stated previously, he also had connections to Rosellini, the foremost authority of the day in such matters. A consideration for Vyse with Walne's request may have been the fact that the good doctor had been on the ground at Cairo since before and during the colonel's 1837 explorations and would almost certainly have visited the Giza pyramids (probably on more than one occasion), perhaps pursuing his own antiquarian interest by searching for hieroglyphic marks on the pyramid's core stones or within the rubble around the base of the monuments.

Thus, the reason for Vyse's reluctance to give copies of the quarry marks to Walne may not have been so much to do with any concerns Vyse may have harbored with the marks coming under the scrutiny of the learned Rosellini but rather that Walne, who had been on the ground in Cairo and Giza and who possessed a great interest and knowledge in hieroglyphic script, might have recognized that the inscriptions presented to him by Vyse were identical to markings that Walne had perhaps seen himself on stone blocks around the Great Pyramid; as such, Walne could have become suspicious of Vyse's activities. Vyse simply could not know just how extensive Walne's knowledge was or what he may have seen around the Great Pyramid. As such, Vyse, in such a circumstance, would have had little choice but to refuse the one man in Egypt at that time who may well have possessed the potential to investigate and expose what Vyse was really doing inside the Great Pyramid. In short, Walne may have represented a risk that Vyse simply didn't need to take—and clearly opted not to. But there's a second possibility.

THE "W FIGURES"

As stated earlier, there is a second possible reading of Vyse's private journal entry of April 27, in which he writes ". . . [?], the Sheikh was inside, [& drew] figures."

Such are the vagaries of Vyse's handwriting style that it is possible that this passage could also be read as follows:

. . . [?], the Sheikh was inside, [the W] figures,

on the western side of calcerous stones as [?]

If this second possible reading is correct, then we are left wondering what Vyse means by "the W figures."

It is possible that this somewhat vague statement, "the W," might, if correct, be a clue to a wider conspiracy. The comments of Pückler-Muskau that Vyse wrote about in his private journal, whereby the Prussian predicted back in February that Vyse would find an inscription in "our apartment" (i.e., Wellington's Chamber) is certainly suggestive that Vyse's intentions may have been known beyond Vyse alone. Pückler-Muskau even published in at least two books his accusation that the marks Vyse presented to the world were likely only to have been painted recently and that the colonel had merely pretended to have discovered them in these chambers.

Vyse, as we know, spent a considerable sum of money buying books by Champollion and Rosellini and makes the curious comment "*our first books*" in his journal, suggesting that others were involved and thus potentially indicating a wider conspiracy. If that was the case, then who else might have been involved? Does "the W figures" refer to a person? Certainly, it would have been helpful to Vyse to have had someone who was knowledgeable in matters of ancient Egyptian hieroglyphics. And, as we have learned, Walne was just such a person. Was it then Walne who supplied Vyse with appropriate inscriptions to paint inside the Vyse Chambers? Is Walne the mysterious "W" that Vyse is referring to when he (possibly) writes, "the W figures" in his private journal entry of April 27? Of course, if there was such a relationship between Vyse and Walne, we might expect other comments regarding Walne to appear in Vyse's private journal, comments that would indicate a much closer association between them. And we do.

On May 8, 1837, two days after having breached Lady Arbuthnot's Chamber, Vyse writes the following curious passage in his private journal, where the currency would likely have been Egyptian pounds, which were first introduced to Egypt in 1836.

M. 8
. . . Wrote to Dr Walne about money, Mr Hill's Bill up 830 £ [?] but had about 15 [?]. Mr Raven 250 £ from [?] Paid Mr Hill 150 £ . . .

It has long been assumed that Vyse was the sole funder of his explorations at Giza, supposedly spending something in the order of £10,000 of his personal fortune—a not inconsiderable sum in 1837. Why on earth then is Vyse writing to Walne, seeking from him, it seems, money for Hill and Raven? Helping to fund Vyse's two closest assistants strongly suggests that Walne had some interest in Vyse's enterprise.

And, of course, if there was a wider conspiracy with Vyse that involved Walne, then we have another possible reason why Walne would have wanted to see the chamber hieroglyphics and why Vyse would have been reluctant to send them to him. Walne, if he *was* the source for the quarry marks Vyse subsequently had painted into the various chambers, may simply have been wanting to check that the hieratic inscriptions he had theoretically given Vyse had been copied correctly. Vyse, on the other hand, would have wished to keep himself and his operations distant from Walne (his possible source) to perhaps ensure plausible deniability. Had a third party seen Walne's original source marks alongside copies of the marks Vyse supposedly discovered and noticed that they were virtually identical, then eyebrows would surely have been raised. To eliminate such a risk, one must simply keep control of the discovery and entirely avoid sending copies back to your original source, where a third party might catch sight of them.

Admittedly, Walne's possible clandestine participation in Vyse's dubious activities at Giza is entirely speculative here; we will likely never know with any certainty to what extent, if any, Walne was involved with Vyse's nefarious activities. But it remains, nevertheless, curious indeed that there evidently existed some level of financial involvement between the soon-to-be British vice consul and Vyse (as well as Vyse's two closest assistants) and that not a single word of this partnership is ever even hinted at in Vyse's published account.

BURNING TRUTH

Critics of the Vyse forgery hypothesis often insist that if the colonel had indeed perpetrated this fraud within the Great Pyramid and that the truth of this could be shown on various incriminating pages of his private journal, then the first thing Vyse would have done upon returning to England would have been to destroy his diary—the evidence—perhaps by throwing it into the fire (fig. A2.36).

It may be, of course, that Vyse fully intended to do this, but he most certainly could not have done so immediately upon returning to England from Giza as he needed these pages of his private journal as the basis to write up his manuscript for publication, which, as a result of a number of delays, did not occur until 1840, some three years or so

Figure A2.36. The parlor with its open hearth in Vyse's ancestral home at Stoke Poges, Buckinghamshire, England. (Photo: Scott Creighton)

after departing Egypt. And he would likely have felt the need to hold on to his journal for some time afterward should any matter have arisen from the published account that perhaps needed clarification from his private notes; not every detail in his private journal, as we know, went into print. As such, there would have been good practical reasons for him to hold on to his private journal long after publication.

Furthermore, these pages were private and intended for the colonel's eyes only. He would publish only what he wanted people to know, censor the rest, and quite likely keep the journal locked away in his private writing bureau. And just like anyone's personal diary, Vyse would almost certainly have had an emotional attachment to it, pages filled with fond memories and a tangible reminder to him of an important time in his life. As anyone one who keeps one will know, personal diaries are difficult to let go of.

But even if Vyse *had* planned to destroy his journal, or even just certain pages of it, he may well have held it over the fire in the parlor of his home at Stoke Poges but, in the end, just couldn't bring himself to let go, resolving to do the deed the following day. Alas, however, one day his tomorrow never came when the colonel departed this Earth with his private journal remaining fully intact, locked in the drawer of his writing bureau, an artifact that would eventually find its way into the public domain and the full glare of international scrutiny.

Notes

CHAPTER 1. A TROUBLESOME DISCOVERY

1. El-Akkad, "The Great Pyramid."
2. Winsor and Ali, "Great Pyramid's Previously Hidden 'Void' Hailed."
3. Merriam, "An Idea of Exploring the Hidden Chambers in Egyptian Pyramids through Elementary Particles. "
4. El-Akkad, "The Great Pyramid."
5. Amos, "'Big Void' Identified in Khufu's Great Pyramid at Giza."
6. Amos, "'Big Void' Identified in Khufu's Great Pyramid at Giza."
7. Smith, "Mysterious 'Big Void' in Great Pyramid Revealed."
8. Amos, "'Big Void' Identified in Khufu's Great Pyramid at Giza."
9. Haridy, "Debate Stirs over Mysterious 'Void.'"
10. *Journal of Ancient Egyptian Architecture,* "What Should We Think?"
11. Lightbody, "Is the Great Pyramid's 'Big Void' in Fact Caused by Two Construction Space Zones Flanking the Grand Gallery?"
12. Pahl, "Why Is Egypt Not Allowing Archeologists to Examine the Voids?"
13. Amos, "'Big Void' Identified in Khufu's Great Pyramid at Giza."
14. Amos, "'Big Void' Identified in Khufu's Great Pyramid at Giza."
15. Magli, "Possible Explanation of the Void."
16. Amos, "'Big Void' Identified in Khufu's Great Pyramid at Giza."

CHAPTER 2. EXAMINING THE LEGENDS

1. Nunn, "Oldest True Stories in the World."
2. Morris Guirguis, "Vision of Theophilus," 6, 30.

3. Morris Guirguis, "Vision of Theophilus," 16.

4. Fodor, *Origins of the Arabic Legends,* 350.

5. Vyse, *Operations Carried On at the Pyramids,* vol. II, 328, 332.

6. Vyse, *Operations Carried On at the Pyramids,* vol. II, 322–24.

7. Vyse, *Operations Carried On at the Pyramids,* vol. II, 324.

8. Lehner, *Complete Pyramids,* 40–41.

9. Fodor, *Origins of the Arabic Legends,* 357.

10. Fodor, *Origins of the Arabic Legends,* 350, 362–63.

CHAPTER 3. WANDERING STARS

1. Hedley, ed., *The Apocryphal Old Testament,* 1 Enoch, 247.

2. Isaiah, 24:1, 20, KJV.

3. Amos, 8:8–9, KJV.

4. Werner, *Myths and Legends of China,* 56.

5. Wilkins, *Mysteries of Ancient South America,* 31.

6. Plato, *Timaeus.*

7. White, *Pole Shift,* 277.

8. Velikovsky, *Worlds in Collision,* 105–13, 120.

9. Warlow, "Return to the Tippe-Top," 10.

10. Carlotto, "New Model to Explain the Alignment," 230.

11. Thomas, *Adam and Eve Story,* 14.

12. Barbiero, "On the Possibility of Instantaneous Shifts."

13. Wölfli, Baltensperger, and Nufer, "Additional Planet as a Model."

14. Hapgood, *Path of the Pole,* xvii, author's note.

15. Gaffney, *Deep History,* 52.

16. Carlotto, "New Model to Explain the Alignment," 209.

17. Alison, "Geographic and Geometric Relationships."

18. Bowles, "Alaskan Era Question."

19. Bard, *Introduction to the Archaeology of Ancient Egypt,* 87, 93.

20. Dodwell, "Obliquity of the Ecliptic."

21. Barr, "Why the World Was Created in 4004 BC."

22. Cuvier and Jameson, *Theory of the Earth,* 239.

23. Vyse, *Operations Carried On at the Pyramids,* vol. II, 326.

24. Krupp, "Astronomical Integrity at Giza."

25. Pogo, *The Astronomical Ceiling-Decoration in the Tomb of Senmut (XVIIIth Dynasty),* 306, 316.

26. Matrejek, *Apocalypse of Enoch and Bhusunda,* 106.

27. Warlow, "Return to the Tippe-Top," 9.

28. Velikovsky, *Worlds in Collision,* 109, 113.

CHAPTER 4. THE DELUGE

1. Budge, *From Fetish to God in Ancient Egypt,* 198.

2. Sachau, *Chronology of Ancient Nations,* 28.

3. Gigal and El Morsy, "Discovery of Fossils on the Giza Plateau."

4. Gray, "Great Pyramid of Giza."

5. Jensen, "800' Inundation of the Giza Plateau," 3.

6. Allan and Delair, *Cataclysm!* 68.

7. Alford, *Midnight Sun,* 13.

8. Plato, *Timeaus,* 22c–23bc.

CHAPTER 6. INTO THE VOID

1. Cookson, "Previously Unknown Void Found."

2. Lehner, *The Complete Pyramids,* 26.

3. Vyse, *Operations Carried On at the Pyramids,* vol. II, 324.

4. Alford, *Midnight Sun,* 153.

5. Heath, *Archaeology Hotspot Egypt,* 46.

6. Heath, *Archaeology Hotspot Egypt,* 46.

7. Gabbatiss, "Great Pyramid of Giza May Be Able to Focus Electromagnetic Energy."

8. Gopinath, Nagaraja, and Nagendra, "Effects of Pyramids on Preservation of Milk," 233–36.

9. Schoch and McNally, *Pyramid Quest.*

10. Pochan, *Mysteries of the Great Pyramids.*

11. Remler, *Egyptian Mythology: A to Z.*

12. Mertz, *Temples, Tombs, and Hieroglyphs.*

13. Reisner, *Bulletin of the Museum of Fine Arts,* 76, 78, 81.

14. Lehner, "Pyramid Tomb of Hetep-heres," 1.

15. Lehner, "Pyramid Tomb of Hetep-heres," 2–3.

16. Lehner, "Pyramid Tomb of Hetep-heres," 3.

17. Lehner, "Pyramid Tomb of Hetep-heres," 17.

18. Lehner, "Pyramid Tomb of Hetep-heres," 42.

19. Callender, *Some Notes Concerning Reisner's Royal Family History,* 69.
20. Diodorus, *Library of History, Book 1,* 219.
21. Onvlee, "Mystery of the Pyramids: Part 1," 12.

CHAPTER 7. END OF DAYS: DATING THE NEXT POLE SHIFT

1. Vyse, *Operations Carried On at the Pyramids,* vol. II, 323.
2. Vyse, *Operations Carried On at the Pyramids,* vol. II, 326.
3. Lehner, "Pyramid Tomb of Hetep-heres."
4. Lehner, *Complete Pyramids,* 106.
5. Magli, "Akhet Khufu: Archaeo-astronomical Hints."
6. Bard, *Introduction to the Archaeology of Ancient Egypt,* 41.
7. Gee, *Towards a New History,* 60, 67.
8. Pérez-Accino, "Who Is the Sage Talking About?" 1495.
9. Browne, "Errors Are Feared in Carbon Dating."
10. Wade, "Neanderthals and Early Humans."
11. Cattane, "Egyptian Archeologists Comment on Carbon Dating."

APPENDIX 1: PORTRAIT OF A FRAUD: ANALYSIS OF COLONEL VYSE'S ACTIVITIES

1. Goedicke, *Old Hieratic Palaeography,* xiii–xiv.
2. Ghonim, *Khufu Second Boat.*
3. El-Aref, "Egyptian Archaeologists Refute Claims."
4. Vyse, *Operations Carried On at the Pyramids,* vol. I, 94.
5. Vyse, *Operations Carried On at the Pyramids,* vol. I, 258.
6. Vyse, *Operations Carried On at the Pyramids,* vol. I, 226, 237–38.
7. Rosellini, *I Monumenti Dell' Egitto E Della Nubia',* 130.
8. Wilkinson, *Materia Hieroglyphica,* 3. Item three has been deliberately left out as it is not relevant to the point being made.
9. Wilkinson, *Materia Hieroglyphica,* 4–5.

APPENDIX 2: MOUNTING EVIDENCE: NEW CONFIRMATION OF VYSE'S DECEIT

1. Vyse, *Operations Carried On at the Pyramids,* vol. I, 259.
2. Vyse, *Operations Carried On at the Pyramids,* vol. II, 43–44.

3. Vyse, *Operations Carried On at the Pyramids,* vol. I, 206.

4. Vyse, *Operations Carried On at the Pyramids,* vol. I, 235

5. Vyse, *Operations Carried On at the Pyramids,* vol. I, 259

6. Vyse, *Operations Carried On at the Pyramids,* vol. I, 277

7. Vyse, *Operations Carried On at the Pyramids,* vol. I, 256.

8. Vyse, *Operations Carried On at the Pyramids,* vol. I, 259.

9. Sitchin, *Stairway to Heaven,* 263–64.

10. Vyse, *Operations Carried On at the Pyramids,* vol. I, 207.

11. Vyse, *Operations Carried On at the Pyramids,* vol. I, 278.

12. Vyse, *Operations Carried On at the Pyramids,* vol. I, 259.

13. Vyse, *Operations Carried On at the Pyramids,* vol. I, 238.

14. Pückler-Muskau, *Egypt under Mehemet Ali,* 245.

15. Pückler-Muskau, *Travels and Adventures in Egypt,* 18.

16. Pückler-Muskau, *Egypt under Mehemet Ali,* 237.

17. Pückler-Muskau, *Travels and Adventures in Egypt,* 18.

18. Roth, *Egyptian Phyles in the Old Kingdom,* 128–30.

19. Goedicke, *Old Hieratic Palaeography,* xiii.

20. Chrisomalis, *Numerical Notation,* 46.

21. Gardiner, *Egyptian Grammar,* 191.

22. Vyse, *Operations Carried On at the Pyramids,* vol. I, 264.

23. Omar, "Anglo-Egyptian Relations."

24. *Literary Gazette,* "Egyptian Society," 796.

25. Stephens, *Voyages and Travels,* 131.

Bibliography

Alford, Alan F. *The Midnight Sun: The Death and Rebirth of God in Ancient Egypt.* Walsall, England: Eridu Books, 2004.

Alison, Jim. "Exploring Geographic and Geometric Relationships along a Line of Ancient Sites around the World." The Official Graham Hancock Online Forums, 2001.

Allan, D. S., and J. B. Delair. *Cataclysm! Compelling Evidence of a Cosmic Catastrophe in 9500 B.C.* Rochester, Vt.: Bear & Company, 1997.

Amos, Jonathan. "'Big Void' Identified in Khufu's Great Pyramid at Giza." BBC News, November 2, 2017.

Barbiero, Flavio. "On the Possibility of Instantaneous Shifts of the Poles." The Official Graham Hancock Online Forums, May 17, 2006.

Bard, Kathryn A. *An Introduction to the Archaeology of Ancient Egypt.* Malden, Mass.: Blackwell Publishing, 2008.

Barr, James. "Why the World Was Created in 4004 BC: Archbishop Ussher and Biblical Chronology." *Bulletin of the John Rylands University Library of Manchester* 67:604, 1984–1985.

Bowles, Jim. "Alaskan Era Question." The Official Graham Hancock Online Forums, October 27, 2004.

Browne, Malcolm W. "Errors Are Feared in Carbon Dating." *New York Times,* May 31, 1990.

Brydone, P. *A Tour through Sicily and Malta.* Edinburgh: Wm. and Robert Chambers, 1840.

Budge E. A. Wallis. *From Fetish to God in Ancient Egypt.* Oxford: Oxford University Press, 1934.

Callender, Vivienne Gae. *Some Notes Concerning Reisner's Royal Family History of the Fourth Dynasty.* Sydney: Macquarie University, 2008.

Carlotto, Mark J., "A New Model to Explain the Alignment of Certain Ancient Sites." *Journal of Scientific Exploration* 34, no. 2 (2020).

Cattane, Valentina. "Egyptian Archeologists Comment on Carbon Dating." *Egypt Independent,* July 8, 2010.

Chrisomalis, Stephen. *Numerical Notation: A Comparative History.* New York: Cambridge University Press, 2010.

Cookson, C. "Previously Unknown Void Found Deep inside Great Pyramid of Giza." *Financial Times,* November 2, 2017.

Cuvier, Georges, and Robert Jameson. *Theory of the Earth.* Edinburgh: W. Blackwood, 1827.

Diodorus Siculus. *Library of History, Book 1.* Translated by C. H. Oldfather. London: Harvard University Press, 2004.

Dobrev, Vassil, Miroslav Verner, and Hana Vymazalova. *Old Hieratic Palaeography I: Builders Inscriptions and Masons' Marks from Saqqara and Abusir.* Prague: Charles University, 2011.

Dodwell, George F. "The Obliquity of the Ecliptic. Chapter 1: The Movement of the Earth's Axis of Rotation Is Evidence of a Disturbance of the Earth's Axis in Ancient Times." The Dodwell Papers. barrysetterfield.org.

"Egypt and Thebes." *Quarterly Review.* Vol 53. London: John Murray, 1835.

El-Akkad, Farah, "The Great Pyramid." *Egypt Today,* December 22, 2017.

El-Aref, Nevine. "Egyptian Archaeologists Refute Claims by German Amateurs on Great Pyramid." *Ahram Online,* November 27, 2013.

Fodor, Sándor. *The Origins of the Arabic Legends of the Pyramids.* Budapest: Acta Orientalia Academiae Scientiarum Hungaricae, 1970.

Gabbatiss, Josh, "Great Pyramid of Giza May Be Able to Focus Electromagnetic Energy through Its Hidden Chambers, Physicists Reveal." *Independent,* July 31, 2018.

Gadalla, M. *Historical Deception: The Untold Story of Ancient Egypt.* 2nd ed., revised. Greensboro, N.C.: Tehuti Research Foundation, 2003.

Gaffney, Mark. *Deep History and the Ages of Man.* Independently published, 2020.

Gardiner, Sir Alan, *Egyptian Grammar.* 3rd ed. Oxford, England: Griffith Institute, 1957.

Gee, John. *Towards a New History for the Egyptian Old Kingdom: Perspectives on the Pyramid Age.* Edited by Peter Der Manuelian and Thomas Schneider. Leiden, the Netherlands: Koninklijke NV, 2015.

Ghonim, Afifi Rohim, "Khufu Second Boat: Rediscover and Reassemble." YouTube video, April 11, 2018.

Gigal, Antoine, and Sherif El Morsy. "Discovery of Fossils on the Giza Plateau." Gigal Research website.

Goedicke, Hans. *Old Hieratic Palaeography.* Baltimore, Md.: Halgo Inc., 1988.

Gopinath, R. K., Prem Anand Nagaraja, and Hr Nagendra. "The Effects of Pyramids on Preservation of Milk." *Indian Journal of Traditional Knowledge* 7, no. 2 (April 2008): 233–36.

Gosse, A. Bothwell. *The Civilization of the Ancient Egyptians.* London: T. C. Jack Ltd., 1915.

Gray, Martin. "Great Pyramid of Giza." World Pilgrimage Guide website.

Hapgood, Charles H. *The Path of the Pole.* Philadelphia, Pa.: Chilton Book Co., 1970.

Haridy, Rich. "Debate Stirs over 'Mysterious Void' Found inside Egypt's Great Pyramid." New Atlas website, November 12, 2017.

Heath, Julian. *Archaeology Hotspot Egypt: Unearthing the Past for Armchair Archaeologists.* Lanham, Md.: Rowman & Littlefield, 2015.

Hedley, F. D. Sparks, ed. *The Apocryphal Old Testament.* Oxford: Clarendon Press, 1989.

Jensen, John M., Jr. "800' Inundation of the Giza Plateau 12,800 Years Ago." Academia.edu website, 2015.

Journal of Ancient Egyptian Architecture. "What Should We Think about the So-Called Discovery Made by the Scan Pyramids Mission in the Great Pyramid of Giza? An Independent Review by the JAEA." *Journal of Ancient Egyptian Architecture* Facebook page, November 3, 2017.

Krupp, E. C. "Astronomical Integrity at Giza." In the Hall of Ma'at website, October 16, 2001.

Lehner, Mark. *The Complete Pyramids.* London: Thames & Hudson, 1997.

———. "The Pyramid Tomb of Hetep-heres and the Satellite Pyramid of Khufu." Cairo: German Archaeological Institute, 1985.

Lightbody, David Ian. "Is the Great Pyramid's 'Big Void' in Fact Caused by Two Construction Space Zones Flanking the Grand Gallery? Looking for Plausible Interpretations of the ScanPyramids Data Set." Academia.edu website, April 2018.

Literary Gazette. "Egyptian Society," 20 (December 1836).

Magli, Giulio. "Akhet Khufu: Archaeo-astronomical Hints at a Common Project of the Two Main Pyramids of Giza, Egypt." Dipartimento di Matematica del Politecnico di Milano. Available on the ArXiv open-access archive through Cornell University.

————. "A Possible Explanation of the Void in the Pyramid of Khufu on the Basis of the Pyramid Texts." Available on the ArXiv open-access archive.

Matrejek, Peter. *The Apocalypse of Enoch and Bhuśunda.* Minnetonka, Minn.: Apkallu Press, 2018.

Merriam, Areeba. "An Idea of Exploring the Hidden Chambers in Egyptian Pyramids through Elementary Particles." November 23, 2020. Predict website.

Mertz, Barbara. *Temples, Tombs, and Hieroglyphs: A Brief History of Ancient Egypt.* London: Constable and Robinson Ltd., 2010.

Morris Guirguis, Fatin. "The Vision of Theophilus: Resistance through Orality among the Persecuted Copts." Ph.D. diss., Florida Atlantic University, May 2010. Florida Atlantic University Digital Library.

Nunn, Patrick D. "The Oldest True Stories in the World." *Anthropology Magazine,* October 18, 2018.

Omar, Abdel-Aziz. "Anglo-Egyptian Relations and the Construction of the Alexandria-Cairo-Suez Railway (1833–1858)." Ph.D. diss., University of London, September 1966. University of London, SOAS Research Online.

Onvlee, Ian. "Mystery of the Pyramids: Part 1." Academia.edu, July 17, 2016.

Pahl, Larry. "Why Is Egypt Not Allowing Archeologists to Examine the Voids under the Sphinx and in the Great Pyramid, and Have Closed Off Access to Many Other Sites?" Quora website, December 28, 2019.

Pérez-Accino, J. R. "Who Is the Sage Talking About? Neferty and the Egyptian Sense of History." In *Proceedings of the Tenth International Congress of Egyptologists,* University of the Aegean, Rhodes, Greece, May 22–29, 2008. Edited by P. Kousoulis and N. Lazaridis. Vol. II, 2011.

Plato. *Timeaus and Critias.* Translated by Benjamin Jowett. Overland Park, Kans.: Digireads Publishing, 2009.

Pochan, A. *The Mysteries of the Great Pyramids: The Luminous Horizons of Khoufou.* New York: Avon, 1978.

Pogo, Alexander, "The Astronomical Ceiling-Decoration in the Tomb of Senmut (XVIIIth Dynasty)," *Isis* 14, no. 2. Chicago: University of Chicago Press, 1930.

Pückler-Muskau. Hermann Von. *Egypt under Mehemet Ali.* Vol. I. London: Henry Colburn, 1845.

————. *Travels and Adventures in Egypt: With Anecdotes of Mehemet Ali.* Vol. II. London: Parry, Blenkarn and Co., 1847.

Reisner, George. *Bulletin of the Museum of Fine Arts,* no. 157. Boston, 1928.

Remler, P. *Egyptian Mythology: A to Z.* New York: Chelsea House Books, 2010.

Rosellini, Ippolito. *I Monumenti Dell' Egitto E Della Nubia.* 1832. Digital image available through Universitätsbibliothek Heidelberg.

Roth, Ann Macy, *Egyptian Phyles in the Old Kingdom*. Chicago: University of Chicago, 1991.

Sachau, C. Edward. *The Chronology of Ancient Nations: Arabic Text of the Athár-Ul-Bákiya of Albírúní*. London: William H. Allan and Company, 1879. Digital image available at Gallica website.

Schoch, R. M., and R. A. McNally. *Pyramid Quest: Secrets of the Great Pyramid and the Dawn of Civilization*. New York: Jeremy P. Tarcher, 2005.

Siliotti, Alberto. *Guide to the Pyramids of Egypt*. New York: Barnes and Noble Books, 1997.

Sitchin, Zecharia. *The Stairway to Heaven*. Rochester, Vt.: Bear & Company, 1992.

Smith, Belinda. "Mysterious 'Big Void' in Great Pyramid Revealed by Cosmic Rays." ABC News, November 2, 2017.

Stephens, J. L. *Voyages and Travels in Egypt, Arabia Petræa, and the Holy Land*. London: William Smith, 1840.

Thomas, Chan. *The Adam and Eve Story."* South Chatham, Mass.: Bengal Tiger Press, 1993. Digital copy available at the Internet Archive website, see page 51.

Velikovsky, Immanuel. *Worlds in Collision*. Garden City, N.Y.: Doubleday, 1950.

Vyse, Richard W. H. H., Colonel. *Operations Carried On at the Pyramids of Gizeh in 1837*. Vols. I–III. London, James Fraser, 1840.

———. *Private Journal*. D121/2/35. Aylesbury, England: Centre for Buckinghamshire Studies.

Wade, Nicholas. "Neanderthals and Early Humans May Not Have Mingled Much." *New York Times,* May 9, 2011.

Warlow, Peter, "Return to the Tippe-Top." *Chronology & Catastrophism Review* IX (1987). Available at Society for Interdisciplinary Studies website.

Werner, E. T. C. *Myths and Legends of China*. Mineola, New York: Dover Publications, 1994.

White, John. *Pole Shift*. Virginia Beach, Va.: A.R.E Press, 2000.

Wilkins, Harold T. *Mysteries of Ancient South America*. London: Forgotten Books, 2012.

Wilkinson, Sir John Gardner. *Materia Hieroglyphica: Succession of the Pharaohs*. Malta: n.p., 1828.

Winsor, Morgan, and Randi Ali. "Great Pyramid's Previously Hidden 'Void' Hailed by Some Scientists, Dismissed by Egyptian Experts." ABC News, November 3, 2017.

Wölfli, W., W. Baltensperger, and R. Nufer. "An Additional Planet as a Model for the Pleistocene Ice Age." April 2, 2002. Available from CERN Document Server.

Index